D0989943

CHILD PROTECTION ASSESSMENT FOLLOWING SERIOUS INJURIES TO INFANTS

Fine Judgments

THE NSPCC/WILEY SERIES
in
PROTECTING CHILDREN

The multi-professional approach

Series Editors: Christopher Cloke,
NSPCC, 42 Curtain Road,
London EC2A 3NX

Jan Horwath,
Department of Sociological Studies,
University of Sheffield,
Sheffield S10 2TU

Peter Sidebotham,
Warwick Medical School,
University of Warwick,
Coventry CV4 7AL

This NSPCC/Wiley series explores current issues relating to the prevention of child abuse and the protection of children. The series aims to publish titles that focus on professional practice and policy, and the practical application of research. The books are leading edge and innovative and reflect a multi-disciplinary and inter-agency approach to the prevention of child abuse and the protection of children.

All books have a policy or practice orientation with referenced information from theory and research. The series is essential reading for all professionals and researchers concerned with the prevention of child abuse and the protection of children.

362.76
D15

CHILD PROTECTION ASSESSMENT FOLLOWING SERIOUS INJURIES TO INFANTS

Fine Judgments

Peter Dale, Richard Green and Ron Fellows

John Wiley & Sons, Ltd

Copyright © 2005   John Wiley & Sons Ltd, The Atrium, Southern Gate, Chichester,
West Sussex PO19 8SQ, England

Telephone   (+44) 1243 779777

Email (for orders and customer service enquiries): cs-books@wiley.co.uk
Visit our Home Page on www.wiley.com

The case studies reproduced on pp. 17–19 in Chapter 2 and pp. 66–69 and 74–75 in Chapter 5 are reproduced from Dale et al. (2002) What Really Happened? Child Protection Case Management of Infants with Serious Injuries and Discrepant Parental Explanations. London: HMSO. Reproduced by permission of the NSPCC.

All Rights Reserved. No part of this publication may be reproduced, stored in a retrieval system or transmitted in any form or by any means, electronic, mechanical, photocopying, recording, scanning or otherwise, except under the terms of the Copyright, Designs and Patents Act 1988 or under the terms of a licence issued by the Copyright Licensing Agency Ltd, 90 Tottenham Court Road, London W1T 4LP, UK, without the permission in writing of the Publisher. Requests to the Publisher should be addressed to the Permissions Department, John Wiley & Sons Ltd, The Atrium, Southern Gate, Chichester, West Sussex PO19 8SQ, England, or emailed to permreq@wiley.co.uk, or faxed to (+44) 1243 770620.

Designations used by companies to distinguish their products are often claimed as trademarks. All brand names and product names used in this book are trade names, service marks, trademarks or registered trademarks of their respective owners. The Publisher is not associated with any product or vendor mentioned in this book.

This publication is designed to provide accurate and authoritative information in regard to the subject matter covered. It is sold on the understanding that the Publisher is not engaged in rendering professional services. If professional advice or other expert assistance is required, the services of a competent professional should be sought.

Other Wiley Editorial Offices

John Wiley & Sons Inc., 111 River Street, Hoboken, NJ 07030, USA

Jossey-Bass, 989 Market Street, San Francisco, CA 94103-1741, USA

Wiley-VCH Verlag GmbH, Boschstr. 12, D-69469 Weinheim, Germany

John Wiley & Sons Australia Ltd, 33 Park Road, Milton, Queensland 4064, Australia

John Wiley & Sons (Asia) Pte Ltd, 2 Clementi Loop #02-01, Jin Xing Distripark, Singapore 129809

John Wiley & Sons Canada Ltd, 22 Worcester Road, Etobicoke, Ontario, Canada M9W 1L1

Wiley also publishes its books in a variety of electronic formats. Some content that appears in print may not be available in electronic books.

Library of Congress Cataloging in Publication Data

Dale, Peter, 1953–
    Child protection assessment following serious injuries to infants : fine judgments / Peter Dale, Richard Green, and Ron Fellows.
        p.   cm. — (The NSPCC/Wiley series in protecting children: the multi-professional approach.)
    Includes bibliographical references and index.
    ISBN 0-470-85353-0 (cloth : alk. paper) — ISBN 0-470-85354-9 (pbk. : alk. paper)
    1. Child welfare—Great Britain.   2. Infants (Newborn)—Wounds and injuries—Great Britain.   3. Child abuse—Law and legislation—Great Britain.   4. Family social work—Great Britain.   I. Green, Richard, 1954 Mar. 24–   II. Fellows, Ron, 1952–   III. Title.   IV. Wiley series in child protection and policy
    HV751.A6D35 2005
    362.76'65—dc22

                                                                                                    2005008669

British Library Cataloguing in Publication Data

A catalogue record for this book is available from the British Library

ISBN-13 978-0-470-85353-5 (hbk)   978-0-470-85354-2 (pbk)
ISBN-10 0-470-85353-0 (hbk)   0-470-85354-9 (pbk)

Typeset in 10/12pt Palatino by Integra Software Services Pvt. Ltd, Pondicherry, India
Printed and bound in Great Britain by TJ International Ltd, Padstow, Cornwall
This book is printed on acid-free paper responsibly manufactured from sustainable forestry in which at least two trees are planted for each one used for paper production.

#S9003357

CONTENTS

ABOUT THE AUTHORS

Dr Peter Dale trained originally as a psychiatric social worker, and subsequently as a counsellor/psychotherapist. His PhD research was a qualitative study focused on the perceptions of clients and therapists of the therapeutic process for adults who were abused as children (Dale 1999). Peter Dale worked in child and family psychiatric services before joining the NSPCC in 1980, where he was a practitioner, manager and Senior Research Officer until 2002. An established researcher and author, Dr Dale now acts as an independent social work expert witness throughout the UK in care proceedings – specialising in cases where there are serious suspicious injuries to infants. For further information, visit: www.peterdale.co.uk.

Contact details: info@peterdale.co.uk

Richard Green trained as a social worker and family therapist. He has held a number of posts in both local authorities and the NSPCC, including practitioner, manager and evaluation officer. He is currently employed as Senior Consultant within the NSPCC, working with a range of statutory and voluntary agencies to improve the safeguarding of children.

Contact details: rgreen@nspcc.org.uk

Ron Fellows trained originally as a social worker, and subsequently as a family/brief therapist. He worked in mental health and children and family services for various London boroughs. Since joining the NSPCC, he has held posts as a practitioner and manager.

Contact details: rfellows@nspcc.org.uk

FOREWORD

This book is about a dilemma at the very heart of child protection practice – how is it possible to avoid 'false-negative' and 'false-positive' attributions, in which professionals either miss evidence of child abuse or else erroneously accuse parents of maltreatment when none has occurred? On the one hand, 30 years of fatal child abuse inquiries or serious case reviews has revealed recurrent deficiencies in professionals' approaches to assessment and their management of information about families. There is also evidence of wide variations in practice, with essentially similar cases being handled in very different ways by respective systems. On the other hand, many families report negative experiences of child protection services, in which care planning and care proceedings seem neither fair nor effective. Furthermore, medical diagnostic opinions can be fallible, the risk indicators which are available are not particularly sophisticated, and focusing attention on the dangers of children dying at the hands of their caretakers may distort approaches to everyday practice. Social workers in particular have been criticised over the years for both inaction and overreaction.

This dilemma is brought into sharp relief by cases in which infants have sustained serious, even fatal, injuries, yet their parents deny responsibility for having caused them. Protection of an infant who survives, and of any siblings, depends on expert medical evidence, detailed family assessment, effective care planning and balanced legal proceedings. However, limitations can be found in all of these procedures, as illustrated by well-publicised conundrums surrounding diagnoses of 'sudden infant death syndrome' and 'induced illness'.

The authors base discussions of all these issues on their long practice experience, wide literature reviews, and studies they have undertaken. Therefore, this book is especially welcome because of the scholarship and thoughtfulness that are evident throughout. These are particularly exemplified by their consideration of parental denial, which is said to have multiple possible origins, including the numbing and amnesia associated with post-traumatic stress and, of course, genuine absence of responsibility because the accusation is incorrect. The context of 'denial' (a term they recommend should be abandoned) needs greater understanding, and this leads them to discuss further the complexities of assessment.

Numerous case examples illustrate the demands inherent in the assessment and decision-taking processes, for which the Department of Health's Assessment Framework guidance is considered inadequate. It is suggested that the prevalence of both false-negative and false-positive attributions is too high and can be reduced by greater consistency in child protection practice. The authors' wide-ranging discussions go beyond the issue of assessment and into the even more intricate realm of making fine judgments. For example, practice experience has taught the authors that parents' initial responses to abuse allegations may be crisis oriented and not necessarily indicative of their general level of functioning.

The many recommendations for improvement include better written explanations to parents about the professional system assessing them, greater use of independent, therapeutically oriented expert assessments, a tighter use of attachment concepts, and attempts to appraise parent's capacity to change by an integrative approach.

This book will probably have the most immediate resonance with social workers, who regularly face the practice dilemmas discussed. They are guided to be reasonable, honest and humane in engaging with parents, but also to be well informed about psychological and family processes so that their assessments are thorough and balanced. This is a valuable message for all other practitioners involved with child protection.

Peter Reder
(*Child Psychiatrist, London*)

ACKNOWLEDGEMENTS

There are too many people to thank individually for the support they have given over many years in respect of the various projects that underpin this book. However, we wish to acknowledge the long-standing support of the NSPCC for resourcing large parts of the research; and the NSPCC library, in particular, for a service which remains unsurpassed.

This book contains material relating to many family tragedies. We wish to pause to reflect upon this; and to acknowledge that we have illustrated and analysed tragic family details in the hope that we can have a small impact in helping avert future similar family catastrophes.

At a personal level, our own families have had to put up with our preoccupation. Thanks go to Veronica and the Dale/Locke children; to Karen, Laura and Alex Green; and to Pauline, Lawrence and Alice Fellows.

1

INTRODUCTION

Child protection involvement with families after the discovery of serious injuries to infants is a matter of continual public concern and controversy. How do child protection professionals and courts undertake assessments and make judgments whether injuries are due to abuse? If injuries are considered to be the consequence of abuse, in what circumstances can it be considered safe for the infant to return home?

In the modern history of child protection practice, countless numbers of vulnerable infants have been protected from further harm through the provision of effective support and therapeutic interventions to enable their parents to care for them more appropriately. Moreover, the lives of innumerable children have undoubtedly been saved by decisions that it could not be considered safe for them to remain within their natural families. Such effective practice in child protection is largely invisible.

In contrast, child protection errors have a continual high profile as matters of public concern. Over the past four decades, tragedies have regularly made headlines in cases where children have been re-injured and even killed when parental violence recurred notwithstanding (inadequate) child protection interventions. More recently, public concern has become acute regarding miscarriages of justice in cases where child abuse was wrongly believed to be the cause of injuries or deaths of infants. Concern is also growing about the increased use of compulsory adoption as an alternative to the provision of sophisticated family support and therapeutic services.

In this book we are concerned with promoting good practice in child protection interventions in cases where infants have suffered serious injuries that give rise to child protection concerns. We assert that the consistency and quality of child protection work needs to improve in two ways:

1. Infants need more effective protection from sources of real risk.
2. Child protection systems need to be more consistent in not intervening in families in unnecessary, inappropriate, disproportionate and damaging ways.

We will highlight a conclusion from this book at this early stage in our introduction: in our view, child protection systems currently are far too inconsistent in the ways that cases of serious injuries to infants are dealt with – particularly the cases where there are 'uncertain perpetrators' or discrepant explanations of the cause of the injury. Essentially similar cases can be handled in contradictory ways. For example, in our own research sample (see Chapter 5), the outcomes for two seriously injured babies in very similar family circumstances were quite different although based on the same rationale: one baby was returned home to natural parents explicitly *because there was no understanding how the injuries occurred* (that is, the parents were given the benefit of the doubt). The other baby was compulsorily adopted *because there was no understanding how the injuries occurred* (parents were denied the benefit of the doubt). This cannot be considered to be satisfactory or acceptable.

How do we understand the nature of such discrepancies and inconsistencies in child protection practice? How do we make sense of the continuing level of both types of child protection errors? Just as child abuse itself is the unpredictable result of a volatile interaction of multidimensional factors, the nature of child protection practice is also determined by a range of complex (and often confusing) forces. In particular, child protection services are provided in a context of multiple influences that include political pressures, social policy expectations, legislation, government guidelines, contrasting professional cultures, technical issues relating to risk prediction, resource availability, and the idiosyncratic beliefs and behaviours of individual practitioners and professional groupings. We shall comment on these factors throughout this book.

There will be times in this book when we express our concern about inappropriate and disproportionate child protection interventions and outcomes. We are concerned that a culture of practice is developing whereby families are increasingly mistrusted by professionals, and where both motivation and resources for family support and therapeutic interventions that could keep some families intact are diminishing. Compulsory adoption is a much simpler (and cheaper) 'solution' than the uncertainties and more visible risks that are inevitably attached to more resource-intensive, successful reunification programmes. However, this concern about unreasonable child protection interventions also sits within a context of the undeniable reality of fatal and severe maltreatment of children.

AUTHORS' CREDENTIALS

The professional knowledge and practice experience of the authors upon which this book is based include:

- undertaking initial investigations of reports of abuse
- providing independent specialist assessment services
- providing a range of preventive therapeutic services (e.g. a therapeutic service for adults who were abused as children, and a brief therapy service)
- providing therapeutic services for children and families after reunification
- undertaking child protection research studies
- undertaking commissioned evaluations of child protection services
- chairing and participating in Part 8 Reviews (fatal case reviews)
- management of assessment services and supervision of practitioners
- providing expert-witness, independent social work reports in care proceedings.

The views expressed are the result of the cumulative professional experience of the three authors, all of whom have been involved in various facets of child protection work for nearly three decades.

THE STRUCTURE OF THE BOOK

Chapter 2 illustrates the graphic nature of severe physical maltreatment of infants, and outlines the types and consequences of errors that occur in child protection practice. *False-negative* errors result in failure to intervene effectively to protect infants in real danger. *False-positive* errors occur when child protection interventions are mistaken, unnecessary or disproportionate.

Chapter 3 is a selective research review of factors known to be associated with serious and fatal physical abuse. It considers what is known about the individual personality and family characteristics of parents who are found to be responsible for such events.

Chapter 4 discusses research into the effectiveness and ineffectiveness of child protection systems. It examines the processes and outcomes of child protection interventions after referral to social services, the issues that arise when cases become subject to legal proceedings, and communication problems between professionals and agencies that are noted to arise (in fatal cases). Finally, research is discussed that provides knowledge about *reunification rates* (the proportion of injured infants who are subsequently returned to the care of their parents) and *re-injury rates* (the proportion of such infants who are subsequently re-injured).

Chapter 5 focuses on the authors' own research in child protection case management of infants with serious injuries where there are discrepant parent/carer explanations. This was a research project sponsored by the National Society for the Prevention of Cruelty to Children (NSPCC) which examined the characteristics of two samples: first, a sample of 17 families where 19 infants had died from suspicious injuries; second, a clinical sample of 21 families referred to an independent assessment service.

Chapter 6 examines the views of parents and other family members about child protection interventions they have been subjected to. Key themes from the body of parental perceptions research are presented and discussed, and space is provided for the voices of parents and family members to convey their (predominantly critical) views about child protection services. Some professionals will find this chapter to be an uncomfortable read.

Chapter 7 discusses diagnostic issues and dilemmas in relation to expert medical witnesses concluding whether serious injuries were caused by abuse, or whether there are less probable non-abuse explanations in certain cases where otherwise the injuries to the infant mimic abuse. This chapter also considers the varied reasons why some parents/carers 'deny' responsibility for the injuries to the infant (one of these being that they are wrongly accused on the basis of a 'false-positive' error). The chapter concludes that the notion of 'denial' is unhelpful and often counter-productive in child protection assessment and case management.

Chapter 8 outlines key approaches to undertaking child protection assessments in cases where infants have sustained serious suspicious injuries. It is noted that the Assessment Framework (the government-promoted assessment tool in England and Wales) is inadequate in this context, and specialist assessment interventions are required. We outline common specialist assessment contexts, and discuss necessary professional skills for intervening effectively with families in specialist assessment practice.

Chapter 9 highlights the necessity of assessing *potential for change*, and considers to what extent are identified family problems that are commonly associated with serious suspicious injuries amenable to change. It also considers what theories, approaches, skills and services can help facilitate such changes. The chapter provides indicators of positive change potential from assessment interventions, and outlines the factors that suggest that potential for change is absent or significantly limited.

Chapter 10 describes how in the course of child protection interventions families and child protection services may behave in either reasonable or unreasonable ways. We conclude in view of this that courts should take into account the *reasonableness* and *unreasonableness* of child protection interventions and case-management practice when forming judgments about the long-term futures of seriously harmed infants. We review the options open to courts at the final stage of care proceedings, and critically discuss the apparently increasing trend toward enforcing compulsory adoptions.

Drawing on original practice-based research and extensive experience of undertaking independent child protection assessments, this book provides an essential reference for all professionals involved in the child protection process in cases where infants have suffered serious suspicious injuries. The book is written for a wide audience, including social workers, health workers, solicitors, barristers and the judiciary. It is hoped that it will also be a valuable resource for parents and families who find themselves involved in child protection and legal proceedings after injuries to their child.

2

CHILD ABUSE AND CHILD PROTECTION ERRORS

In this chapter we consider the nature of serious and fatal physical abuse of infants, illustrating this with several highly unpleasant examples that are in the public domain. We go on to consider the nature of child protection errors that arise from professional interventions – or the absence of them.

In a book with a commitment to effective and proportionate child protection practice, it is important to keep in mind that babies, infants and children of all ages are injured and even killed by accidental events on a far greater scale than by being abused. Underlining this point, in a major UK medical child abuse handbook, a leading paediatrician reminded readers that 'accidental injury is extremely common in childhood' (Hobbs et al. 1999, p. 101). Given the prevalence of accidental injuries to infants, it is essential that professionals undertaking child protection investigations of serious suspicious injuries to infants consider carefully the possibility of unusual accidental events and rare medical conditions that can mimic signs of abuse. We shall discuss non-abuse explanations for suspicious serious injuries in more detail in Chapter 7.

While accidental injuries to infants are common, research also indicates that certain types and combinations of injury have a much higher likelihood of being the result of maltreatment than accident. Statistically, the first year of life reflects a peak risk level for being non-accidentally killed or seriously harmed, and this occurrence is most likely to be at the hands of a parent/carer. A major study in Wales recently concluded that 1:880 babies of this age is subject to serious physical abuse (Sibert et al. 2002). Across England and Wales, there is a consistent figure of approximately 30 recorded homicides of infants aged 0–12 months per year. Several commentators estimate the actual figure to be at least double (e.g. Wilczynski 1997). It is also estimated that 200 children are killed each year by their parents or carers (NSPCC 2001).

In addition, unknown numbers of adults live with physical, intellectual and neurological impairments stemming from abuse-related brain injuries acquired in infancy. One study reported that 78% of infants with non-fatal, abuse-related head injuries were left with significant long-term neurological and developmental abnormalities (Barlow & Minns 2000). One of our concerns in this book is to consider to what extent such tragedies could be preventable with improvements to the efficacy and consistency of child protection practice.

Public health campaigns have had notable successes in reducing the incidence of certain types of serious and fatal accidental injuries to infants. For example, the incidence of sudden infant death syndrome (SIDS) in many countries has diminished significantly after 'Back to Sleep' campaigns. The numbers of toddlers drowning in unguarded domestic swimming pools has been reduced in Australia and the USA by public awareness campaigns coupled with regulatory and legislative changes. Such campaigns are demonstrably more effective in reducing infant deaths from accidents than from abuse (Kemp & Coles 2003). The incidence of child abuse has proved to be stubbornly less susceptible to public health prevention activities.

In the UK, no national figures are collated regarding the incidence and severity of serious (but non-fatal) physical injuries (or re-injuries) to young children. Child protection registers do not record the severity of injuries or rates of re-injury to children. There are no reliable data by which to monitor incidence and re-injury trends and the effectiveness of prevention and intervention programmes. Consequently, it is not known to what extent young children have been effectively and appropriately 'rescued' from further acute risks. Nor is it known to what extent infants have been unnecessarily separated from their natural families in the name of 'protection', or the proportion who subsequently have had disrupted experiences in adoptive families. The reason why the answers to such fundamental questions are not known is that (notwithstanding their massive overall financial cost) the nature and ratio of benefits/harms stemming from child protection services are significantly underevaluated.

SEVERE MALTREATMENT OF INFANTS

Some infants are subjected to extreme forms of maltreatment. In contrast to more obvious single-factor reasons for many accidental deaths (such as children being unrestrained in motor vehicles), the cause of serious child abuse is complex, multifactorial and debatable. There is no doubt that some infants are chronically maltreated in sadistic ways in seriously disturbed families where there can be very little potential for sustained genuine positive changes. As the following international, public domain examples illustrate, the phenomenon of much fatal and serious abuse of infants can be difficult to comprehend, let alone to anticipate and prevent.

The UK

'Baby tossed 'like a rag doll' '. A mother told yesterday of her horror after the man she caught hurling her one-year-old baby around like a rag doll walked free from court. Jamie Thompson, 28, was secretly filmed tormenting the child after the mother left a video camera running in the lounge of her home. . . . The video shows Thompson walking into the room and yanking the child from where it [sic] was sitting on the sofa. Clutching one of her legs, he swung the child around as she screamed hysterically. (*The Times*, 19/5/04)

A father who punched his baby son to death, and afterwards blamed a gang of youths for the attack, was yesterday convicted of manslaughter. . . . MacDonald (25) gave no explanation of why he turned on his five-month-old child Connor while waiting at a station. . . . The baby's mother said she no longer had any feelings for MacDonald, but acknowledged that he had been a 'very good father'. (*The Guardian*, 9/2/01)

A man from Loughborough who headbutted his eight-month-old baby has been jailed for three years. . . . Leicester Crown Court heard how the child suffered several bouts of abuse at the hands of her father and was violently shaken when her crying became too much. The man said he was sorry, and said he had been unable to cope when the child would not stop making a noise. (BBC News website, 20/9/02)

A mother has been jailed for life for deliberately pouring boiling water over her two-year-old daughter – ten years after injuring her son with an iron. The 39-year-old took a full saucepan and tipped it over her little girl's chest and thighs. The youngster suffered horrific injuries needing weeks of hospital treatment which need more surgery when she gets older. (*Hastings Observer*, 31/1/03)

A mentally-ill mother who killed her two babies by smothering them was ordered to be detained in hospital. The mother, 29, put her hands over the face of her nine-month-old daughter. Years later, she did the same thing with her eight-month-old son. (*The Guardian*, 2/2/01)

A mother killed her baby daughter while under the supervision of a social services department. The eleven-week-old baby died after being punched. The mother put make-up on the baby's bruised head as she tried to conceal her crime. (*Daily Mail*, 24/11/01)

The USA

A woman has been jailed for five years in New York for killing her month-old son by putting him in a microwave oven and turning it on. . . . Relatives told police that she appeared detached from her son but there were no signs that she wanted to harm him. (*The Guardian*, 15/12/00)

After a long and moving speech in which he touched on personal responsibility, human nature and why people hurt one another, Cook County Judge

John J. Moran sentenced a young father to 20 years in prison for shaking his 4-month-old infant son to death. Authorities said he died from such violent and sustained shaking that his left leg was fractured in two places and dozens of blood vessels in his eyes and brain had burst. The defense attorney had argued that the baby had been choking due to a severe cold and the father had unintentionally injured him while performing 'lifesaving techniques'. (*Chicago Tribune*, Internet Edition, 8/12/01)

The father of a 7-week-old boy clinging to life at Children's Hospital admitted he shook the child hours before the infant was found convulsing from a head injury, court records show. Mark Schnabel, 32, told investigators he shook his son, Cadin, because the boy was fussy during his 3 a.m. feed. Doctors found the boy's twin sister Kylie, also had a broken arm and leg. Schnabel said he was rougher with Cadin than Kylie because 'he is a boy'. (*Denver Post*, 11/7/02)

New Zealand

Another child has been bashed to death in a bleak 'family' home.... The pathologist's evidence showed that over 20-odd minutes 3-year-old Tangaroa Matiu's stepfather hit the child around 100 times. Favourite spots were places that hurt terribly but would not kill – until he miscalculated and whacked Tangaroa's head so hard that blood spattered the toilet walls. When the child's bottom slipped into the toilet, Mahanga hauled him out and hit him again. When the boy's mother came down the hall, far from saving him, she slapped him a couple of times too, then stepped back to let her boyfriend carry on... (*New Zealand Herald Online*, 29/8/00)

These disturbing accounts highlight the extent of catastrophic violence endured by some very unfortunate babies and young children. The cases demonstrate that both male and female parents can inflict severe, sadistic injuries on their children. Assaults may be sudden and single incidents. Alternatively, infants may be subjected to prolonged torture and fatal neglect. Such cases of appalling abuse and neglect of young children understandably stir powerful emotional reactions. However, it is important that general child protection policy and practice are not overdetermined by such relatively rare 'hard cases'. To do so leads to overzealous forms of child protection practice that also can result in ruinous harm to families.

FOUR OUTCOMES OF CHILD PROTECTION INTERVENTIONS

There is general social consent that child protection services should intervene promptly and appropriately to make enquiries when a report is

True-positive	True-negative
• Abuse is detected • Risk is real • Child is protected	• No abuse • Risk is appropriately discounted • Enquiry is sensitive and proportionate
False-positive	False-negative
• No abuse • Risk is overestimated • Interventions are inappropriate and disproportionate • Family is harmed by inappropriate child protection interventions	• Abuse is undetected • Risk is underestimated • Interventions are absent/inadequate • Child is re-injured in context of inadequate child protection interventions

Figure 2.1   Desirable and undesirable outcomes of child protection interventions.

received that a child has been harmed or is thought to be at risk. As shown in Figure 2.1, there are theoretically four types of outcome of child protection interventions – two of which are desirable (true-positives and true-negatives), and two of which generate adverse outcomes (false-positives and false-negatives). We shall consider and illustrate each of these in turn.

DESIRABLE OUTCOMES OF CHILD PROTECTION INTERVENTIONS

True-positive Outcomes

Ideally, the desired outcome of the child protection system is to prevent abuse and re-abuse. Family needs and stresses are identified at an early stage, and effective interventions are offered which prevent difficulties escalating into episodes of child abuse. This requires the provision of easy access, non-stigmatising family support and therapeutic services. Children at acute risk of significant harm and those who have been harmed are quickly identified. Their circumstances are promptly and competently investigated and assessed. Interagency protection plans are instigated which secure children's safety either in their own homes or, if necessary, in appropriate substitute care. Risk is acute and protection is effective. True-positive outcomes are largely invisible, as they involve interventions that prevent children re-experiencing serious and escalating abuse. The generally low public reputation of child protection services is in part due to a lack of published material and media attention which illustrates effective child protection practice. The public is largely unaware that child protection systems which have developed over the past three decades do work well for thousands of children each year.

For example, an independent survey in Victoria, Australia, found that 80% of children interviewed reported that their 'life had got better' as a consequence of child protection interventions (Gleeson et al. 2001). Another study of 282 parents who had received child protection interventions (also in Victoria), reported significant positive progress in many parents who, at the beginning of interventions, were not highly motivated to change (Trotter 2004). In 2002, in the south of England, the first author undertook a file review audit of a very busy social services intake and assessment team. The report (Dale 2002b) commented on significant aspects of good practice:

> I have noted what appeared to be high levels of good practice in two-thirds of the closed cases. I felt that one-third of these amounted to excellent practice. 'Good practice' in this context predominantly represents combinations of the following factors:
>
> - Prompt and effective response to referral
> - Very effective inter-agency liaison
> - Demonstrable good skills in working with parents and children
> - Good recorded observations (developmental and behavioural) of relevant children
> - Provision of effective practical advice and support to families. (p. 2)

Out of sight, skilled and diligent professionals arrange vital protection for vulnerable children and provide or organise effective support for their parents and wider families. As we shall discuss in more detail in Chapter 6, views of parents who have benefited from child protection services are not often publicly heard. A small parents' perceptions research project, also conducted by the first author, concluded:

> In the study reported in this paper half of the participants reported that their experiences of child protection interventions had been either very helpful or helpful to some extent. Some of these cases involved remarkable stories of the lives of parents and children being transformed through

well-coordinated, sophisticated inter-agency packages of assessment and support; delivered by groups of sensitive and highly-skilled professionals. It is a real disadvantage for the image of public services that successes rarely achieve widespread recognition and have minimal impact on service development. (Dale 2004, p. 154)

Without this level and nature of successful but hidden child protection practice, the rates of serious and fatal child abuse in the UK would undoubtedly be substantially higher than they are.

True-negative Outcomes

A common example of true-negative situations arises when concerns about the safety of a child are referred to child protection agencies, enquiries reveal no problems with the care or welfare of the child, and it is concluded that the referral was either mistaken or malicious. There is little public dissent from the view that when a referral is received alleging that a child is being abused, child protection agencies have a duty to make enquiries and investigate the child's circumstances and welfare. When enquiries are conducted sensitively, most parent/carers (while being understandably upset by the referral) are able to accept that it was reasonable that the enquiries had to be made. However, when enquiries are not conducted sensitively, parents may be left feeling very angry, offended, unsettled and undermined by the experience.

True-negative outcomes are also reflected when abuse does not occur in susceptible families (where it otherwise would have done so) as a consequence of the preventive effect of universal or targeted family support services. These are the unknown numbers of hidden preventive successes that are notoriously difficult to identify and evaluate. True-positive and true-negative positions represent successful outcomes of child protection interventions. In the first position, a child has been appropriately protected. In the second, inappropriate interventions into family life have been avoided. The other two positions – false-positives and false-negatives – encompass the two major types of child protection errors. It is a major premise of this book that, with more systematic and consistent practice, it is possible to reduce these two types of child protection error. We shall now focus in more detail on both of these types of error.

UNDESIRABLE OUTCOMES OF CHILD PROTECTION INTERVENTIONS: FALSE-NEGATIVE ERRORS

The killing or serious injury causing permanent disability of a baby by parents/carers that should have been prevented (by any reasonable judgment) is one of the most tragic outcomes of the failure of the child protection system. This is the 'false-negative' error. False-negative errors arise when the child protection system does not recognise signs of risk, or respond appropriately with rapid action to protect the children concerned. We will argue that more constructive and consistent child protection interventions could save more children from abuse-related deaths and serious injury (many of which cause permanent disability).

High-profile criminal trials and public judicial enquiries into fatal child abuse, and (usually confidential) Part 8 Review reports repeatedly illustrate false-negative child protection errors. These sources frequently highlight professional inexperience and naivety in not recognising the danger that some parents can present to their children. The inquiries into the deaths of Ainlee Labonte and Victoria Climbié both provided detailed descriptions of the nature and context of false-negative child protection errors.

Ainlee Labonte: Born 24 June 1999, Died 7 January 2002

The role of child protection agencies with the family of Ainlee Labonte, who was killed by her parents in London at the age of 2 ½ years, was examined in a Part 8 Review published by Newham Area Child Protection Committee (ACPC) in December 2002. The report is a striking example of a classic collection of professional errors and failures of communication in relation to two parents that manifested high levels of visible acute risk factors. These included incidents of violent attacks by the parents on professional staff to the extent that:

> One by one the agencies withdrew for personal safety reasons... the children were living in a environment that adults were not prepared to visit... it seemed that this couple became so powerful through their manipulation, aggression and refusal to co-operate that the focus on the needs of the children became lost. (Newham ACPC 2002, pp. 15–16)

Notwithstanding the earlier child protection registration of Ainlee's elder brother, Ainlee herself, at her birth, was not incorporated into child protection procedures. Although the levels of concern were high enough to merit the provision of a residential family assessment facility, social services provided substitute care for the older child on a voluntary basis (Section 20, Children Act 1989). As the Part 8 Review report points out, this avoided care proceedings that would have necessitated a pause for overview (and independent representation for the children) of the case that is manifestly missing throughout. Social services closed the case before Ainlee's death on the rationale that this was a case of a 'child in need' whose parents were not accepting social services family support interventions:

> It is recorded that in February 1999 there was a debate within social services as to who would take responsibility for the family. A management decision was made that it should be within the Family Support team. It is at this point that the focus of the work with the family shifted. The efforts became directed towards parenting skills and rehabilitation.... A comprehensive assessment was not undertaken then or at any other time. As a result of this, it was not reasonable to shift the focus of work...away from (his) protection toward an assumption that rehabilitation and 'family support' were the plan. (Newham ACPC 2002, pp. 24 and 43)

It is difficult to read the Part 8 Review report into the death of Ainlee without some bewilderment as to why the combination of incidents of concern and known high-risk factors had not, on a number of occasions, resulted in Emergency Protection Orders and care proceedings. Such action was clearly necessary to facilitate careful assessment of the immediate safety and long-term needs of the children in the family given the parents' manifest severe psychosocial problems, and lack of cooperation with agencies. The known concerns should have triggered urgent alerts to practitioners and managers in all of the key agencies. These concerns included the following facts:

> Ainlee's mother (Leanne Labonte) had been on the child protection register as a child because of sexual and physical abuse as a child. There was serious domestic violence in her family when she was a child. She became pregnant the first time at the age of 14 by a man who was believed to be aged 27. Following this baby's birth she was homeless (with the baby) with no income and no family support. Age 15 she began a relationship with her co-convicted partner Dennis Henry. Dennis Henry was aged 40 and had a criminal history which included imprisonment. Leanne Labonte had an abortion for her next pregnancy at age 16. She considered abortion for her third pregnancy (baby Ainlee).

> The first child was removed on a Police Protection Order having been left alone. A residential assessment was arranged to consider the prospects of rehabilitation of that child (Leanne Labonte gave birth to Ainlee during that time). Parents refused to comply with the assessment and returned home with both children when Ainlee was one week old. Parents had refused to allow assessment staff to observe the new baby, claiming that staff 'had the evil eye'. Staff were under the erroneous impression that the new baby was male.

> A period of increasing avoidance of and conflict with professionals developed. Several staff were physically threatened and assaulted by Leanne Labonte.

Violent disputes with neighbours were reported, and the police were called on a number of occasions following violent arguments between the couple. Housing and Health staff refused to visit the home because of the degree of threats and actual violence. Hospital and clinic staff made extra security arrangements when the couple were due for appointments.

Baby Ainlee was presented at hospital Accident & Emergency on a number of occasions, with parents reporting breathing difficulties, rash, rigid limbs and shaking. Mother discharged her on these occasions following admission. Medical concerns were recorded that Ainlee was failing to thrive. Mother became pregnant again (with third child), and did not cooperate with her own health care. Drug paraphernalia was observed in the flat during one contact. Parents begin refusing developmental checks for Ainlee.

As with many previous fatal abuse enquiries, there were major communication failures between the professionals involved. No professional from any agency had a fully informed 'bird's eye view' of all the factors that were only partially known to different professionals:

The communication between agencies was not constructive...no-one appears to have taken a step back and evaluated the situation...there is no evidence on file of a thorough Risk Assessment, nor of housing officials contributing to the knowledge base of this family. The extent of police involvement was not evident in social work files. There was failure to bring together all the information known about a clearly dangerous family....Perhaps one of the most distressing findings of this review has been the amount and depth of information available to agencies and the failure to share it. (Newham ACPC 2002, pp. 15 and 44)

The Death of Victoria Climbié

On 25 February 2000, 8-year-old Victoria Climbié died in London, having arrived in March 1999 from the Ivory Coast, via France, to live in the care of her great-aunt Marie-Therese Kouao. Victoria's lonely, drawn-out death from multiple injuries, neglect and hypothermia was the culmination of a long period of systematic torture and neglect at the hands of Kouao and her boyfriend Carl Manning. Both were sentenced in January 2001 to life imprisonment for her murder. Following their convictions, public horror about revelations of the prolonged sadistic abuse of Victoria, and the failure of several hospitals, police and social services to intervene effectively resulted in the establishment of a statutory public inquiry. In January 2003 the report of the inquiry chaired by Lord Laming was published (Laming 2003).

The Laming inquiry focused first on the specific role of agencies in their failure to protect Victoria, and in a second stage extended its remit to review the child protection system in England and Wales as a whole. The recommendations relating to the death of Victoria were depressingly familiar from the swathe of public inquiries and Part 8 Reviews that had preceded it: significant failures in the performance of individuals and agencies, confused interagency responsibilities and communication, and the absence of anyone's having a overview perspective of the accumulation of events.

High-profile child protection errors, such as those concerning Ainlee Labonte and Victoria Climbié, provoke public outrage that children continue to die in such grotesque ways as a consequence of the combination of parental sadism and false-negative child protection system failures. Yet, a puzzle remains regarding what raises the death of a particular child into a case with extensive media coverage. When sadistic child abuse is not in the news, children continue to be fatally abused in the context of child protection failures, as the following non-high-profile cases from our own research illustrate:

'James'

Child and family characteristics:
Baby boy aged 6 weeks. Natural parents both aged 17. First and only child.

Circumstances and official cause of death:
Post-mortem report: 'Extensive bruising to chest and buttocks, fractures to seven ribs plus a brain injury leading to fatal subdural haemorrhaging: most likely from shaking.'

Family and injury circumstances:
Father (aged 17) had experienced a traumatic and very disturbed childhood. He had demonstrated extremely violent behaviour as a child and adolescent, including physical assaults on teachers. Father was involved in violence with alcohol during pregnancy. No information given regarding mother's background.

A violent argument was observed between the parents during the delivery of baby. Father punched a hole in the wall outside the delivery room (fracturing a bone in his hand). James did not gain weight appropriately. Midwife and health visitor recorded concerns regarding poor hygiene. At age 3 weeks James was admitted to hospital via GP for concern regarding weight. James gained weight quickly while in hospital.

At age 5 weeks mother reported to her health visitor and GP that father had lost his temper with James and had put his hands round his throat on a couple of occasions. The social worker was informed. Two days later father told his GP that he has 'bad thoughts' about the baby – saying that he wished him dead sometimes. The following day a social worker visited but focused on the couple's accommodation problems, organising a small flat for father to 'give him some space'. Five days later father moved into bed-sitter. Mother and James however are observed to have moved there as well.

Three days later mother left father alone with James while she visited her mother. Less than one hour later father phoned for an emergency ambulance. James was found to be dead on arrival at hospital. Father was subsequently charged with his murder.

Part 8 Review conclusions regarding role of child protection agencies:
Part 8 Review was critical of social services for not calling a pre-birth child protection conference and for not commencing a child protection enquiry when the report was made about father putting his hand around James's throat. It was noted that the social worker was very newly qualified with no child protection experience whatsoever.

'Chloe'

Child and family characteristics:
Baby girl, died aged 6 months. First child of single mother, aged 20

Circumstances and official cause of death:
The final, fatal hospital admission was the culmination of four Accident and Emergency hospital attendances and two previous hospital admissions. History given of baby going pale and floppy while being fed and stopping breathing. Diagnosis of bi-lateral retinal haemorrhages (but no external signs of bruising or trauma). Chloe died when her life support system was switched off. Post-mortem findings were: death from head injury consistent with forceful impact onto a firm surface. Additional possibility of shaking contributing to the head injury.

Family and injury circumstances:
Social Services had extensive records of mental health and child protection concerns about mother when she was a child. The pregnancy was unplanned and mother was reported to be very apprehensive. Little family support. Concerns regarding finance and housing.

At age 3 weeks Chloe had been taken to hospital with a torn frenulum. The hospital paediatric department was not informed. No child protection referral was made to social services. At age four weeks mother told her health visitor and GP that baby Chloe was rejecting her and crying all the time. GP prescribed anti-depressants for post-natal depression. At age four months there was a second hospital Accident & Emergency attendance with a history given by mother of the baby having episodes of apnoea (stopping breathing).

Chloe was admitted to the paediatric unit and discharged the following day. Four days later she was readmitted to hospital by ambulance following a further reported apnoea attack. She was discharged later the same day without a follow-up appointment. The final, fatal hospital admission occurred six weeks later.

Mother was charged with murder and remanded to a psychiatric unit. At the time of the Part 8 Review she was considered mentally unfit to plead in relation to this charge.

Part 8 Review conclusions regarding role of child protection agencies:
Review was critical of community health services (midwifery, health visiting, GP) and hospital services (Accident & Emergency and Paediatric Department) for failure to assess whole picture; and for not referring to social services at key moments.

The review process was problematic particularly in respect of stated criticism of inaccuracies and contradictions in the health service management reports submitted to the review.

Part 8 Reviews (such as those into the deaths of James and Chloe) regularly (albeit with the benefit of hindsight) conclude that the deaths of the children concerned would have been preventable if warning signs had been recognised and acted on appropriately. Few readers will doubt that the parents of James and Chloe needed more systematic and effective support, and that both children were clearly in need of urgent protection from known risks prior to the fatal events. Interagency child protection practice needs to be much more consistent in the identification, protection and family assessment in cases such as those of James and Chloe to reduce the incidence and impact of false-negative errors.

UNDESIRABLE OUTCOMES OF CHILD PROTECTION INTERVENTIONS: FALSE-POSITIVE ERRORS

The other major unintended consequence of child protection interventions is the occurrence and nature of false-positive errors. These occur where it is wrongly believed that a child has been abused, or where the child protection intervention is disproportionate and inappropriate to the degree and nature of abuse. Profound irrevocable damage to children and families can result, as when children are permanently removed from their natural families on the basis of mistaken medical diagnoses and erroneous judicial 'findings of fact' regarding child abuse.

There are also cases where abuse has occurred, but the damage is compounded by harsh and sometimes draconian child protection interventions and outcomes. We mention as a particular concern the use of compulsory adoption in cases where there is a reasonable chance that with effective family support and therapeutic services the child could have been reunited with the natural family (or kinship network) with appropriate monitoring. Because findings of 'not guilty' in criminal child abuse cases rarely attract significant publicity, and as family proceedings courts are not open to members of the public or the press, it is unusual for details of false-positive cases to be available in the public domain. However, significant exceptions to this have been the following:

- the public judicial enquiry into the extensive misdiagnosis of sexual abuse in Cleveland in 1987/8
- the acquittal of Sally Clark on her second appeal in 2003 from the conviction for the murders of her two baby sons
- the acquittal on appeal of Angela Cannings in 2003 from the conviction for murder of her two baby sons
- the finding of 'not guilty' at the trial in 2003 of Trupti Patel, who was charged with the murder of her three babies
- three cases subject to public Court of Appeal judgments in July 2003.

Cleveland, England

In 1987/88 more than 100 children were removed from their parents by social services over a very brief period of time on the basis of mistaken diagnoses of sexual abuse by a team of paediatricians who believed over-confidently in a diagnostic procedure for sexual abuse that subsequently proved to be invalid. This provoked unprecedented public concern about inappropriate and disproportionate child protection interventions. In the UK, the place names of Cleveland, Rochdale, Orkney and Broxtowe in Nottingham became synonymous with false-positive child protection errors stemming from an era which was marked by the sudden emergence of a belief system where some professionals in certain areas began crusading in the search for sexual and 'ritualistic' abuse.

The resultant public judicial enquiry (DHSS 1988) highlighted the enormous harm caused to children and families by the nature and extent of these inappropriate and highly damaging false-positive child protection interventions. Readers in New Zealand will be aware of similar controversies surrounding the conviction of a children's day-care worker, Peter Ellis, in 1993 for sexual offences against children in the *Christchurch civic crèche* case. Major concerns continue about the potentially false-positive nature of much of the evidence that resulted in Ellis' conviction. These have been highlighted in the *New Zealand Law Journal*, and expounded in detail in a remarkable book, *A City Possessed* (Hood 2001).

Sally Clark

Two successive babies of solicitors Sally and Steve Clark died in the early weeks of their lives in 1996 and 1998, aged 11 and 8 weeks, respectively. In November 1999 Sally Clark was found guilty by majority verdicts of murdering both babies. She was sentenced to life imprisonment. In October 2000 the case was heard by the Court of Appeal. The Appeal Court judges accepted that expert-witness evidence presented by the prosecution at the original trial was now understood to be unreliable. This flawed evidence had stated that the statistical chance of two cot deaths occurring in the same family was 73 million to one. Nevertheless, the Appeal Court in 2000 rejected Sally Clark's first appeal, reasserting that there was other overwhelming evidence of her guilt.

In July 2002, the Criminal Cases Review Commission confirmed that it was sending the case back to the Court of Appeal for a second time, having been made aware of fresh evidence in relation to the original trial. The second Appeal Court heard that vital evidence from a pathologist (indicative of the deaths being due to meningitis) had been withheld from the original trial. Sally Clark's convictions for both murders were quashed at this second appeal in January 2003, and she was released after three years in prison. The book written by one of Sally Clark's solicitors, *Stolen Innocence*, provides a very informative account of the complex (false-positive) diagnostic and legal issues that were central to this case (Batt 2004).

Angela Cannings

In April 2002 at Winchester Crown Court, Angela Cannings was found guilty of the murder of her two baby sons. The first baby boy had died in 1991, aged 7 weeks; the second baby boy in 1999, aged 18 weeks. The jury was also aware that Angela Cannings's first child, a daughter, had died at the age of 3 months in 1989. The cause of death of her baby daughter had been recorded as sudden infant death syndrome (SIDS), and Mrs Cannings did not face any criminal charges in respect of her death.

In December 2003 the Court of Appeal overturned the convictions of Angela Cannings in relation to the murder of her two sons. Mrs Cannings and her family had always maintained that both boys had also died as a consequence of SIDS – not as a result of suffocation by Mrs Cannings, as the original jury had been persuaded. Giving reasons for the successful appeal, the court heavily criticised the nature of the expert evidence in favour of the prosecution at the trial. In particular, the original evidence of consultant paediatrician Professor Sir Roy Meadow was held by the appeal judges to have been 'simply wrong'. The essence of Meadow's evidence had reflected his theory about the incidence of cot deaths in families: 'one is a tragedy, two is suspicious, three is murder unless proven otherwise' (Meadow 1997). Reference in the appeal was also made to Meadow's statistical evidence given for the prosecution in the case of Sally Clark, that the chances of two babies dying of SIDS in the same family was one in 73 million. This evidence had been rejected in the Clark appeal.

Trupti Patel

In May 2002 (one month after the original conviction of Angela Cannings), pharmacist Trupti Patel was charged with the successive murders of three of her babies. A central part of the prosecution case was that the third baby to die was discovered to have several fractured ribs. It was alleged that these must have been caused by Mrs Patel squeezing and suffocating the baby. Several expert medical witnesses for the defence gave evidence that the rib fractures were more likely to have been caused by attempts at resuscitation. The prosecution also highlighted that the babies had died without a natural cause being found, despite extensive medical tests. A key defence witness was Mrs Patel's maternal grandmother, who gave evidence that five of her own 12 children had died without explanation in infancy. After a 6-week trial at Reading Crown Court ending in June 2003, the jury (no doubt very aware of the recent, successful second appeal by Sally Clark), took only 90 minutes to unanimously find Trupti Patel not guilty on each charge.

In the aftermath of the cases of Sally Clark, Angela Cannings and Trupti Patel, there has been much public concern about assumptions of murder in families where there have been multiple cot deaths. The role and the nature of medical expert-witness evidence has come under particular scrutiny. Following this sequence of acquittals, the government announced that it would review all cases of parents convicted of killing their children where evidence for the prosecution had been given by Professor Meadow. In January 2004 the government also announced that cases of civil proceedings in the family courts where children had been removed from families on the basis of such evidence would also be reviewed.

Court of Appeal Judgments, July 2003

Details of a further three false-positive cases, this time in the civil courts, were made available after Court of Appeal hearings and judgments issued on 31 July 2003. These cases are particularly significant, as they shed light on the judicial processes within Family Courts, which ordinarily are immune from public scrutiny. (There is a difference of view between those who regard the proceedings in the Family Court as being 'private' and those who regard them as being 'secret'.)

The legal issue at question in these three cases was whether parents and children could sue social services and health authorities in relation to psychiatric harm caused to them by erroneous accusations of abuse (the Appeal Court determined in favour of children but against parents on this question – this judgment was upheld in April 2005 by the House of Lords). However, for our purposes, it is the illustration of the confirmed false-positive nature of the cases that is particularly pertinent:

Case of JD

A mother, referred to as JD, claimed damages in relation to harm caused to herself though being diagnosed by a paediatrician as suffering from Munchausen's Syndrome by Proxy (MSBP). According to the paediatrician, the mother was exaggerating the symptoms of her child, and the child's condition was a case of illness fabricated by the mother. Eventually, following further medical investigations, it was determined and accepted by all parties that the nine-year-old child concerned was suffering from extensive and severe allergies. The child's name was consequently removed from the child protection register.

Case of MAK and RK

In this case a father and his nine-year-old daughter claimed damages for psychiatric injury and financial loss resulting from unfounded allegations that the father might have sexually abused his daughter. The erroneous allegation had resulted in the father being denied contact with his daughter for a short period of time. Following a minor accident (while riding a bicycle), the GP referred the child to the paediatrician at the local hospital. On examination the paediatrician concluded that the girl had been sexually abused and social services were informed. The child was detained in hospital for 10 days, with the father prohibited from visiting during this time. At the end of 10 days the diagnosis of Schamberg's disease (which produces discoloured skin patches) was made and it was accepted that there was no evidence of abuse. The implications of the allegation of abuse had had significant damaging ramifications for the father within his local Gujerati community.

Case of baby M

In this case, a mother and father issued a claim for damages for psychological distress having been wrongly accused of inflicting serious physical injury to their two-month-old daughter. At the age of two months, while being looked after by her grandmother, the baby began to scream and appeared to be in pain. She was taken to hospital where examination revealed an oblique displaced fracture of her left thigh. The consultant paediatrician concluded that this was an 'inflicted injury' and the police and social services were informed.

Care proceedings were brought in respect of the baby by the Local Authority and the judge hearing the case ruled that the injuries were not accidental. A Care Order was made and it was determined that the baby would be cared for by an aunt. Subsequently, at the age of eight months (while in the care of the aunt) the baby suffered bi-lateral femoral fractures (fractures to both legs). Subsequent medical investigations revealed that the baby was suffering from osteogenesis imperfecta, a bone condition which results in a predisposition to accidental fractures. On this basis an application for the revocation of the original care order was made and granted. Baby M was returned to the care of her parents after an absence of over nine months.

These three examples have been judicially determined to be false-positive child protection errors. In fact, such errors can have even more serious outcomes than is demonstrated by these examples. It is fortunate for 'baby M' and her family that she had been placed within her extended family following the making of the Care Order. Tragically, many other 'baby Ms' have been compulsorily and irrevocably adopted.

INEVITABILITY OF CHILD PROTECTION ERROR

We have emphasised that we are concerned with child protection errors of two types. Having illustrated the serious nature and tragic consequences of *both* false-positive and false-negative child protection errors, we find it salutary to recognise in child protection practice that a certain level of error is unavoidable. Human behaviour is inherently unpredictable, and human (professional) judgments are fallible. Fortunately, serious child abuse is a relatively rare event. When it occurs, it often stems from the interplay of relatively common personality, relational and social factors. Occasionally, and quite unpredictably, these combinations can suddenly become volatile.

In this context, given that a degree of child protection error is inevitable, the question arises: which type of error is preferable? This is a very uncomfortable ethical question which is rarely explicitly addressed by social and legal policy makers. To do so would require a statement as to what incidence of child abuse fatalities society is prepared to accept as 'normal' or tolerable. It would also require recognition of the levels of resources required to provide consistently effective preventive, identification, protection and support services for families and children. From the reverse perspective, the question arises as to what level of inappropriate enforced permanent separation of children from families (compulsory adoption) is acceptable in the greater interest of minimising false-negative tragedies. This latter dilemma is more explicitly reflected upon in criminal justice matters, where it is generally accepted that the balance of rules of evidence should be in favour of allowing a proportion of guilty people to be acquitted in the interests of minimising the greater injustice of wrongful convictions.

The ratio of false-positive errors to false-negative errors in child protection practice and criminal justice raises profound social and legal policy questions. Policies and laws to reduce false-negative errors (e.g. preventable re-abuse) invariably increase false-positive errors (e.g. unnecessary compulsory adoptions). Consequently, there will always be a ratio of errors, depending on prevailing political attitudes, social policies and interpretations of the law. However, it is a premise of this book that the general level of both types of error in child protection practice is inordinately high, and that with more consistent child protection practice and effective family support provision, there is definite scope for both types of error to be reduced.

3

CHILD ABUSE RESEARCH

Sadly, serious and fatal injuries to infants can be the result of abuse and mal-treatment. There is an extensive history of international research identifying family factors that are often associated with serious and fatal child abuse. In this chapter we shall focus on key issues arising from this literature that are particularly important when undertaking child protection assessments.

RESEARCH REVIEWS OF SAMPLES OF CHILD ABUSE DEATHS: 'RISK RESEARCH'

Research reviews of child abuse fatalities in the UK have developed through a sequence of studies of collections of statutory (sometimes public) inquiry reports, samples of clinical reports on offenders, and Part 8 Reviews under-taken in England and Wales by Area Child Protection Committees (ACPCs). The Department of Health in England and Wales is committed to publishing a biannual meta-review of all Part 8 Reviews undertaken in each successive 2-year period. The most recent such report was by Sinclair and Bullock (2002).

Internationally, reviews of fatal cases are undertaken via two main methods. In the USA and parts of Australia, Child Death Review Teams (CDRTs) review all child deaths and report on an annual basis with a summary of key findings relating to prevention (e.g. NSW CDRT 2004; Victoria CDRT 2004). In England and Wales (still lacking the benefits of a CDRT system), there have been a number of meta-reviews of statutory inquiries into child abuse deaths (e.g. Munro 1999; Reder et al. 1993); and samples of Part 8 Review reports (e.g. Reder & Duncan 1999; Sinclair & Bullock 2002). Scotland so far has not had a formal system for reviewing child abuse deaths, although devel-opment of such a system has been recommended (Scottish Executive 2002).

We shall refer to the group of studies of child abuse fatalities together as the 'risk research', intending in doing so to raise its profile in relation to the 'needs research' reflected in 'Messages from Research' (Department of

Table 3.1   Risk research studies

Samples of statutory inquiry reports	Samples of Part 8 Reviews	Samples of clinical reports
Department of Health (1991) Reder et al. (1993) Munro (1999, 2002)	James (1994) Falkov (1996) Sanders et al. (1999)	Resnick (1969) Scott (1973) Greenland (1980)
	Reder & Duncan (1999)	Wilczynski (1995, 1997)
	Arthurs & Ruddick (2001)	Stroud (1997)
	Dale et al. (2002a and b)	Fleming et al. (2000)
	Sinclair & Bullock (2002)	Stroud & Pritchard (2001)
		Dale et al. (2002a and b)

Health 1995), which underpins the Assessment Framework (Department of Health 2000). Our argument is that it is important for the 'risk research' to become better integrated within the Assessment Framework – a framework that curiously contains very little explicit perspective on risks of harm to children. The risk research studies we shall draw upon in this chapter and the next are listed in date order in three groups in Table 3.1.

KEY FINDINGS FROM RISK RESEARCH – FAMILY FACTORS

The risk research focuses on the factors and relationships within families that are found retrospectively to be closely associated with serious and fatal child abuse to infants. These can be grouped under the following headings:

● family structure
● child characteristics
● parent factors
● parental motivations for causing harm to the child
● the nature of the incident.

Family Structure

Research consistently indicates that it is the first baby, or the youngest child in a family, that is most susceptible to serious or fatal physical abuse. In the first year of life (and especially the early months), infants cannot avoid or escape from threatening situations and physiologically are most fragile in relation to the consequences of a physical assault. Apart from such vulner-abilities stemming from being the youngest, or only child, there is little in respect of family *structure* that is notably associated with serious physical risk to a young child. Fatal and serious abuse of infants occurs in families that have typical structures: either both natural parents living together, or an infant living with a single mother. Stepparents are not disproportionately implicated in the serious/fatal physical abuse of babies. Their role (particu-larly stepfathers) becomes more prominent in the abuse of older children – partly because the composition of families with toddlers and school-age children is more likely to include stepparents.

Child Characteristics

To what extent are the characteristics of infants themselves (sometimes referred to as *victim characteristics*) associated with a greater likelihood of being subject to serious harm by their parents? A general consensus from research indicates that infants who manifest combinations of the following characteristics may be more vulnerable to parental abuse:

- unwanted pregnancy
- born prematurely
- low birth weight
- only child or youngest child
- male
- illness/disability
- poor sleeping patterns
- poor feeding patterns
- propensity for prolonged, high-pitch screaming.

Infants with combinations of these characteristics may understandably be more 'difficult to rear' (Greenland 1980). However, it is often not easy to be clear what is cause and effect in terms of an infant being 'difficult', and the parents feeling inadequate, unrewarded and responding angrily – thereby provoking and sustaining the unsettled behaviour of the infant. Tragically, the 'difficult' behaviour of a baby can be the consequence of brain damage already sustained from an earlier assault (e.g. shaking), and this can be present without any external signs of injury. One peak age for the amount of crying by babies is 6–8 weeks (Barr 1990; Raiha etal. 2002). This also corres-ponds with the onset of post-natal depression and is a peak age for babies to be seriously harmed by their parents. Across fatality research studies, it is also clear that baby boys are consistently more likely to be seriously/fatally abused than baby girls – although there is no generally agreed understanding of why this is so.

Parent Factors

The parents of infants who sustain serious/fatal suspicious injuries are in the same age range as all parents: in general, they are not especially young parents. The most significant parental factors that arise are mental health concerns (including personality disorders and alcohol/substance abuse) and violence between parents. There is some inconsistency in terminology in research reports that have considered the significance of mental health problems of parents in relation to serious/fatal child abuse. Some use the term 'psychiatric disorder' to denote those parents who meet the criteria for psychiatric diagnoses in accordance with the two formal classification systems, *DSM-IV* (APA 1994) and *ICD-10* (World Health Organisation 1992). Others use the term 'significant mental health problems' in a wider sense that includes parents with such diagnostic conditions, as well as parents who manifest major emotional, relational and behavioural difficulties that do not meet formal psychiatric diagnostic criteria.

Psychiatric Disorder

There is a considerable research and literature base about the course of formal psychiatric disorders, their impact on parenting, the nature and level of risks they present, and the appropriateness of specific treatment and support/management strategies (Cassell & Coleman 1995; Fitzpatrick 1995). The major most relevant psychiatric conditions include: organic/neurological disorders, intellectual impairments, mood disorders (including post-natal depression), cognitive disorders, schizophrenia and other psychotic disorders (including puerperal psychosis), neurotic/anxiety disorders, personality disorders, dissociative disorders, substance-related disorders and impulse-control disorders (especially intermittent explosive disorder) (APA 1994).

All of these psychiatric conditions can have a considerable negative impact on the style and safety of parenting. The level of risk ('dangerousness') that stems from psychiatric disorders relates to history and mental state. Previous violence, substance misuse, poor compliance with (and recent discontinuation of) psychiatric treatment, recent severe stress and unstable lifestyles are high-risk indicators of repeated violence. With regard to mental state, high-risk factors are agitated, hostile, or suspicious behaviour; angry mood; thought disturbances (such as delusions of persecution/ jealousy); and auditory hallucinations (which issue commands). The prognosis for psychiatric disorders varies with diagnosis, previous history of recurrence, personality, social or family circumstances, and degree of compliance with recommended treatments (and their availability).

The psychiatrist Adrian Falkov was commissioned by the Department of Health to review 100 Part 8 Review reports exploring the significance of parental psychiatric disorder. His study found that one-third (32%) of the cases provided evidence of significant parental psychiatric illness. The parental psychiatric disorders included likely diagnoses of:

- psychosis – 40%
- depression – 20%
- personality disorder – 28%, including Munchausen's syndrome by proxy (8%).

Three-quarters of the parents with psychiatric disorders were the mothers of the children who were killed, and nearly 40% of them had had contact with adult psychiatric services in the month prior to the fatal incident. It was noteworthy that their utilisation and compliance with psychiatric services was variable and poor. Notwithstanding this, Falkov found that the level of participation by adult psychiatric services in interagency child protection practice was minimal (Falkov 1996).

The academic psychiatric social workers Julia Stroud and Colin Pritchard have also researched the relationship of parental psychiatric disorder to child homicide. Stroud & Pritchard (2001) reviewed psychiatric reports in the UK concerning 68 adults (42 female) who were charged with killing or attempting to kill a child. While asserting that the 'vast majority of psychiatrically disturbed people pose no threat to their children', the authors echoed Falkov's conclusion that adult psychiatric services often overlook the welfare of the children of their patients. They also highlighted that in general most social workers are inadequately trained in relation to psychiatric issues. In most social services departments, 'child protection workers are unlikely to have adequate knowledge and experience of mental disorder to undertake the difficult and demanding risk assessments required' (Stroud & Pritchard 2001, p. 263).

It is particularly important that assessments are multidisciplinary with families where a serious suspicious injury to an infant has occurred in the context of a parent with a formal psychiatric illness. It is vital, for example, that social workers understand the significance of future risks related to particular psychiatric diagnoses (and also the impact on parenting abilities of psychiatric conditions and medications). It is equally vital that psychiatrists understand the psychosocial context of the patient/parent insofar as this contributes important stressors, or buffers, regarding precipitating factors for psychiatric illnesses.

In the graphic context of child abuse tragedies, it is important to highlight that the vast majority of parents with formal psychiatric disorders do not cause harm to their children (Stroud & Pritchard 2001). Multidisciplinary mental health services are continually working to assist and support parents with mental illnesses of many forms to care appropriately for their children. Undoubtedly, such services ensure that unknown numbers of children who might otherwise be adversely affected do not come to significant harm.

Post-natal Depression

There are three noted forms of depression that can affect mothers after childbirth: 'baby blues', post-natal depression and post-natal psychosis (also referred to as 'puerperal depression'). Baby blues is so common that it is considered a normal (but unpleasant) transient reaction to childbirth. Symptoms include being weepy and irritable with low mood, starting around the third day after the birth, and lasting usually for about 1 week before resolving. Informal support, reassurance and rest are indicated, and medical, psychological or psychotherapeutic treatment is not required.

Post-natal depression develops within 2–6 weeks after giving birth, and affects up to 15% of new mothers within 1 year of their child's birth (Warner et al. 1996). Symptoms are more pronounced and prolonged than with 'baby blues' and include combinations of low mood, continual tearfulness, irritability, feelings of rejection and aggression toward the baby, feelings of guilt and inadequacy, and poor concentration. These symptoms are likely to have a significantly deleterious impact on the developing bond with the baby, may impair parenting skills and commitment, and adversely affect family relationship and general ability to cope with life. Other factors such as ambivalence about having a baby, traumatic birth experience, relationship tensions and lack of support can exacerbate the condition. Some mothers deny their inner desperate feelings to significant others (and often to themselves) and therefore do not receive adequate support or seek necessary help. Post-natal depression can be a significant contributory factor to 'out of character' impulsive and aggressive responses to a baby. As this period coexists with a peak incidence for babies' crying, this potent, stressful combination may overwhelm coping mechanisms. Consequently, post-natal depression can contribute to high-risk situations, and medical and psychotherapeutic interventions are necessary: a combination of antidepressant medication and counselling is most effective (Puri 1995).

Post-natal/puerperal psychosis is a very serious, acute condition that is fortunately rare; it affects approximately one in every 1000 pregnancies. The onset is rapid (usually at 3–14 days after birth), and the psychotic symptoms include confusion, delirium, hallucinations, irrational behaviour and suicidal thoughts. Delusions relating to the baby may occur. These can create severe risk, as the delusional thinking may involve the baby having to be killed either for his/her own protection (psychotic altruism) or because the baby is misperceived as a threat to the parent. Psychiatric inpatient treatment (sometimes in the mother–baby unit) is usually indicated for post-natal psychosis, and the prospects for full recovery can be very good.

Personality Disorders

In stressing the need for child protection workers to have improved levels of psychiatric understanding, Stroud & Pritchard (2001) emphasised the importance of including specific knowledge of the impact of personality disorders. As defined in ICD-10 (WHO 1992), personality disorders are 'deeply ingrained and enduring behavioural patterns manifesting as inflexible responses to a broad range of personal and social situations'. People with serious personality disorders (especially the 'dissocial', 'psychopathic' or 'sociopathic' types) demonstrate a range of distinct psychological and behavioural features (Puri 1995). These include combinations of the following: distortions in perceptions of themselves; impaired emotional expression; inhibited impulse control; frequent outbursts of aggression; lack of empathy, remorse and conscience; highly manipulative and exploitative behaviour; and inability to have successful sustained relationships. These disturbances are expressed in behaviours that appear more dramatic than the social norm and often result in significant interpersonal conflict.

It is estimated that 10% of the general population is affected by some form of personality disorder (Cordess 2003). Falkov (1996) reported that 28% of the parents in his sample of fatal abuse had an identifiable personality disorder. A generation earlier, Steele and colleagues (Steele & Pollock 1968) had concluded that 5–10% of abusing parents possess personality disorders of such severity that they are likely to abuse children repeatedly and cruelly. As can be deduced from some of the graphic examples in Chapter 2, parents with such personality disorders are likely to be responsible for the most violent and sadistic child killings. They can pose particular challenges (including intimidation and violence) to child protection workers. They and their children rarely benefit from a 'lighter touch'.

Mental Health Problems Without Formal Psychiatric Disorder

One of the most challenging problems that arises in assessments is the presence of concerns about parental mental health that do not appear to meet criteria for formal psychiatric diagnosis. A well-reported assessment error in such situations is to conclude that the absence of a formal psychiatric disorder means that the level of risk is not as high as it otherwise might be. As several studies have highlighted (Falkov 1996; Reder et al. 1993), parents can demonstrate alarming levels of attitudinal, emotional, relational and behavioural disturbances without fitting into any formal psychiatric diagnostic category. Predicting future behaviour and outcomes in such a situation can be harder than with parents who have formal psychiatric disorders (Gallwey 1997).

Such problems include grossly inconsistent attitudes toward others (e.g. children, partners and professionals); highly unpredictable hostile behaviour; significant emotional lability, flatness or incongruity; lack of impulse control (frequent physical and verbal aggression); disabling apathy; substance misuse; and suicide attempts and self-harming. These behaviours impact negatively on adult and parenting relationships, contribute to domestic violence, and affect the nature of parents' relationships with professionals. In one memorable case in the NSPCC research (to be discussed in Chapter 5), a mother who had set herself on fire in front of her children was diagnosed as having 'no formal psychiatric disorder'. We reiterate the conclusions of Reder & Duncan (1999): it is parental behaviour, rather than psychiatric diagnosis or lack of it, that is the key child protection assessment factor. Consequently, psychiatric assessments must be complemented by risk assessments focused on the psychosocial context of parental behaviour, and the potential for change regarding these concerns.

Alcohol/Substance Abuse

A 4-week-old baby was found dead in bed by a family friend next to both parents who were deep in heroin-induced sleep. The baby had been born with opiate withdrawal symptoms and had only been home in parents' care for two days following discharge from hospital. Official cause of death was given as Sudden Infant Death Syndrome (SIDS) which seems questionable given the context of major concerns (especially parental drug usage) revealed in the Part 8 enquiry. The Part 8 Review concluded that this death was preventable and social services had failed to act protectively despite expressed medical concerns. The case had been designated as 'child in need'.

At age 4 weeks a baby boy was found dead by his parents. Initial post-mortem findings were indicative of cot death. Several weeks later toxicology reports revealed large amounts of heroin and distalgesic in the baby's blood. Both parents were charged with murder and eventually (half-way through trial) pleaded guilty to manslaughter. The baby had been placed on the child protection register at birth in relation to serious pre-natal concerns including parental mental health issues, domestic violence and emotional neglect of two siblings. However, care and development of the baby prior to death was consistently noted to be good throughout regular observations, and agencies had no knowledge or suspicion of parental use of non-prescribed drugs.

These two cases from the NSPCC research (discussed in Chapter 5) illustrate the presence of a significant pattern of alcohol/substance abuse sometimes featured in cases of severe child maltreatment and neglect. Assessment of this factor will affect decisions regarding reunification and outcomes (Coleman & Cassell 1995; Terling 1999). The effects of substance misuse relevant to child welfare and abuse can include the following:

● parental disinhibition and poor impulse control (e.g. poor tolerance of frustration, violent outbursts)
● distorted parental perceptions and cognitions (e.g. lack of awareness of impact on child, lack of empathy)
● parental mood dysfunction/swings (ranging across depression, agitation, panic and manic to euphoria)
● impact on parental memory (e.g. poor recall of behaviour and events – including violence – when intoxicated)
● parental preoccupation with immediate adult needs (e.g. lack of attention to child's needs and routine)
● inadequate supervision of child (e.g. child left alone or supervised by unsuitable others; or parent(s) unconscious)
● parental preoccupation and dependence on drug/alcohol subculture (e.g. exposure of child to disinhibited, disturbed and criminal behaviour of a range of adults)
● dangerous criminal activity and high-risk prostitution to obtain money for supplies
● degeneration of parental self-care that affects care of child and household
● deliberate or accidental ingestion of parents' drugs by child (e.g. through lack of supervision or intentionally administered to subdue the demands of the child).

Much of this behaviour and its effects can be concealed from child protection workers. Parental denials of the extent and effects of their substance misuse can be highly plausible yet contrast markedly with reality. This is a very difficult issue to assess from a child protection standpoint. Children of many parents who use, and misuse, substances do not come to great harm. Substance misuse in itself is not predictive of serious child abuse. However, when it is known to have been a factor in previous abuse or significant neglect, it must be considered as a potential indicator of risk of recurrence. Courts can now order hair strand toxicology tests, which are a valuable way of confirming (and disconfirming) parental self-reports about drug use and abstinence.

Domestic Violence

Some infants are killed or seriously injured in the context of violent family relationships – especially violence between their parents. This is referred to in the literature as intimate partner violence or domestic violence. A body of research evidence suggests that there can be a strong association between domestic violence and child abuse (Hester et al. 2000; Sturge 2000). Edleson (1999) reviewed 35 studies which examined both child abuse and domestic violence, finding an 'overlap' between the two types of violence of 30–60% in a majority of the studies. Cleaver et al. (1998) noted that at the point of referral to social services, domestic violence was recorded in 27% of child protection cases, rising to 51% in cases that became subject to care proceedings. Similar findings were made by Farmer and Owen (1995) and Brandon and Lewis (1996). Three studies of child fatalities recorded domestic violence in just under one-third of cases (Reder & Duncan 1999), in at least one-half of cases (Reder et al. 1993), and in two-thirds of cases (Sinclair & Bullock 2002).

Is domestic violence predominantly a manifestation of unidirectional violence directed at women by men, or is the expression of conflict within intimate relationships a more complex and multivariate process? This is a contentious issue which can give rise to significant bias and errors in child protection assessments (Sturge 2000). A feminist stance construes domestic violence as almost exclusively male to female (Dobash & Dobash 1992).

Other research has noted that fathers involved in domestic violence are rarely effectively engaged in a constructive way by professionals, who tend to focus individually on the mothers in the family (Farmer & Owen 1995; O'Hagan 1997). Stanley & Goddard (2002) reflected that as, increasingly, most front-line child protection professionals are women, actual (or feared) intimidation could result in fathers being avoided in such situations from feelings of personal discomfort or lack of safety. Consequently, male accounts of the dynamics of intimate partner violence tend to be unheard.

Most experienced child protection practitioners will be familiar with cases where mothers have serial, mutually aggressive relationships with men of established violent histories. Fatal case reviews often note backgrounds of serious domestic violence involving mutually provocative and retaliatory behaviour by both parents, including repeated separations and reconciliations. In these cases, repeated reconciliations are often mystifying and dismaying to child protection workers when they have invested considerable commitment and resources in assisting mothers to separate from violent partners and to establish themselves as single parents. For children, it results in highly disturbed lifestyles and confused attachments in unpredictable violent environments to which, sometimes, social workers appear to have become resigned or desensitised.

Child protection assessment errors can arise when there is inadequate professional recognition and understanding that women can and do initiate serious violence to their adult partners and children. Generally, research on domestic violence (see Tomison 2000, for a thorough review) tends to ignore the type of situation we are drawing attention to in which women have a significant role in either initiating, reciprocating or escalating physical expression of conflict in relationships. However, Archer (2000) recently drew attention to the actively violent female role in some dynamics of intimate partner violence.

Many years ago, the founder of Chiswick Women's Refuge, Erin Pizzey, noted that 62% of women seeking refuge in a domestic violence shelter were in fact as violent as the partner they had just left (Pizzey 1982). These important findings were (and remain) deeply unpopular in the domestic violence 'movement', from which Ms Pizzey was unceremoniously excommunicated (Pizzey 1998). Pizzey's experiences have more recent support from O'Keefe (1995), who found, in a study conducted in a women's refuge, that 35% of the children had been abused within the past 12 months by both parents. More research is needed to understand the complexities of intimate partner violence, particularly in respect of potential for change – and the most effective interventions to promote this.

Parents Who Were Abused as Children

A major retrospective prevalence study into levels of child abuse in the UK was undertaken by the NSPCC at the end of the 1990s (Cawson et al. 2000). The results revealed that 7% of children suffer serious physical abuse, 6% serious neglect, 6% serious emotional abuse and 4% serious sexual abuse by a parent or relative. These figures are much lower than expected from previous prevalence studies.

Retrospective research and clinical material suggest that approximately 70% of parents who seriously harm their own children were themselves abused as children (Dale & Fellows 1999; Oliver 1993). It is important not to misinterpret this figure. It does *not* mean that 70% of people who were abused as children *will* abuse their children in some form of 'intergenerational transmission of abuse'. The small number of relevant studies estimate that approximately 30% of abused children will eventually become abusing parents (Egeland 1988; Kaufman & Zigler 1987).

There is a significant research base (and not inconsiderable controversy) regarding the nature and extent of consequences in adult life for people who were abused as children:

> Research demonstrates that significant lasting problems are most likely for people who experienced chronic multiple abuse, beginning at an early age in the context of a significantly dysfunctional family. While no symptoms or clusters of adult problems are specific to childhood abuse, extensive empirical and clinical material highlights clear categories of difficulties that are likely to be experienced by people who were seriously abused as children. These include psychiatric symptoms (especially depression) and a range of physical, cognitive, existential, relational, sexual and social problems. (Dale 2002a, p. 37)

This often presents a crucial and challenging aspect of assessments of parents when serious suspicious injuries to infants occur (Dale & Fellows 1999). The continuing consequences of their own childhood abuse can contribute to parents experiencing serious depression, substance misuse, preoccupation with their own extensive, unmet emotional needs, and tendency to form short-lived, impulsive, intimate relationships. They may also be particularly suspicious of and hostile towards professionals. Given sufficient motivation, problems in parenting for adults who were abused as children is an area where significant positive changes are sometimes possible (Dale 1999, 2002a). However, the poignant question often arises in court cases of whether the timescale needed for parental change and maturation is in keeping with the infant's need for stable and secure parenting arrangements to promote optimal attachments and development.

Parents Who Have Adverse Experiences of Being Brought Up in 'Care'

There are particularly poignant cases of young parents brought up in care following abuse and neglect by their own parents who cause serious harm to their own infants by maltreatment or neglect. While many young parents were significantly emotionally damaged by the abuse and neglect they experienced in their families before being taken into care, some cases present damning indictments of the additional harm that can be done to children and young people in inadequate care systems involving multiple, inappropriate and sometimes abusive placements.

Few adults are more bitter than those who have experienced serious and chronic abuse and neglect within their families, only to be neglected and sometimes maltreated in 'care'. In an independent assessment undertaken by the first author, the father's level of detestation of social services was vehement (all names changed):

Mr Aubrey's most negative feelings in relation to his disturbed childhood are focused on social services. There is considerable depth of feeling in his resentment of the way he was dealt with by social services as a child. He feels that his career in the 'care system' involved significant lack of recognition of his needs, and lack of professional skill and commitment to help him appropriately. He resents that (despite a good level of innate intelligence) his skills in reading and writing are not good. He is bitter at being confined to a secure unit for three months at age 13. . . . It is in the context of a long history of dissatisfaction with the role of social services in his life that Mr Aubrey does not conceal his lack of confidence and trust in relation to the fairness of social services' interventions and intentions in relation to baby Aaron. The couple feel that the approach of the social workers toward them in the recent social services assessment has been one of negative pre-judgment.

This assessment begged the crucial question of whether the lack of cooperation of the parents reflected a generalised avoidance of scrutiny indicative of intent to conceal real risk factors, or whether it was specific to the relationship with social services. To what extent was Mr Aubrey unreasonably hostile to social services, or was his behaviour understandable (and reasonable) given the history and the way in which social services had approached their task? The assessment concluded:

It seems clear that an effective working relationship has not been achieved between the social workers and Mr Aubrey and Ms Jones. The Core Assessment report does not take into account ways in which the highly contentious relationship between the parents and social services may have affected the parents' responses to the social workers' interventions. In essence, the social workers were key players in one of the dynamics they were attempting to assess (the willingness of Mr Aubrey and Ms Jones to cooperate with social services; but the report does not indicate any recognition of this, or include any comment on ways in which the social workers attempted to improve the difficult relationship with the couple. In such circumstances the (perceived negative) style of social services interventions can create unnecessary levels of anxiety for parents and reinforce hostility and non-cooperation; as opposed to providing the encouragement and support that well-motivated young parents from disadvantaged backgrounds can often significantly benefit from.

Social workers who have the unenviable task of assessing the safety of infants, at times face the wrath of vulnerable, agitated, petrified and sometimes highly unstable parents whose competence, self-esteem and family survival are being threatened by (in their experience) the very people who did not provide for them properly during their own childhood in 'care'. The imminent threat of or actual removal of their own infant into the same system that damaged the parents so badly can generate an abhorrence of social workers that sometimes can escalate to a dangerous level. Management support and attention to necessary and appropriate health and safety strategies for social workers in such circumstances are vital. However, it does not help if the interventions are unskilled, patronising and provocative. When such levels of feelings are aroused, assessments independent of social services can be particularly helpful in enabling parents to take a less hostile and oppositional stance.

Parental Motivations for Causing Harm to the Infant

There is a fascinating history of forensic research into motives for murders and other unlawful killings, including fatal child abuse (e.g. d'Orban 1979; Resnick 1969; Scott 1973; Wilczynski 1997). Establishing the motives of people who kill other people is a complex research and legal challenge. To what extent is it valid to rely on self-reports of offenders as to what their intentions and motivations were? To what extent will such self-reports be accurate? Or is it inevitable that they will be consciously or unconsciously reconstructed over time due to subsequent influences and interests? This is particularly likely to be an issue in criminal proceedings, where the chance of conviction (and type and length of sentence) may be substantially influenced by the cogency of accounts regarding motive and degrees of intent and responsibility.

Research studies provide typologies of parental motivations for killing children that are valuable in highlighting the variety of psychosocial circumstances that may lie behind such tragedies. One thorough review of motives was provided by the Australian criminologist Ania Wilczynski. Wilczynski (1997) undertook three detailed reviews into the unlawful deaths of 95 children (in the UK and Australia), using documents made available by the crown prosecutor (now called the Crown Prosecution Service) in the UK, and a Child Death Review Team and the Judicial Commission in Australia. Building on previous research into motives, Wilczynski outlined the following 10-point classification. The percentage figure in brackets records the primary established motivation in Wilczynski's UK study into the deaths of 48 children:

- unwanted child (27%)
- retaliatory killing (21%)
- parental psychosis (19%)
- discipline (12.5%)
- jealousy of or rejection by the victim (8%)
- altruism (8%)
- munchausen syndrome by proxy (2%)
- unknown motive (2%)

- killings secondary to sexual or ritual abuse (0%)
- no intent to kill or injure (0%).

From this sample of cases where parents faced criminal prosecution, the most frequently identified parental motives for killing a child were the *child being unwanted*; the killing being motivated by *retaliation*; and parental mental illness involving *psychosis*. (It is likely that these results would be different in samples of cases where criminal charges were not brought – for example, the 'no intent to kill or injure' rate would certainly be higher.)

Killing an unwanted child is most specifically a maternal motivation (Spinelli 2003). All of the nine neonaticides (killing of a baby within 24 hours of birth) in Wilczynski's study were killed by their mothers. Wilczynski notes that 'denial and concealment of the pregnancy is a classic feature of neonaticides' (p. 49). Of the four older unwanted children in her study, three were killed by their mothers. The circumstances of conception, the planned or unplanned nature of a pregnancy, and the personal and family implications of having a child highlight the importance of the findings of Peter Reder and colleagues relating to understanding the meaning of the child for the parents (Reder & Duncan 1999; Reder et al. 1993). The motivation for intentionally killing a child is inextricably linked with the particular meaning of the child for the parent and family concerned.

The second most common motive reported by Wilczynski – that of the killing being an expression of retaliatory feelings toward the child – has been described in a long history of psychiatric research (e.g. d'Orban 1979; Scott 1973). One parent kills a child in an act intended to hurt or 'punish' the other parent, as in the context of severe relationship disharmony, sexual infidelity, threats to leave the relationship, or separations from a relationship. For example:

> Two girls died in a car driven and deliberately crashed by their father who had driven off telling his wife that he intended to kill himself and the three children following an intense marital row. In fact the father was uninjured, and the third child recovered after major surgery. The father was convicted of two offences of manslaughter and sentenced to four years imprisonment. (Dale et al. 1986, p. 173)

> A former soldier who stabbed his two sons to death with a screwdriver 'to teach his wife a lesson she would never forget' was jailed for life yesterday. Steven Wilson, 44, murdered Brad, seven, and Brett, eight, in revenge for his wife's decisions to end their violent marriage... (*Daily Telegraph*, 26/03/2003; one week later Wilson committed suicide in prison)

In Wilczynski's study, the sex ratio of perpetrators of retaliatory child killings was 60% male, 40% female. Other child deaths occur in the context of severe parental psychotic illness. In this context the meaning of the child can become significantly distorted. For example, the child may be misperceived as a malevolent force that, for parental self-preservation, has to be extinguished. Or, similarly intense paranoid delusions may lead the child to be misperceived as facing such a level of threat and adversity in the world that death is the best form of protection for the child. This latter perspective has a (distorted) altruistic motivation; that is, the intent of the parent at the time is 'mercy killing'. Research into child deaths in the context of parental psychotic illness indicates that both mothers and fathers can be susceptible to this.

It is important to reiterate that risks remain during the course of psychiatric recovery. In cases of suicidal depression, the risk of suicide actually occurring is at its peak when the depression begins to lift (as the person has greater volition to carry out the suicidal intent). The same is true in cases where the parent has psychotic delusions about harming their child. We are aware of one tragic case of a mother, admitted to a psychiatric hospital with puerperal depression, who several times stated that she feared she would kill her children. In hospital, her mood improved in response to treatment, and she was considered well enough to be discharged. Shortly after returning home, she drowned her twin infants.

Finally, on the question of motive, some serious and fatal assaults occur in the context of offenders having high levels of psychological disorientation where there is significant confusion and little awareness of events (or motive) at the time (Porter et al. 2001). As we shall discuss in some detail in Chapter 7, such disorientation may occur due to neurological (e.g. epilepsy/organic amnesic states) and/or psychological processes (such as psychogenic amnesia/dissociation), or as a consequence of intoxication (McLeod et al. 2004).

The Nature of the Incident

A number of relevant points have arisen from research which has focused on the context and dynamics of the violent incident itself. For example, there are indications that the circumstances and methods of killing of children by male and female parent/carers are generally somewhat different. Fatal assaults by women are more likely to involve asphyxiation, strangulation, poisoning, burning and neglect. Killings by men tend to be assaults with fists, swinging by limbs and shaking (Falkov 1996; Greenland 1980; Wilczynski 1997). According to Wilczynski's analysis, the methods used by women indicate a clearer specific intent to kill, more so than attacks by men (where death or survival may be more a matter of chance). It has been argued that *motive* rather than *severity* of injury is the key assessment factor, as the latter can be significantly affected by chance factors (Southall et al. 2003).

Falkov (1996) contrasted the methods of killing between cases where parents had a formal psychiatric disorder and those who did not, reporting greater incidence of asphyxia, use of implements, poisoning and drowning in the former group. Reder & Duncan (1999) and Pritchard & Stroud (2002) concluded that such types of killings of children by severely mentally ill parents are qualitatively different from other forms of fatal child abuse. While fatality research supports the finding that infants aged 0–12 months are at greatest risk, it is also the case that where parents have psychiatric illness, the risk age for children in the families extends for several years beyond the first birthday (Falkov 1996; Reder et al. 1993; Stroud & Pritchard 2001).

Combinations of the child, parent and family factors discussed in this chapter are often identified retrospectively in investigations of child abuse deaths. In many assessments relating to potential reunification (or future children) they will be key issues to be explored. However, it is important to stress that these factors in themselves are not accurate and reliable predictors of abuse. Nor does their presence (even in significant combinations) prove that the cause of a suspicious injury or death was abuse. It is a fundamental mistake to assume that because, say, such factors are found in 75% of fatal abuse cases, that in 75% of families with such factors a child will be abused. To make this assumption generates an extremely high level of false-positive identifications.

4

CHILD PROTECTION RESEARCH

Five main areas of research are relevant to understanding the effectiveness of child protection interventions with infants who have sustained suspicious serious injuries. We shall focus on four of these in this chapter:

- studies which focus on the process and outcomes of general child protection practice in relation to large samples of referrals to social services
- research into the processes and outcomes of care proceedings in the family courts
- studies that analyse problems in interagency communication and professional practice in cases that have had fatal outcomes
- research that identifies successful and unsuccessful outcomes in relation to reunification and re-injury rates.

The fifth area of research into child protection system processes and outcomes – that which focuses on eliciting and analysing family perceptions of child protection interventions – is discussed in Chapter 6 of this book.

ANALYSES OF GENERAL CHILD PROTECTION PRACTICE

The most substantial collection of studies focused on the processes and outcomes of large samples of child protection/welfare referrals to social services was commissioned in England and Wales by the Department of Health, following public concerns about overcoercive child protection practice revealed by the inquiry into the events in Cleveland in 1987 (DHSS 1988). It is this collection of studies (e.g. Farmer & Owen 1995; Gibbons et al. 1995; Thoburn et al. 1995) that informed the policy of 'refocusing' promoted in the UK government summary publication *Child Protection: Messages from Research*

(Department of Health 1995). This publication generally highlighted the false-positive aspect of child protection practice in that too many families needing support were being drawn unnecessarily into formal child protection procedures. Once caught in the child protection 'net', many families were damaged by the experience, and in fact often still did not receive the help that they required. *Messages from Research* summarised these findings as follows: 'The emphasis on abuse was too great in many cases dealt with under a child protection banner, especially as one third of families were well known to social workers and could be approached without the spectre of child abuse being raised' (Department of Health 1995, p. 35).

Consequently, it was concluded that the threshold for entry into the child protection system was too low, and that in general a 'lighter touch' policy was needed to *refocus* formal child protection interventions on the more serious cases. In the interests of encouraging child protection systems to focus more specifically on abused children to minimise false-positive identifications (and wasted resources), this makes much sense.

Unfortunately, the *Messages* research programme methodology and analysis did not attend equally to the need for child protection interventions to become more consistent and specifically effective with actual cases of serious abuse which do need to be in the child protection system. In this chapter we are particularly interested in what these studies tell us (and do not tell us) about risk factors associated with serious physical abuse, and about child protection outcomes – especially successful reunification and re-injury rates.

PROCESSES AND OUTCOMES OF CARE PROCEEDINGS IN THE FAMILY COURTS

> We have to do something. It's unbearable the research that shows how badly children have done in care. (lawyer, in Hunt & Macleod 1999, p. 228)

In the court arena, child protection practice involves the interplay of two distinct professional cultures and traditions (King & Trowell 1992):

- law, policing and justice
- the various 'helping' professions (e.g. psychiatry, psychology, social work, counselling/psychotherapy).

The predominant culture of law and justice is *dichotomous*: lawyers and the judiciary search for certainties, consistency, regularity, predictability, linear development and identification of individual responsibility (Coles & Veiel

2001). In contrast professionals with a change-promoting purpose are accustomed to working in a *continuous* culture: contexts of uncertainty, contradiction, ambivalence, ambiguity, intuition, dynamic development and diffuse responsibilities. Consequently, the courtroom is not natural territory for most therapeutic professionals, and it can feel uncomfortable, alien, undermining and occasionally intimidating (Wall 2000).

Several publications have addressed the need for legal systems and therapeutic systems to work more effectively together in ways that produce better outcomes for cases that end up in courts. There is a need to halt an identified process where therapeutic professionals are increasingly reluctant to become involved in forensic work because of the unpleasant nature of the experience (Brophy & Bates 1998; King & Trowell 1992). This is not to say that therapeutic culture cannot benefit from utilising some of the specific principles of legal practice. For example, some major therapeutic misadventures of recent times might have been avoided or minimised if therapeutic practice had been more firmly rooted in the *rights* of patients/clients, and the need to have *evidence* to justify the likely benefits of certain approaches (Dale 1999; Pendergrast 1995).

Cases of serious suspicious injuries to infants are highly likely to result in care proceedings initiated by local authorities. What, then, is known from research about the processes and outcomes of care proceedings in family courts? Unfortunately, there have been no studies focused specifically on legal proceedings relating to seriously injured infants (and their present and future siblings). However, there are several important publications that inform us about key process and outcome issues in care proceedings relating to *general* serious childcare concerns. We shall discuss a selection of this material; first, issues arising from five judicial studies conferences held between 1995 and 2003, and second, some specific studies of samples of families subject to care proceedings.

Judicial Studies Conferences

Between 1995 and 2003, a series of conferences held at Dartington were sponsored jointly by the Judicial Studies Board and the Department of Health. These events brought together senior figures in the legal establishment and nationally prominent therapists (mostly psychiatrists and psychologists with experience of forensic work), all of whom had an active and shared interest in legal proceedings affecting children and families. The proceedings of these conferences are referred to in the following titles: *Rooted Sorrows* (Wall 1997), *Divided Duties* (Thorpe & Clarke 1998), *No Fault or Flaw* (Thorpe et al. 2000), *Delight and Dole* (Thorpe & Cowton

2002) and *Hearing the Children* (Thorpe & Cadbury 2004). These publications provide a fascinating insight into the complex interaction between legal and psychotherapeutic culture and practice, in the context of a shared aim to increase mutual understanding and establish a clearer and more effective role for therapeutic insights and input into court proceedings concerning children. Issues discussed at the conferences included the function of expert witnesses, the role of courts in ordering necessary assessments, the non-implementation of care plans, and the impact of the Human Rights Act 1998. These discussions had a significant influence on the development of judicial policy, and even on judgments in subsequent individual cases.

One criticism of the Dartington conferences, however, is that the 'therapeutic' contribution was significantly dominated by a *psychoanalytic psychotherapy* perspective (Waller 1997). The fact that this was so is both disappointing and ironic, as (invariably long-term) psychoanalytic psychotherapy is possibly one of the least suited approaches to promoting positive change with parents and families in relation to the often raised criterion in courts of the 'child's timescale'. It is also theoretically abstruse, highly susceptible to the intuition (bias) of the therapist, and almost totally devoid of empirical evaluation. Judging by the contributions to these five conferences, it may still be the case that the judiciary remains overdeferential to psychoanalytically derived assessment and opinion, and insufficiently informed about the wide range of other, more evidence-based therapeutic and psychosocial interventions. This issue is discussed further in Chapter 9, 'Potential for Change'.

In addition to the informative Dartington conference proceedings, there are three specific research studies which focus on the processes and outcomes of care proceedings in the family courts. We shall select key issues from each of these studies in turn.

The Last Resort (Hunt et al. 1999)

This was a large-scale study of nearly 200 cases proceeding through the civil courts both before and after the implementation of the Children Act 1989 (in October 1991). Prior to October 1991, many of the most serious child abuse cases were dealt with under wardship jurisdiction, which, crucially, enabled judges to retain control of local authorities' actions regarding children subsequent to the conclusion of proceedings (as the child remained a ward of court). As we shall see, the inability of courts under the Children Act 1989 to review and direct local authority care plans for children subject to care orders has become and remains a matter of significant concern. This study discussed the following problems in the operation of the court system:

- Social services assessment reports for courts were often inadequate – being overdescriptive with minimal analysis.
- Some families were involved in legal proceedings prematurely, and some families were involved much too late in proceedings.
- The rights of children and parents were much better protected within the legal system than they were within the welfare system (that is to say, in cases that did not go to court but were handled on the superficially attractive basis of the 1989 act philosophy of 'partnership' – which, however, denied parents the right to legal representation and the child access to a guardian *ad litem*).
- Major problems were identified with resources for court time, and in relation to the undertaking of assessments for courts.

The Best-Laid Plans (Hunt & Macleod 1999)

Joan Hunt's second study focused on post-Children Act (1989) cases that were subject to applications to courts from local authorities for care or supervision orders. The sample comprised 131 children from 81 families. Records pertaining to each case were reviewed 3 years after the conclusion of the court proceedings to establish follow-up outcomes. Consequently, the aim of the research was 'to ascertain and document what happens to children subject to care proceedings after the court has made its final decision' (Hunt & Macleod 1999, p. 7). A wide range of child protection concerns were included, and cases involving serious injuries to infants cannot be distinguished. Nevertheless, there are important findings that clearly do apply to this age group, particularly in relation to changes in care plans and placement breakdowns.

Changes in Care Plans

To what extent are social services' care plans that are presented to, and ultimately approved by, courts actually implemented? Are the planned placements for children sustained effectively over time? The researchers found that at the time of the final hearing *firm* care plans for 120/131 of the children presented by the local authorities were as follows:

- placement with at least one parent (61 children – 51%)
- adoption (27 children – 22.5%)

- long-term substitute care – fostering or residential – (17 children – 14%)
- kinship care (15 children – 12.5%).

A significant tension between local authorities and courts was noted in relation to responsibility for ensuring that court-agreed care plans are actually implemented by local authorities after the completion of care proceedings. As we have noted, in the old 'wardship' proceedings, the court could direct the actions and services of the local authority. However, under the Children Act 1989, this judicial role and authority were extinguished. After making the final care order, the court no longer has authority to monitor, regulate or intervene if the local authority (for whatever reason) does not follow its intentions as stated in the care plan.

This study noted that most professionals involved in such court cases (apart from local authorities) felt strongly that there is a need for some form of judicial scrutiny of the implementation of care plans. To what extent is this a problem? *The Best Laid Plans* attended to this question in detail. In the sample in the study, care plans were not implemented (or were significantly changed) in 49/83 cases (59%). In many cases, the researchers concluded that such changes were reasonable and appropriate, given the changed circumstances in the life of each child. However, in a minority of cases, the non-implementation of the original care plan (or its change) resulted from capricious and quite unreasonable behaviour on the part of the local authority – to the extent that the researchers concluded that the court had, in effect, been misled.

Such failures occurred for a number of reasons. First, there was a tendency for a sense of direction to be lost within social services once the court proceedings were completed. Intense social services activity is focused on *obtaining* the care order; but after this is achieved, the momentum can be lost, and cases can drift for long periods within social services systems.

Second was the issue of resources. Staff changes and vacancies mean that family placement work (needed for the implementation of many care plans) has a low priority within social services. Difficulties are also experienced in actually providing services as spelled out in care plans (this is particularly so if such services are expected from separate health departments/agencies).

Third, there were cases where the local authority found itself in the position of having insufficient resources to implement the care plan (including the use of such resources being vetoed by senior social services managers on the grounds of budget constraints).

Fourth, there were a small number of cases where local authorities appeared to change direction radically in complete disregard for the care plan that had been presented to the court.

As far as such examples are likely to relate specifically to infants with suspicious serious injuries, examples of such changed plans noted by Hunt and Macleod (1999) included:

- removal of children placed at home
- adoption of children for whom the plan had been rehabilitation
- long-term fostering rather than adoption and vice versa
- plans to place with relatives changed to placement outside the family
- dramatic reduction in frequency of contact.

Consequently, this research highlighted the concern that local authorities cannot be relied upon to implement care plans: 'Most plan changes were accomplished without any outside scrutiny and the appropriateness of the new plan for the child was left entirely to the judgement of the local authority' (Hunt & Macleod 1999, p. 197).

Placement Breakdowns

By the end of the 3-year follow-up period, approximately one-third of the care plan placements had broken down:

A failure rate of 3 in 10 plans, however, after the lengthy and close scrutiny most had received during the court process, might be regarded as rather disappointing, perhaps suggesting a degree of unwarranted over-optimism on the part of the courts and the professionals advising them. (Hunt & Macleod 1999, p. 43)

Although issues relating to placement breakdown are complex, the authors highlighted the need for appropriate resources in establishing and supporting all forms of placement to have maximum chance of effectiveness. This is especially so in relation to kinship care placements, which are particularly prone to breakdown when there is continuing antagonism between extended family members:

Three continuing (kinship care placements) were characterised by serious and chronic conflict between parents and carers.... Carers described children cowering terrified as they witnessed these angry confrontations.... Accepting the *local authority* having parental responsibility is hard enough for a parent to swallow, accepting *relatives* doing so may be just too much, particularly perhaps if the supplanting relative is a sibling, rather than a parent. (Hunt & Macleod 1999, pp. 98–9)

Kinship care is a very appropriate and effective method of placement for many children who cannot live with their natural parents. However, it should not be seen as a cheap option. Failure of kinship care placements in this study often reflected inadequate levels of support by social services, which, in one case, was described as being 'disgracefully negligent' (Hunt 2001, p. 33).

Harwin & Owen (2002)

The third study we shall discuss focused specifically on the implementation of care plans after the conclusion of care proceedings. The researchers distinguished three components of care plans:

- the planned placement
- the planned contact
- the planned services.

The sample comprised 100 children from 57 families who were placed on care orders in 1997. Follow-up information was obtained from files and interviews with professionals 21 months after the making of the care order. Overall, 60% of care plans had been implemented fully by follow-up – but not all of these cases had outcomes that could be considered to be successful. Conversely, 40% of care plans had not been implemented fully at follow-up – and not all of these outcomes were considered to be unsuccessful.

A number of findings in the Harwin and Owen study (about placements, contact and services) are very relevant to our concern in this book about seriously injured infants. In the sample the biggest change in care *placement* plans was a significant change in direction from an initial commitment to reunification – this being replaced by plans for adoption. This change in direction stemmed particularly from the influence of the guardian *ad litem* and expert witness. The family feature that weighed most heavily against reunification was parental substance abuse. In this sample, this factor had far greater adverse impact on the potential for reunification than did parental learning difficulties, mental health problems and domestic violence.

While many commentators are justifiably concerned about non-implementation of court-endorsed care plans by local authorities (Hunt & Macleod 1999), Harwin and Owen are gentler in their analysis of the local authorities' perspective. First, they note that sometimes care plans are changed for very good reasons, to reflect continually evolving circumstances or unexpected events. As such, care plans should not be 'set in stone'. Second, they note that much non-fulfilment occurs in relation to the *services* aspects of some care plans. For example, local authorities are having increasing difficulty in recruiting specialist foster and adoptive parents for children with special needs. Third, local authorities may find that they do not have the financial resources to commission the specified specialist services or that other service providers (especially health) refuse to deliver. In this context it would be sensible for courts not to agree care plans unless a senior manager of the local authority has confirmed to the court that the necessary resources for the plan will be made available.

PROBLEMS IN INTERAGENCY COMMUNICATION AND PROFESSIONAL PRACTICE

The third major area of research on the efficacy of child protection systems focuses on problems in interagency communication and professional practice. Research findings consistently highlight the false-negative aspect of child protection practice – where risk factors are not recognised, and where assessments of risk are either absent or significantly inadequate. The body of risk research has repeatedly drawn the same conclusions about the shortcomings of interagency communication, coordination and professional practice associated with fatal cases of child abuse. These concerns divide into three main areas:

- absent or inadequate assessments undertaken by professionals
- poor coordination and communication between agencies
- family-agency dynamics.

This research stems predominantly from overviews of statutory inquiry and Part 8 Review reports. The findings are familiar and repetitive over more than two decades, giving rise to the questions: why do such significant errors continue to be made? why do interagency coordination procedures not identify such failings more effectively at an early stage?

Absent or Inadequate Assessments

One of the most striking findings in the risk research into professional practice and interagency communication is that in most fatal cases where concerns had been known to appropriate agencies, adequate and appropriate assessments of risk were not undertaken. A long list of research publications have drawn this conclusion (virtually all of the publications in Table 3.1 on page 28). The conclusion of Reder and Duncan after their second review of a sample of child abuse fatalities in the 1990s can speak for the conclusions of these studies as a whole on this issue:

> The most common assessment problem in the cases reviewed was that assessments were not undertaken following notification of a child maltreatment concern. Sometimes this meant that a referral received no specific response at all or that minimal information was sought from unreliable sources. Alternatively, interventions were planned and decisions taken but they did not appear to have been guided by any assessment. We wondered whether this might have been due to omissions by the reviewers when compiling the chronology, so that assessments had been performed but were simply not recorded. However, there were so many examples of this absence of reported assessments that we believe a more likely explanation is that they were, indeed, not performed. (Reder & Duncan 1999, pp. 84–5)

Statutory inquiries and Part 8 Reviews have concluded repeatedly that front-line agencies fail to recognise the significance of danger signs in families. Consequently, families with known, significant, high-risk indicators are not referred to social services by universal services such as health visitors, police, paediatricians and GPs. As we have noted from our own research:

> In 13/17 of the fatal cases, the baby had died in the absence of formal child protection interventions. This signifies that serious and fatal violence to babies, on occasions, can erupt quite unpredictably in families where there have been few or no previously recorded significant concerns. However, in all but two of these 13 cases, the *Part 8 Review* reports concluded (or intimated) that the level of concerns known to professionals prior to the fatal SIDE [serious injury – discrepant explanation] injury *should have led* to child protection procedures being invoked to assess the safety needs of the children prior to the fatal incidents. A quite inappropriate level of professional tolerance of observed harm or threat to babies/infants without child protection interventions being triggered was apparent in some cases. (Dale et al. 2002, p. 306)

In other cases, universal services did refer high-risk families to social services, but these referrals resulted in either a very delayed, low-level, 'child in need' response – or no response at all:

> The major failings in professional judgements identified by the *Part 8 Reviews* involved the absence of appropriate assessment of situations of concern (apparent in 9/17 cases) and the practice of social services in categorising referrals as 'child in need' rather than 'child at risk'. In effect, 'child in need' designations virtually guaranteed that no assessment of the child or family would occur, and may have falsely reassured other professionals (particularly Health) that the welfare of the child about whom they had expressed concern would be looked into. (Dale et al. 2002, p. 306)

Such cases reflect insufficient urgency to assess the immediate safety/protection needs of the injured infant – separate from the fuller comprehensive/core/independent assessments of the risk of recurrence of injury and the prospects for reunification. Research consistently notes that assessments often reflect inadequate analysis of the information obtained or the influence of significant biases in the interpretation of the information (Holland 2004; Macdonald 2001; Munro 1999; Scott 1998). These researchers conclude that this is a sign that the education and training of social workers may be ineffective in developing skills relating to the synopsis and analysis of complex information, and also that significant biases can be undetected in the process of thinking (and forming opinions) that is overreliant on intuition, as in emotional contamination, fixed views and fundamental errors in reasoning (Arthurs & Ruddick 2001; Dale et al. 2002; Macdonald 2001; Munro 1999, 2002; Reder et al. 1993; Scott 1998).

Basic Communication and Coordination Between Agencies

In 1974, the inquiry into the death of Maria Colwell stated:

> There was no question at any time in our view of anyone deliberately shirking a task; there was no shortage of devotion to duty. What has clearly emerged, at least to us, is a failure of systems compounded of [sic] several factors of which the greatest and most obvious must be that of the lack of, or ineffectiveness of, communication and liaison. A system should so far as possible be able to absorb individual errors and yet function adequately. (Secretary of State 1974, p. 86)

One outcome of the Colwell inquiry was the initial establishment of the current structure of local interagency child protection procedures under the auspices of Area Child Protection Committees (ACPCs). Since this issue was highlighted by the Colwell inquiry, virtually every statutory inquiry into child abuse deaths, and significant proportions of Part 8 Reviews, have continued to make recommendations about improving interagency communication and coordination. Continuing problems include:

- failure to follow established child protection procedures
- poor professional recording of information, activities and rationales for actions/inactions
- absent, inadequate and distorted communication between professionals
- poor coordination of agency activities and responsibilities
- role confusion and conflicts between professionals.

Part 8 Reviews often conclude that deaths were not predictable or preventable, and many criminal child abuse trials have concluded with judges making similar comments. It is not now common for a Part 8 Review to conclude that errors or gaps in the procedures themselves had a significant role in the circumstances of the death of a child. The recurrent major problem is that the procedures are not followed (Arthurs & Ruddick 2001; Sanders et al. 1999). To our knowledge, no research has explored in detail the baffling question of why professionals do not more consistently follow established procedures in child protection cases.

Family–Agency Dynamics

Understanding (and influencing) the dynamics that arise in the domain where families and professionals interact is crucial with regard to maximising the potential for services to achieve their aims. In an earlier book, *Dangerous Families*, this dynamic was construed systemically as the 'family–agency' system (Dale et al. 1986). *Dangerous Families* pointed to the need in some cases (especially those that were 'stuck') for an intervention into this system as a whole to clarify roles, processes and desired outcomes.

The kernel of child protection practice is found in the interaction between families and the network of professionals and agencies – a context of complex dynamics and motives (Crenshaw 2004). Families and professionals encounter each other with positive, mixed, uncertain and occasionally disastrous results. As we shall discuss in Chapter 10, families and professionals behave both reasonably and unreasonably. Surprisingly, the dynamics of these crucial interactions have not been subject to a great deal of research. One exception to this is the study led by Peter Reder (Reder et al. 1993).

Beyond Blame – The Reder Research

Consultant child and family psychiatrist Dr Peter Reder and colleagues have undertaken the most detailed systematic exploration of the dynamics between families and the child protection system through their analysis of a sample of 35 statutory inquiries into fatal child abuse as reported in the influential book *Beyond Blame* (Reder et al. 1993). (The second study, *Lost Innocents* (Reder & Duncan 1999), analysed a sample of Part 8 Review reports and did not focus specifically on the operation of the family–professional system.)

The *Beyond Blame* sample of inquiry reports was published between 1973 and 1989. As such reports tended, on average, to be published 2 years after the death of the child concerned, the era of child protection practice which is the focus of the *Beyond Blame* analysis can be placed roughly between 1970 and 1987. It is important to locate criticisms of practice in the context of contemporaneous professional knowledge. As two Australian social work researchers have pointed out: 'There was . . . little to guide the social workers in the 1970s working with the assault, abuse and neglect of children, at a time when inquiries into child deaths were gaining widespread media coverage' (Stanley & Goddard 2002, p. 71).

Reder et al. (1993) use the term 'family–professional systems' to refer to the dynamics between families and professionals from child protection/welfare services. Their analysis of these dynamics is grounded in a conceptual base that reflects both psychodynamic and systems theories. The psychodynamic perspective portrays parents who were unable to resolve care and control conflicts in their families of origin, replaying these unresolved tensions in their relations with professionals and agencies. A categorisation of family-professional dynamics is presented under four main headings: processes of dependency, closure, disguised compliance and double-binds.

The dependency dynamic is one where the family–professional system is skewed toward interventions that are prolonged and focused on the unmet emotional needs of the parents:

professionals were then unwillingly drawn into meeting more and more demands from the parents for practical and emotional support and became as much stuck in the process of giving as the families did in asking. Attention to the parents often obscured the children's needs and the parents sometimes subtly vied with their children to be the main focus of input and concern. (Reder et al. 1993, pp. 97–8)

This dynamic is evocative of the unintended consequences of the 'reparenting' models of child abuse interventions that were predominant in the 1960s and 1970s (Baher et al. 1976). In the current public service era, it is much more likely that families will be unable to obtain any services at all (professional neglect rather than dependency), rather than receiving a confusing surfeit of them. However, the dynamic of professionals' responses to parents' distress blinkering awareness of significant risks to a child does still arise in tragic cases.

Reder et al. also described a pattern of behaviour observed retrospectively in some fatal cases in families who had withdrawn and avoided professional attention, intervention and surveillance. They conceptualised this behaviour as 'closure':

the family attempted to tighten the boundary around themselves so that they reduced their contact with the external world and few people were able to meet or speak to them. For example, their curtains were always drawn, the children stopped playing outside and no longer attended school or nursery. The parents failed appointments with professionals, the children were not taken to scheduled visits to health clinics and social workers and health visitors could not obtain entry to the home when they called. (Reder et al. 1993, p. 99)

'Closure' was noted in over half of the 35 families in the *Beyond Blame* sample. Such was the authors' concern about the possible implications of this behaviour that they recommended that 'all episodes of closure should be considered as potentially fatal' (Reder et al. 1993, p. 132). The term 'closure' is potentially open to misunderstanding as there is now a psycho-jargon use of the word to connote a constructive ending or satisfactory completion of a process – which is manifestly not what Reder et al. intended to convey.

We agree that in respect of families where there are known, significant risks this behaviour is a signal that should raise levels of concern. However, the warning that all 'closure' is indicative of potential fatality is potentially disproportionate. In particular, it does not take into account the 'reasonableness' of the child protection interventions, and the unknown (but probably large) number of cases in which parents retreat from the attention of child protection interventions but their children do not come to any further harm.

The third dynamic between families and the child protection system described by Reder et al. is 'disguised compliance'. This refers to cases where professionals adopted a more assertive (and controlling) stance with families who were moving into a 'closure' position. Parents then, in effect, pretended to cooperate with professional requirements. In return, the professionals perceived this apparently increased cooperation as a sign of progress, relaxing the degree of the controlling aspect of their interventions with the family accordingly. Having manipulated the professionals to withdraw in this way, the abusive dynamics in the home continued to escalate toward the ultimate fatal outcome. We recognise this dynamic as being a significant one within the family–professional system, and one that is important in fatal abuse cases where professionals were essentially deceived by parents. We also agree with the comment of Stanley & Goddard (2002) that what is actually portrayed here is disguised non-compliance.

The work of Reder and colleagues regarding 'family–professional systems' is valuable and thought-provoking. A limitation of their analysis is that the model is based on a specific sample of cases where the parents were clearly very dangerous, and where the child protection system interventions were inadequate to protect the children from ultimate death. However, cases with such severe outcomes constitute a minute proportion of child protection work as a whole. Reder and colleagues portray the 'family–professional systems' as a dynamic of (very) unreasonable families reacting to (attempting to avoid or deceive) essentially reasonable child protection services. The *Beyond Blame* analysis does not extend to construing how *reasonable* families may respond to *unreasonable* child protection interventions. As we shall discuss in Chapter 10, in conceptualising how families behave within the 'family–professional system', it is vital to take the 'reasonableness' of the child protection interventions into account.

SUCCESSFUL REUNIFICATION AND RE-INJURY RATES

Given the human consequences of effective and ineffective child protection practice, and the huge financial costs of child protection services, it is lamentable that so little routine evaluation of the process and outcome is built into the operation of child protection systems in the UK. For example, data are not systematically collected in relation to type and severity of suspicious injuries to children, nor are rates and severity of re-injuries recorded. In a previous publication, we recommended that ACPCs should routinely collect and review specific process and outcomes data as part of a strategy to reduce the incidence of serious injury (and re-injury) cases (Dale et al. 2002a).

Without such data being routinely and systematically collected, knowledge of successful reunifications and re-injury rates stems mostly from occasional studies on the operation of specific child protection systems. For example, Farmer and Owen (1995) observed 120 initial child protection conferences, and focused in detail on a sample of 44 children on the child protection register. At the follow-up point of 20 months, one-quarter of the children had been re-abused. Farmer (1997) highlighted the risk factors in these cases:

> The outstanding feature of these unprotected children was that the dangers to children were minimised by professionals. This happened either because the social workers' commitment to keeping the children in the family led them to underestimate problems, or because the workers had come to accept low standards of child care and believe that continuing risks to the children were unavoidable. (Farmer 1997, p. 151)

The collection of studies within *Messages from Research* (Department of Health 1995), taken as a whole, indicate that re-injury rates to children (of all ages) subject to child protection interventions (with follow-up periods ranging from 6 months to 10 years) are fairly consistently in the range of 25–33% (Cleaver & Freeman 1995; Farmer & Owen 1995; Gibbons et al. 1995): 'The conclusion that between a quarter and a third of the children studied were re-abused is disquieting but concern is tempered somewhat by the low incidence of severe maltreatment' (Department of Health 1995, p. 44).

Wishing to promote a 'lighter touch', the government highlighted the conclusion of Thoburn et al. (1995):

> The child protection process works as well as it can with the most severe cases, it works reasonably well when there is an unproved allegation of serious abuse (especially if services are sensitively offered) but it works less well with needy families who resent being brought in to the 'abuse' system. (Thoburn et al. cited in Department of Health 1995, p. 35)

This view, endorsed by the Department of Health, should not pass without pause for reflection. We have reservations about the conclusion that 'the child protection system process works as well as it can with the most serious cases' (Thoburn et al. 1995, p. 35). It is difficult to understand that such a view can be reached in the context of the 'risk research' that shows repeatedly that a major problem with child protection practice is the extent to which adequate assessments are not undertaken, and the nature of false-negative risk assessment that is repeatedly revealed in Part 8 Reviews. Moreover, the statement is incompatible with the views of parents who are subject to false-positive and/or disproportionate child protection interventions (see Chapter 6). It is a significant limitation of *Messages from Research* and the associated Assessment Framework that attention has not been specifically focused on how child protection systems can work *more* effectively with the most serious cases.

Concern about ineffective child protection, of course, is not specific to England and Wales. Following public concern about a child abuse death in Scotland, a national audit of 188 child protection cases was undertaken in 2001. Re-injury rates were not specifically identified, but in relation to 179 cases where information was obtainable, 40 children (22%) were considered either not to have been appropriately protected, or not to have had their identified needs met by interventions (Scottish Executive 2002).

In Ireland, Ferguson and O'Reilly (2001) reported on a study undertaken in 1996 of a consecutive sample of 319 referrals of children about whom there were concerns about abuse or welfare. Investigations occurred in 262 of the cases, and abuse (predominantly neglect) was substantiated in 61%. At the end of the 1-year follow-up period, re-referrals had been made in almost one-third of the cases, 10% of these in relation to physical abuse. Overall, the authors concluded: 'In 16% of officially defined and substantiated child protection cases the system is known to have been unable to prevent further child protection concern being substantiated within 12 months of initial case substantiation' (Ferguson & O'Reilly 2001, p. 242).

In Australia, Stanley & Goddard (2002) analysed a random sample of social work case files relating to 50 children who were known to have been abused. The children had all been subject to a legal protection order indicative of serious abuse and family disturbance. Follow-up information was available for a period from 3 months to 15 years. In addition to the case file reviews, interviews were undertaken with 50 child protection workers in the State of Victoria. Of 38 children in the sample who had been physically abused, 29 (76%) were recorded in files as having been subject to further physical abuse subsequent to the initial child protection referral. The authors concluded that child protection interventions had not been adequate to prevent re-abuse:

> It is apparent that the protection offered to the more severely abused children was inadequate. These children were not protected from re-abuse. Indeed, many children were re-abused on more than one occasion. Further, the severity of abuse suffered by these children did not appear to be diminished. (Stanley & Goddard 2002, p. 60)

These findings raise concerns about the levels of re-injuries of abused children notwithstanding child protection interventions.

In Wales (Cardiff), a 3-year follow-up study led by Professor Jo Sibert was undertaken in relation to 69 infants (aged 0–1 years) presenting consecutively to hospital (between 1996 and 1998) with non-accidental injuries (Ellaway et al. 2004). Sadly, five of the babies died from their injuries. Of the surviving 64 infants (information about outcome was not available in one case), 14 were permanently separated from their parents/carers, and 49 were returned home at some point after child protection investigations. The researchers had access to police and social services records to gather information about follow-up after 3 years. At follow-up, it was reported that 15 of the 49 infants who had been returned home had been re-abused – a re-abuse rate of 31%. This conclusion received national press attention in the UK in August 2004.

However, the research report (Ellaway et al. 2004) states specifically that eight of these 15 're-abused' infants had suffered further physical abuse injuries. The other seven had been subject to neglect. The researchers combined re-injury and subsequent neglect to reach the reported 're-abuse' rate of 31%. However, while both have serious consequences, the distinction between re-injury and neglect is a very important one. Neglect subsequent to reunification after a serious, inflicted injury to an infant should be preventable by appropriate family support and child protection monitoring services. Consequently, the 14% (7/49) incidence of neglect after reunification in this study raises questions about the child protection system failure as well as parental inadequacy. If the neglect cases are excluded, the *re-injury* rate in this study is 16% (8/49). Although the researchers are unable to be specific (Sibert 2004 personal communication), it is likely that only one of these re-injuries would be classifiable as 'serious'. On this basis, the *serious re-injury rate* in the Ellaway et al. (2004) study is actually 2% (1/49).

Unfortunately, this important study by Ellaway et al. was not able to analyse re-abuse and re-injury rates to the infants in the context of the nature, types and appropriateness of child protection interventions. It is not known how many of the re-abuse cases reflect inadequate assessments and interagency communication deficiencies (as is so often highlighted in Part 8 Review findings). Nor is it known to what extent appropriate assessments and family support/therapeutic services were provided for these families, with reunifications being endorsed by care proceedings judgments.

Another interpretation of the Ellaway et al. (2004) data is that 98% of the initially injured infants who were returned home were not subsequently seriously re-injured over a period of 3 years. To what extent this is due to effective child protection and family support measures, or the passing of a transient phase of high risk within such families (or combinations of both) is not known. This is an area where there is an urgent need for further research into successful reunifications and the effects on re-injury rates of reasonable and unreasonable child protection interventions.

5

THE NSPCC SERIOUS INJURY–DISCREPANT EXPLANATION RESEARCH

In this chapter we describe an NSPCC research project exploring child protection case management of infants with serious suspicious injuries from the perspective of two samples: one sample of 17 families where 19 infants had died, and a clinical sample of 21 families referred to an independent assessment service.

THE INDEPENDENT SPECIALIST ASSESSMENT SERVICE

Between 1986 and 2000, two of the authors (PD and RF) led an independent assessment service in the south of England which received referrals in relation to all types of child protection concerns. The service was used extensively with referrals being made by social services, guardians *ad litem* and solicitors representing parents. Of 203 major assessments undertaken during that period, 21 cases involved serious suspicious injuries (or previous fatalities) to 26 infants (0–2 years) where there were absent or discrepant explanations from parents/carers of the cause of the injuries. For shorthand purposes, we use the acronym 'SIDE' (serious *i*njury–*d*iscrepant *e*xplanation) to refer to such situations. These cases present particularly perplexing problems for child protection systems and courts (Cobley 2004, Cousins 2002), and throughout our clinical assessment practice we often felt unease about inconsistencies in outcomes between similar cases.

In undertaking assessments, it was often unclear why social services, guardians *ad litem*, and courts formed 'hard' or 'soft' views in relation to individual cases. Chance factors determining which particular social worker and guardian *ad litem* became involved often affected processes and outcomes: *child-protectionist* social workers and guardians pushed for compulsory adoption; *family-preservationist* social workers and guardians promoted the case for reunification (Fox Harding 1997). If a chance combination of a *child-protectionist* social worker and a *family-preservationist* guardian *ad litem* (or vice versa) arose, the stage could be set for drawn-out professional disagreements that, on occasion, could become highly contentious.

It was satisfying that one common outcome of the service was that recommendations could often be made (usually after intensive work with the family) that were acceptable to all parties (parents, social services, and guardians *ad litem*), thus obviating the need for emotional, stressful and very expensive contested court hearings. When agreements could not be reached in this way, the recommendations of the independent assessment service differed from those of social services and guardians *ad litem* on a roughly equal basis. In some cases the independent assessment service did not support reunification when this was the preference of either social services or the guardian *ad litem*. In others the service would support reunification when this was opposed by either social services or the guardian *ad litem*.

In providing this independent specialist assessment service, we developed a particular interest in the cases that are the subject of this book: serious/fatal injuries to infants where there are absent, inconsistent or parent/carer explanations discrepant with medical opinion. Because of the complexity of assessments in such cases, the inconsistencies in case-management process and outcomes, and the nature of professional disagreements that arise, we developed a research project to examine systematically the child protection case management process with this clinical sample. In addition to the 21 families referred to the assessment service, the research project also included a comparison sample of predominantly fatal cases derived from 17 Part 8 Reviews undertaken by several Area Child Protection Committees (ACPCs). This was an opportunity sample of cases (occurring between 1996 and 2001) obtained mostly via NSPCC membership of ACPCs in the south of England. In total, the sample was as shown in Table 5.1.

In this chapter we describe family factors, assessment issues and outcomes that are apparent from a retrospective reappraisal of the voluminous

Table 5.1 Characteristics of samples

	No. of families	Infants aged 0–2 years		
		Male	Total	Female
Assessment sample	21	17 (65%)	26	9 (35%)
Part 8 sample	17	14 (74%)	19	5 (26%)
Total sample	38	31 (69%)	45	14 (31%)

documents on file in relation to each assessment case. We also reflect on similar issues that were identifiable in the cases with very poor outcomes – the tragic cases of 17 infant deaths recorded in the Part 8 Review sample.

ASSESSMENT SAMPLE

The assessment sample involved families where the injuries to the infants were predominantly serious, but not fatal. However, three cases involved assessments of the safety of unborn babies conceived some time after the suspicious death of an earlier child in the family. Such assessments have to consider the dire necessity of 'removal at birth' of a new baby (or the futures of babies that have been removed at birth). Another case involved a consultation assessment (opinion from reading papers) regarding the surviving sibling of an infant who had been fatally re-injured after reunification.

Family Structure

As sufficient information was not available about the circumstances of previously injured children in two families (these were assessments of unborn babies where the concerns were related to serious and fatal injuries to previous children), information about family structure at the time of the first SIDE injuries relates to 19 families in the assessment sample as follows:

- in 8/19 cases, the injured child was living with both natural parents, and in six of these cases was the only child in the family
- in 6/19 cases, the mother was living as a single parent
- in 5/19 cases, the natural mother was living with a boyfriend who was not the father of the child
- in 11/19 cases, the injured child was the only child in the family
- in every case with more than one child in the family, it was the youngest child who was injured.

Examples follow of six of the families where serious suspicious injuries had occurred. The outcomes recorded are not necessarily in accordance with the recommendations of the assessment service. These examples amended from the NSPCC research report (Dale et al. 2002b) are chosen to illustrate cases where there are significant psychosocial factors of concern, and also those perplexing cases where serious suspicious injuries occurred to very young infants in the context of families that appeared to be well-functioning, resourceful and problem-free.

Sophia   First injuries: age 2 weeks

Injuries: fractures to both legs (tibia × 2, fibula × 1)

Parent context: 2 natural parents (together)

Child's position in family: first and only child

History of known previous injury concerns: none

Significant combination of other contextual concerns: no

Parental explanation for the injuries was that father had caused these accidentally whilst passing the baby to mother for a feed in the middle of the night. This was firmly discounted by the paediatrician.

After a few days in hospital Sophia was discharged home to her parents' care, ahead of the child protection conference. The day after the child protection conference she sustained a further injury, a bruise to the cheek, whilst in her father's care. The explanation was again deemed inadequate by the paediatrician. This time Sophia was removed from her parents' care and placed with extended family under an Interim Care Order.

Conflicts emerged within the professional network, specifically around whether child protection intervention was counter-productive. Within 6 months Sophia was reunified with her parents under the terms of a Supervision Order.

David   First injuries: age < 6 weeks

Injuries: 14 fractured ribs (of at least three different ages), fractured fibula, bilateral retinal haemorrhages

Parent context: 2 natural parents (together)

Child's position in family: first and only child

History of known previous injury concerns: none

Significant combination of other contextual concerns: no

Baby taken to hospital unwell. No external signs of injury. Diagnosis of NAI made a week after hospital admission upon review of x-rays. David was placed with foster parents under an Interim Care Order. Early in the assessment father admitted that he had caused the injuries but maintained that this was 'accidental'. Shortly afterwards, his wife left him and made a statement to the police which acknowledged she had been aware of his maltreatment of the baby. Father then committed suicide. Following assessment (which included a mother–baby residential component) there was consensus that mother was able to provide proper care for her son. It remained unclear at this stage whether David would suffer permanent disability. Seven months after the original hospital admission he returned to her care.

Graham   First injuries: age 8 weeks

Injuries: multiple fractures, of different ages to femur, clavicle and ribs

Parent context: natural parents (together)

Child's position in family: youngest of 3

History of known previous injury concerns: (see below)

Significant combination of other contextual concerns: no

A paediatrician and forensic pathologist diagnosed NAI (non-accidental injury). The parents offered a number of explanations, including the injury being caused either by a boisterous elder brother or hospital staff holding the baby down to complete a medical procedure.

A retrospective examination of medical records uncovered previous injuries to elder siblings, at least one of which (a fractured ankle at age 6 months) was also thought to be an uninvestigated potential NAI.

Graham was placed with extended family for several months under a Residence Order while several assessments took place. Further medical opinion was sought by parents, who contested the application by social services for a Care Order. This opinion was that the injuries were caused by 'temporary brittle bone disease'. This diagnosis was disputed by paediatricians and was rejected by the judge, who made the boy subject to a Care Order. Further assessment work was undertaken following the care proceedings. Graham was returned to his parents' care.

Mary   First injury: age 11 weeks

Injuries: bleeding from nose

Parent context: single parent

Child's position in family: only child

History of known previous injury concerns: none

Significant combination of other contextual concerns: yes

Teenage single mother gradually admitted attempting to smother her baby by holding her face down in the cot mattress for 3–5 minutes. No explanation regarding motivation. The baby was adopted.

Assessment referral was precipitated by rapid subsequent second pregnancy, regarding protection of new baby at birth.

The new baby was removed at birth and made subject to a Care Order. Assessments pointed to both parents' capacity to mature, to work cooperatively with agencies and to care appropriately for the baby. Major social problems significant at time of birth of first baby had substantially resolved. Contact was increased, leading to Mary being placed at 'home on trial', followed in turn by revocation of the Care Order.

Sally   First SIDE presentation: age 8 months

Injuries: multiple fractures (femurs, tibia, radius and ulna). Extensive bodily bruising. Injuries of different ages.

Parent context: mother and boyfriend (stepfather)

Child's position in family: youngest of 2

History of known previous injury concerns: bruising to temple observed at age 7 1/2 months

Significant combination of other contextual concerns: yes

Paediatric opinion was of four, discrete, non-accidental injuries occurring on at least three occasions. Sally and her sibling were taken into care for protection and assessment. Initial explanations were given by mother, boyfriend and extended family member of various accidental causes. Paediatric opinion was that these were mechanically insufficient to cause the nature and extent of the injuries.

Mother and boyfriend were tried on charges of cruelty but acquitted on the judge's instruction, as it was impossible to determine who was responsible. Mother then separated from her boyfriend. Following further assessment the children were returned to mother's care.

Neil   First injuries: age 9 months

Injuries: fractures to skull, brain and retinal haemorrhages

Parent context: parents recently separated, child living with mother

Child's position in family: only child

History of known previous injury concerns: Neil had been presented some 3 weeks prior to hospital with vomiting. The explanation then, as with the index injury, was that he had fallen and hit his head.

Significant combination of other contextual concerns: yes

Paediatric opinion was that the injuries were consistent with Neil having been shaken and that the skull fracture suggested impact with a wall. Both parents were initially charged with GBH but a prosecution did not proceed, as it was thought impossible to establish in a court which parent was responsible. Neil was accommodated within the extended family for almost a year. An adult psychiatric report (no formal psychiatric illness) was influential in the decision to rehabilitate him with his mother.

Nature of Injuries

These cases are illustrative of many of the challenges that non-fatal SIDE cases present to child protection services. In the assessment sample as a whole, the gender of injured infants was 65% boys and 35% girls. This is consistent with the known disproportionate vulnerability of males to serious and fatal injury in infancy reported by other studies (e.g. Wilczynski 1997). There is no generally accepted understanding of why this consistent gender imbalance exists.

Many families (such as those of Neil, Mary and Sally) lived in a context of significant psychosocial concerns. Less commonly, and perplexingly, as in the cases of Sophia, David and Graham, with some families there are no or few apparent such problems. In some cases (e.g. Sophia, David and Mary), the serious injury is the first known injury. In others (e.g. Neil and Graham), a history of a more minor precursor or harbinger injury (often a bruise) is apparent prior to the serious injury. It is also common for medical investigations at the time of the discovered serious injury to reveal a pattern of older serious injuries, including brain injuries and fractures of different ages.

The number of separate injuries to the infants in the assessment sample ranged from a single event – to one child with an extraordinary sequence of 23 injury incidents. (This child's mother has since been sentenced to life imprisonment for causing grievous bodily harm to a later infant.) The most common were bone fractures (71% of cases). Fifteen babies sustained a total of 58 fractures, including four babies with a total of 28 rib fractures between them. A striking feature was the very young age at which SIDE injuries occurred. Just under half of the cases (9/21) involved at least 18 fracture injuries to babies who were 3–12 weeks old. The earliest was three fractures (one femur and two tibia) to a baby girl aged 2 weeks. Another baby in this highly vulnerable age group suffered bilateral retinal haemorrhages and brain damage, apparently from being shaken at age 8 weeks.

One-third (7/21) of the cases involved injuries that had been recorded at the time to be life-threatening or the cause of permanent disability. These involved brain damage (three cases), suffocation (three cases) and poisoning (one case). Lack of follow-up information (especially regarding developmental problems that would become apparent only over time) means that this is almost certainly an underrecording of abuse-related permanent disability. There had been four child fatalities in the past in three families within the assessment sample, two of which had been classified as cot deaths. In one case, retrospective analysis of the circumstances, including subsequent serious abuse to other children in the family, raised queries about this conclusion. One case involved assessment of a family where the father of a new baby had in the past been charged (and acquitted) of the murder of an 8-week-old baby.

Explanations for Injuries

The defining characteristic of SIDE cases is the nature of parent/carer explanations, which are absent, inconsistent, implausible or discrepant with expert medical opinion. Legal parlance refers to 'uncertain perpetrator' or 'uncertain attribution' cases (Hayes 2004).

Types of recorded parent/carer explanations (or lack of them) were reviewed from the documents in relation to each injury. In two-thirds (14/21) of cases, at the point of initial investigation, *no explanations* regarding any untoward event were forthcoming. Most commonly, parents/carers asserted that the baby had suddenly become seriously unwell. When initial explanations were provided, these were mostly based on some form of reported *accident*. These were split roughly equally between accidents involving the parent and those that did not. Two examples stated inadvertent parental involvement as follows:

A 2-week-old baby girl sustained three leg fractures (both tibiae and one fibula). Her young parents maintained that the injuries had occurred accidentally while the baby was being passed between them during the night.

The parents of an 8-week-old baby maintained (after initially offering no explanation) that the multiple rib fractures must have been caused inadvertently by the mother in a hospital while she was holding the baby for eye drops to be administered.

Both of these cases generated strongly held different views between professionals regarding the extent to which the explanations were feasible. The fact that these were both what would be considered middle-class families with apparently few significant psychosocial stresses, added to the complexity of assessment and case management.

In six situations, parents/carers insisted that the injuries must have been *self-inflicted accidents*:

A 6-week-old baby boy sustained a spiral fracture to his tibia. Parents stated that this must have been caused by the boisterous baby trapping his leg in an awkward position while sleeping.

Social services gave the parents the benefit of the doubt, and the baby was discharged home from hospital without any assessment being undertaken. The child was re-injured at age 17 months having sustained a fractured humerus. In response to the second injury, his parents were again adamant that he had caused this himself by 'doing acrobatics' in his cot. At this point, an independent assessment was requested.

The fourth most common type of explanation was where one parent (either immediately or subsequently) *accused the other*:

In a family where a previous baby had died (in circumstances that we consider suspicious), a 10-week-old baby lived with both natural parents. Shortly after the father left home, the baby sustained five fractured ribs. Mother claimed that these must have been caused by the baby's father during contact.

During an assessment interview she subsequently tacitly acknowledged that she must have caused the injuries by 'squeezing him too hard'. She later withdrew this explanation.

In a small number of cases, parents stated that a boisterous elder sibling must have caused the injuries. One case involved a grandmother who threw the child protection system into further confusion by suddenly asserting in the middle of a child protection conference that she had caused the injuries inadvertently. This was subsequently discounted as not being physically possible in the manner described, and seems to amount to an unusual *false confession* (presumably to distract the focus of suspicion).

A notable pattern (7/21 of cases) was for a lack of initial explanation to be followed by the emergence of a *sequence of different accounts* as criminal and child protection enquiries continued. Explanations evolved as (depending on interpretation) parents strived either to identify the unknown actual cause of the injuries, or endeavoured to concoct a plausible explanation that the child protection system would accept, without implicating themselves criminally.

In only four cases, did admission of responsibility emerge over time that could be construed as being fairly explicit:

- A 5-week-old baby was found to have multiple fractures of different ages and bi-lateral retinal haemorrhages. Both parents initially denied having any knowledge how these injuries had occurred. Several weeks later in an assessment interview the father acknowledged that he might have 'unintentionally' caused the injuries. He committed suicide a week later.
- In a police interview the mother of a 4-month-old baby who sustained serious brain damage stated: 'I said to the baby "I always get it in the neck when you cry." He kept on crying so I shook him . . .'

We noted in a small number of cases a process that we construed as the development of tentative or *tacit admissions* – as if the parent/carer was attempting indirectly to clarify the consequences of making a confession prior to committing herself/himself to this. One mother, for example, stated in an assessment session: *'Whoever did it, knowing how serious it was, would be unlikely to do it again.'*

It was, however, uncommon for 'confessions' to emerge during the course of child protection system involvement. The exact circumstances of the injuries remained, in most cases, poorly understood years later. There are few incentives for parents to acknowledge responsibility when they have caused an abuse-related serious injury, and many reasons (psychological, social and legal) to adopt and reinforce a stance of 'denial'. 'Denial' is a complex and often contentious feature of these cases. In Chapter 7 we discuss the issue of 'denial' in more detail (noting that the term itself is unhelpful) and outline a range of hypothetical dynamics that can result in responsibility and motivation for injuries remaining opaque.

At this stage we only note the significant fact that remaining silent is likely to impede criminal prosecutions and convictions in both non-fatal and fatal cases, especially if both parents were present in the home when the events occurred. This is because of the long-standing legal principle that *individual culpability* for causing harm must be proved beyond reasonable doubt – convictions have been overturned when it could not be proved which of two (or several) individuals were responsible. A national survey undertaken in 2002 by Sussex police of 492 children who were thought to have been unlawfully killed or seriously injured by their carers revealed that only one-third of these cases resulted in criminal prosecution – and the conviction rate would be even lower (NSPCC 2002). A change in the law on this matter has been subject to a long campaign (NSPPC 2002, 2003). The Domestic Violence, Crime and Victims Bill (2003) proposes a new offence of *familial homicide* for causing or allowing the death of a child or vulnerable adult, which is intended to address this concern.

At this point it is important to pause and remind ourselves of a key issue that is an important theme of this book: that it is not unknown for parents to find themselves under scrutiny in criminal investigations and child protection assessments when they genuinely have no idea how their baby was harmed. In some cases, they are not aware that another person has assaulted the baby. In others (as we shall discuss in Chapter 7), there can be unrecognised medical causes for the symptoms that mimic suspicious injuries, and also unknown accidental causes. This reinforces the view that it is imperative that the professional approach to parents in investigation and assessment practice is one of 'respectful uncertainty' (Laming 2003). As we shall discuss in Chapter 6, parents feel strongly that assumptions about their guilt are too often made at the outset of the child protection process, leaving them with the impossible onus of proving their innocence, or falsely confessing as the basis upon which their child might be returned.

FATAL CASES: THE PART 8 REVIEW SAMPLE

We analysed 17 Part 8 Review reports which focused on cases of suspicious injuries to 19 injured infants. Seventeen of these infants died from these injuries. We were interested to identify the characteristics of fatal abuse cases, and to see how these compare and contrast with the predominantly non-fatal cases in the assessment sample. Are there any striking differences in the family factors between serious injury cases that are fatal and those where the child survives? To what extent are the actions and inactions of professionals and health/welfare agencies crucial in affecting the different outcomes?

In a quarter of cases (4/17), the deaths occurred 'out of the blue' in families where general health monitoring services had detected no cause for concern and no significant family/social problems. As we discussed earlier, these cases remain particularly perplexing. In two-thirds of cases, the deaths occurred before any involvement of child protection services. However, in over half of these, it was concluded that the concerns known to some professionals at the time should have resulted in child protection assessment and interventions.

'Daniel'

Child and family characteristics:
Male infant aged 18 months. Only child of 17-year-old single mother.

Circumstances and official cause of death:
Sudden infant death syndrome (SIDS)

Family and injury circumstances:
Mother was in care as child. She had very disturbed childhood and adolescence including suicide attempts and cutting herself. The pregnancy with Daniel was unplanned and unwanted, occurring shortly after she left care aged 16. Arrangements initially were made for termination of the pregnancy but mother withdrew from this action under pressure from her own mother. Mother called social services twice during pregnancy asking them to look after baby when born.

Significant concerns were recorded about the care of Daniel from birth and throughout his life. Mother recorded a high post-natal depression score. Several referrals to social services were made by community health professionals. Social services responded to these by writing to mother advising her to get in touch if she required any help (this with a young mother who had herself had very negative experiences growing up in the care of social services).

The fatal chain of events started with a sequence of reported apnoeic events, and hospital Accident and Emergency Department contacts. The hospital response to these was subject to significant criticism: including discharging the baby home 'in error' when it had been decided appropriate to admit Daniel for observation. Also on another occasion a social services note says '*The hospital were unable to establish why Daniel had stopped breathing and discharged him.*'

The final, fatal hospital admission occurred following several earlier admissions with reported apnoea. Mother said she had 'put the baby to sleep in the normal way'. When she returned later she found him not breathing and without a pulse. Toxicology tests revealed a high level of caffeine in the Daniel's urine. Cause of death given as SIDS.

Part 8 Review conclusions regarding role of child protection agencies:
It was concluded that there were a significant number of events and concerns during Daniel's life that should have triggered formal child in need and/or child

protection assessment. Instead health and social services focused predominantly on practical matters such as monitoring his weight and helping with housing needs. The indicators of the mother's disturbed and despairing state of mind were not recognised or responded to. This amounted to major failings by health and social services regarding assessment, support and protection.

This was not a good-quality Part 8 Review report. The review process itself was clearly problematic. Specific conclusions state that resources were inadequate for the review group to undertake their task appropriately, and that such reviews require an independent input. The recommendation was made that the ACPC should consider commissioning a further independent enquiry into the case.

Source: Amended from Dale et al. 2002b. Reproduced by permission of the NSPCC.

In at least 9/15 cases where concerns had been identified by professionals and formal child protection interventions had commenced, the child protection assessment was either inadequate or absent. In one disconcerting fatal case, the child was receiving injuries on such a frequent basis that social services acknowledged they had simply given up responding. The internal management report provided for the Part 8 Review included the observation: 'It should be noted that injuries were occurring to Luke constantly and it would have been unnecessarily burdensome to pursue each occurrence through procedural channels...' This is an extraordinary explanation from a senior social services manager for the failure to investigate re-injuries to a child who had been reunified after a previous serious injury.

In at least one-third of cases, social services had designated a referral about an infant as a 'child in need', rather than a 'child at risk'. This stems from an era in the late 1990s/early 2000s when some understaffed social services initial assessment teams developed a gatekeeping tendency to classify referrals inappropriately under Section 17 Children Act 1989 ('child in need'), rather than under Section 47 Children Act 1989 ('child at risk'). This practice was particularly prominent in relation to notifications that began to be received from the police in large volumes about police call-outs to domestic violence incidents (when it became police policy routinely to refer all such calls to social services). Social services initial assessment teams simply could not cope with the extra workload generated by such notifications. For many 'child in need' referrals, the result was either a 'no further action' response, or sometimes a desultory letter to the family enquiring if they needed services (particularly pointless in cases of domestic violence or risk to children in chaotic or avoidant families). It is ironic that the rationalisation often given for such practice was that it was an implementation of the 'lighter touch' promoted by the government in *Messages from Research*.

In the Part 8 Review fatal sample, there was no case where a review concluded that the death of the child concerned could have been *predicted*, but nearly half of the reviews concluded that the death should have been *preventable*. This is a realistic recognition that, because of the rarity of fatal child abuse, it is impossible to predict from within the *general* population of young families who manifest significant contextual concerns (e.g. parental mental heath problems, drug/alcohol misuse, domestic violence) the *actual* very small number of families where an infant will come to serious harm. It is also imperative that assessments of families should be undertaken in such circumstances, with appropriate services being provided to protect children while supporting parents with the identified problems. It is very difficult to comprehend why the *known* concerns in many Part 8 Review cases (such as 'Daniel' and 'Chloe' in Chapter 2) had not prompted urgent child protection/family welfare assessments and interventions.

The most common problem throughout the 15 reviews was that professionals did not follow existing child protection procedures. This was a feature in 11/15 (73%) cases. As was noted in Chapter 4, notwithstanding the fact that this problem is identified repeatedly in the literature, no research has explored why professionals so often fail to follow established procedures in child protection practice. It is a significant missed opportunity that the Part 8 Review system in the UK has not explored why this happens (in addition to noting repeatedly that it does happen).

To what extent is it possible to clarify retrospectively how injuries and deaths to infants really occurred – and who was responsible? We have already noted that, as a general rule, very little information subsequently becomes available (at least to child protection agencies) to answer this question. Another limitation of Part 8 Reviews is that they do not consider this issue, focusing instead solely on the actions (and inactions) of professionals and agencies. Perhaps the most important point for practitioners to bear in mind is that it is clear that both mothers and fathers can cause death or serious injury to their infant (that is, it is not disproportionately a maternal or paternal susceptibility).

Dynamics and Context of Fatal/Serious Injuries

Drawing from the analysis of these samples of fatal and non-fatal cases, there are clearly a wide range of circumstances and dynamics which can result in confirmed serious non-accidental injuries to infants. These include:

● Mishaps stemming from lack of proper supervision (e.g. toddler falling out of a window or on to a fire). The context may include significant and chronic neglect, chaotic parental lifestyles, or alcohol and drug dependence.

● Children injured in the context of serious domestic violence, caught in violent 'crossfire', or intentionally hurt in a revenge attack against the other parent.

● Single serious outbursts of violence – momentary loss of control (guilt). Violence erupts in the context of otherwise good parenting where there are often identifiable recent significant stressors. Control is quickly regained, guilt feelings are immediate and strong, and help is quickly sought.

● Single serious outbursts of violence – momentary loss of control ('denial'). (See Chapter 7 for discussion of 'denial'.) Violence erupts often in the context of otherwise good parenting. There are often signs of long-standing family tensions and stresses below the surface of happy family presentation. Immediate response to the violent incident is 'denial' or displacement onto others (e.g. blaming injured infant's sibling or medical misdiagnosis). Parents (and sometimes whole extended family) unite against child protection agencies.

● Repeated incidents of momentary loss of control.

● Sustained (not momentary) outbursts of violence (male). Serious (and sometimes systematic) abuse to children occurs in households where the male is habitually violent. These fathers or stepfathers tend to abuse others (including partners) and may have psychopathic and sadistic tendencies. Mothers may be terrified and terrorised into passivity (rather than collusion).

● Sustained outbursts of violence (female). These are rarer, but similar to above. Either such mothers are single parents, or the male partner colludes or by-stands.

● Sustained outbursts of violence (both parents jointly). There may be serious serial abuse to children in households where both parents are habitually violent to the children. Attacks on children occur jointly, and separately with collusion. Parents may have psychopathic and sadistic tendencies.

● Psychosis. Serious and fatal attacks on infants and children can occur as a consequence of parental delusions resulting from psychotic illness. A child may be psychotically misperceived as a threat or evil influence, and the parental attack represents a deluded defence against such attack. Or the attack (often fatal) on the child may stem from a psychotically depressed altruistic motivation – that it is an act of love to kill the child to protect him/her from an evil world or other specific imagined misfortune. When psychosis clears, guilt is likely to be great.

- Revenge attacks. Such attacks may occur in the context of seriously enmeshed and conflictual parental relationships with established patterns of mutual provocation and retaliation. The child may be killed (perhaps with perpetrator suicide) in a final raising of the stakes in the bitter parental dispute.
- Munchausen's syndrome by proxy (now known as 'fabricated or induced illness'). A parent (almost always a mother) secretly and deliberately induces illness in her child and repeatedly presents the child for medical attention. A pattern of increasingly serious presentations develops, resulting in a sequence of unnecessary medical procedures. Fatalities occur. This controversial diagnosis is discussed further in Chapter 7.

These (by no means exhaustive) clinically well-established situations illustrate the range of potential psychological, parental and family dynamics that may lie behind a SIDE injury. It is important that assessments are open to all possible explanations. In turn, the evidence to support the existence of one scenario over another must be searched for and considered in a detailed exploration of significant events. This hypothesis-testing, neutral stance avoids the communication of judgmental (or sometimes persecutory) professional attitudes to accused parents and – equally damaging in many ways – inappropriate reassurances to parents that the professional does not believe that they are responsible.

Failure to Protect

In addition to trying to understand the dynamics and motives of the person who caused the injury, assessments invariably have to explore the dynamics between all of the adults in the household at the time of the injury. To what extent did the other parent/carer fail to protect the infant from recognised potential harm? This raises questions about the role of parents as *bystanders* or in *failing to protect* when they are aware of another person ill-treating the child – in some cases systematically and sadistically over a period of time. In much social work thinking, the notions of the 'abusing' and 'non-offending parent' have become a commonplace distinction. In our view, in the context of these SIDE cases, this can be an unhelpful, simplistic and artificial dichotomy – and a potentially dangerous misconception. The behaviour, attitude and potential roles of each parent/carer require an open-minded and careful assessment focus.

Failure-to-protect dynamics are varied and complex. The non-protective parent may also be traumatised and acutely afraid of the abusing parent (who may often also be physically violent). The non-protective parent may calculate that the consequences of intervening to protect the infant would be more disadvantageous than the harm that the infant is experiencing. Psychologically, the non-protective parent may minimise the significance of the assault, choosing to believe that it was an isolated incident, or may even, through a traumatic psychological mechanism, not recognise or remember the event that has been observed. This is a controversial potential post-traumatic response, implying psychological mechanisms of denial, suppression, repression and dissociation are impossible to prove or disprove in any individual case (this is discussed in detail in Chapter 7).

We can note four main scenarios of significant failure to protect:

• Natural parents together, or separately, ill-treat their infants, inflicting single or sequences of injuries. They deny having done so, and cover up for each other (*joint enterprise*).
• One parent mistreats an infant, with the knowledge and condonation of the other. One parent assaults the child repeatedly, in effect, expressing the hostile/rejecting feelings of both parents; and the abuse is emotionally congruent for the other parent (*vicarious assault*).
• One parent mistreats an infant and the other does not take action, despite opportunities, to prevent it (*bystander*).
• Not seeking medical help when an infant is known to have been injured (even seriously) and is in pain is a feature of many (but by no means all) suspicious serious injury cases. The effects of the injury can be made much worse by a failure to seek urgent medical attention. Some infants die (or are permanently disabled) as a consequence of these dynamics that promote delay and sometimes concealment (*delayed help seeking*).

In one of the Part 8 Review cases, it was strongly believed in the child protection system that the mother had regularly abused the child. After the death, on viewing the body, the father was overheard by a coroner's officer to say: 'I knew you had it coming, son...' Police interviews with another father noted his account of the events of the death of his baby:

He said he was angry and shook the child three times. During the third shake, Mr X stated that his son went limp and his breathing became unusual: '*He made this groaning noise. It sounded like he was in pain. I didn't do nothing about it...*' Mr X went on to say that he had checked the baby every 45 minutes and that he was fitting at those times. He took no action, considering that it was more important to get the decorating finished.

The conjoint psychological dynamics of sustained, sadistic, joint-enterprise infant and child abuse are poorly understood. They are not cases where it can be easily envisaged that sufficient genuine positive change can occur (and be sustained) to risk allowing other children (or subsequent children) to remain in the care of such parents.

Readers may recall the case of the severe maltreatment of the New Zealand toddler Tangaroa Matiu reported in Chapter 2 (page 10). The stepfather apparently paused briefly in the midst of his sadistic and ultimately fatal beating of Tangaroa. Then: 'When the boy's mother came down the hall, far from saving him, she slapped him a couple of times too, then stepped back to let her boyfriend carry on...' This is a ghastly example of joint enterprise by two parents in systematic and sustained maltreatment where both actively assault the child, and each encourages (or at least does not discourage) the actions of the other. These cases are severe, but, fortunately, they are rare.

The dynamics of vicarious assaults, bystanding and delayed seeking of medical assistance in cases of fatal and non-fatal SIDEs is an issue that needs to be carefully considered by all professionals involved in child protection assessments. Failing to protect has been described throughout much of the child abuse literature of the last 30 years, including in some detail by one of the present authors from a previous sample of 26 children nearly two decades ago (Dale et al. 1986). However, the psychology and family relationships of the 'failing to protect' parent remain poorly understood and require further research. This behaviour, its implications and susceptibility to change are of fundamental significance in child protection assessment in SIDE cases.

Contextual Psychosocial Concerns

In three-quarters of the cases in the NSPCC SIDE research, families scored highly on the presence of risk factors known from research to be often associated with maltreatment and neglect of children: parental mental health problems, drug/alcohol abuse and domestic violence. When serious suspicious injuries to infants occur in the context of some or all of these concerns, specialist assessments carefully review levels of continuing risk stemming from identified concerns (and the risk factors which stem from their interactions), as well as forming considered views as to the potential of therapeutic change within identified timescales. Such assessments generate a risks/strengths ratio on a continuum with extreme positions at each end: high continuing risks/few identifiable strengths versus low continuing risks/high identifiable strengths. It is our experience that cases do arise at both ends of the spectrum: some families where serious/fatal suspicious injuries to infants have occurred reflect continuing acutely high levels of continuing risks and hopeless prospects of sustained genuine therapeutic change. Others, notwithstanding the circumstances of the serious injury event, are indicative of low continuing risk and excellent prospects of sustained significant therapeutic progress. Many cases lie somewhere in the middle of this continuum.

Cases with Few Identified Psychosocial Factors of Concern

One of the most perplexing types of case where serious suspicious injuries are sustained by a young infant are those where there are no apparently identifiable classic problems associated with child abuse. In the NSPCC SIDE research, approximately one-quarter of families registered very few (if any) of the well-known contextual factors of concern that are often retrospectively associated with serious physical abuse to infants. As the case of 'Bianca' illustrates, in these stable and often middle-class homes, violent (and sometimes fatal) events seemed to have occurred 'out of the blue' to babies/infants who were often developing appropriately and seemed well cared for.

'Bianca'

Child and family characteristics:
Baby girl, died aged 8 weeks. Only child of two natural parents: mother aged 26; father aged 24.

Circumstances and official cause of death:
Post-mortem examination revealed linear fracture of skull; extensive bilateral retinal haemorrhages; and sub-dural and sub-arachnoid haemorrhages. The pathologist's view was that these were caused by two separate injuries with the approximate force of a road traffic accident. Father was acquitted of Bianca's murder.

Family and injury circumstances:
When Bianca was aged 2 weeks, her mother took her to the GP, saying she had noticed bruising on Bianca's face and body. Bianca was admitted to hospital where paediatric examination noted three bruises to her face, three bruises to her abdomen, and four bruises to her legs. Clinical investigations were negative in relation to any likely medical cause. The consultant paediatrician expressed a clear view regarding non-accidental injury.

A multi-disciplinary strategy meeting agreed that Bianca should remain in hospital until after the initial child protection conference. However, shortly after this meeting the social worker and police officers involved in the enquiry came to believe that the consultant paediatrician was wrong, and that instead the injuries were due to some form of unknown accident. They then returned Bianca home against the explicit paediatric advice (and the plan of the initial strategy meeting). Social services cancelled the pending initial child protection conference.

Social services involvement with the family continued on a supportive basis to the parents based on the social worker's newly acquired view that the bruises were in fact mongolian blue spot (and her belief that the consultant paediatrician was failing to recognise this). The police opted out of any further enquiry or involvement. Over the next month, further bruising was noted to Bianca on three further occasions. Mother's explanations were always accepted and no further medical examinations in relation to these further injuries were arranged. Other key professionals were not informed. At age 8 weeks, an emergency ambulance was called to the home. Bianca died the next day in paediatric intensive care.

Part 8 Review conclusions regarding role of child protection agencies:

- inadequate child protection investigation
- social worker and police officer discounting opinion of consultant paedi-atrician on a medical matter (erroneous belief regarding mongolian blue spot)
- social services and police supervision processes not identifying these mistakes
- lack of systematic assessment
- inadequate social services responses to the three observations of further bruising
- poor agency and interagency communication.

There is little knowledge of this phenomenon whereby severe injuries occur within a context of otherwise apparently unremarkable personalities and relationships. To what extent is this a particularly well-concealed form of child abuse with explosive personality and relationship factors beneath a façade of middle-class respectability? How common is it for otherwise loving and competent parents momentarily to lose control when faced by temporary, unexpected intense pressures stemming from caring for a baby? Or, are there as yet little known and accidental medical explanations for severe injuries that have all the traditional hallmarks of abuse? We shall discuss the key diagnostic dilemmas and disputes that often arise in such cases in Chapter 7.

Difficulties can arise for practitioners in responding constructively to the highly articulate, resourceful and influential characteristics of parents in some of these cases. Such families (particularly when socially and professionally successful and financially advantaged) do not expect to become subject to child protection system interventions. They are likely to make clear their deep resentment of this, a response that often provides a great professional (and often emotional) challenge for the social workers who have to undertake initial assessments and implement whatever urgent child protection plans are considered necessary in the circumstances. Practitioners may feel great sympathy for the parents, or be significantly intimidated by them. Either way, it can be difficult to achieve and sustain a confident, neutral-yet-supportive stance without becoming subject to dynamics that promote an overidentification with the parents at one extreme, or mutual antagonism at the other. Consequently, expectations and dynamics of 'partnership' can become problematic and distorted.

Reunification and Re-injuries

We noted in Chapter 4 that, apart from the important recent project in Wales (Ellaway et al. 2004), systematically gathered, long-term, follow-up data specifically about cases of serious suspicious injury to infants are practically non-existent. The studies of general child protection systems (the *Messages from Research* conclusions) indicated that between one-third and one-quarter of children were known to have been re-abused after they had come to the notice of child protection agencies (Department of Health 1995). These studies also noted that when re-injuries did occur, the proportion that was severe was very low.

Outcomes of the Independent Assessment Sample

A number of summary statements can be made about the 17 infants that had been removed from parental care after serious suspicious injuries (the other four babies were removed from their mothers at birth because of injuries to previous children). As we noted earlier, these reunifications were not always in accordance with the recommendations of the assessment service.

Reunifications

- In 15/17 cases, the injured infant was reunified with some combination of family members.
- In just over half of these cases (8/15), the infant was returned to the same parental combinations as at the time of the injuries.

- An almost equal proportion (7/15) returned to a household which had changed by the departure of a parent/carer, or to stay with close relatives.
- In only 2/17 cases was the injured child permanently separated from parents/carers and extended family.

Re-injuries

Re-injuries occurred in seven of the 15 cases of children reunified with parents/carers/extended family. This happened more often when children returned to homes with the same combination of parents/carers as at the time of the original injuries (5/8 cases). Reunification with changed parenting arrangements resulted in fewer known re-injuries (2/7 cases).

The extent and severity of re-injuries were mixed. One child died (cause of death was officially recorded as natural, but the body was badly bruised and neglected). This family had refused to engage in the independent assessment, but the infant was still returned home by social services. Three reunified children in other families sustained further bone fractures; and another three significant bruising. In only two cases (to our knowledge) did any of the reunifications end on child protection grounds. One child who had been returned to a single-birth mother was permanently separated after a re-injury of moderate severity. A later born sibling was seriously injured in another family where a child had been returned to a changed household.

Removals at Birth

In four cases, the child protection task was related to assessment of unborn or new babies where there were histories of serious and fatal suspicious injuries to previous children. Three out of four of these cases involved the removal of the baby from the mother at birth on the basis of an emergency court order. In one of these cases, this was effected only after the parents were caught by the police, having absconded from the hospital with the baby shortly after mother gave birth. In one case, the child was already 9 months old at the time it was learnt that the father had been implicated in the death of a previous baby elsewhere in the country. In this case, a residential placement was obtained, thus preventing the detrimental impact of separating the baby from her mother. The outcomes of these four cases were that three of the children were reunited at some stage with their natural parents (two cases) and single mother (one case). In the other case (the absconding parents), the baby was placed for adoption. Re-injuries are known to have occurred in one of these cases: a subsequently born sibling to the baby of the single mother sustained a SIDE injury several years later.

In the independent assessment sample as a whole, a substantial proportion (18/21) of the children were returned home. This is similar to a high proportion of babies with suspected non-accidental injuries who were returned to their parents in the Welsh study previously discussed (Cobley & Sanders 2003; Ellaway et al. 2004). A study in the USA of SIDE-type situations found that 52% (of 30 injured infants) had been returned to their parents/carers (Miller et al. 1999). While some of these were infants who returned into circumstances that clearly caused the researchers considerable alarm, only one child was known to have suffered another serious injury after reunification at 9-month follow-up.

These figures should not be used as the basis for supporting recommendations about future risk or reunification in any individual case. Apart from the Welsh study, the samples are small, and have less than ideal follow-up information. They are also context specific. In particular, it is not known what assessments were undertaken or what family support/therapeutic services were provided to families in the Welsh study. It is clear in the US study that significant psychotherapeutic and education resources were offered to the parents involved. In the NSPCC assessment sample, most of the cases had arisen in areas that (at the time) were very well resourced in terms of the quality and variety of assessment, therapeutic and family support services. Moreover, generally speaking (there were a few exceptions), the culture of interagency child protection case management (and the courts) was to allow sufficient time for parents to derive benefit from the therapeutic opportunities that independent assessment offered. In any interpretation of the figures we have presented for reunification and re-injury from this assessment sample, these factors relating to service context must be taken into account.

6

PARENTAL PERCEPTIONS OF CHILD PROTECTION INTERVENTIONS

If you are upset they put you down as an emotional wreck. If not, they say you have no feelings. (A mother in an independent assessment interview, 2003)

An accusation that is all in the day's work for professionals such as health visitors, social workers and others, is a cataclysmic life event for parents and wider family. (Cleaver & Freeman 1995, p. 163)

Dealing with the loss and grief of parents who have had their children removed remains an urgent priority. Parents can be far more effective in meeting the needs of their children and achieving positive relationships with carers if their own pain is sensitively acknowledged and worked with. (Thorpe & Thomson, p. 30, 2003)

In contrast to the volume of research that has identified the varied *consequences* of child abuse and the *processes* of the child protection system, there is a modest but significant collection of studies of the experiences of families who have become subject to child protection interventions. This research falls within the tradition of enquiry into the views of consumers of general social and therapeutic services, dating back to the 1970s (e.g. Lishman 1978; Maluccio 1979; Mayer & Timms 1970; Sainsbury 1987). In the 1990s, studies began to explore specifically parental perceptions of child protection services.

Two important conclusions can be drawn from the body of parental perception studies. First, there is a consistently strong tendency for parents to be highly critical of the process and outcomes of child protection interventions. Second, researchers are agreed that the views of many parents can extend beyond the biases of their particular personal experiences and consequently can offer sophisticated and insightful contributions that are of much value in relation to the development of good child protection practice. It is a general failing of child protection services (and one that has a major negative impact on quality and cost-effectiveness) that feedback from families is not routinely sought to facilitate continual adjustment and improvements to the nature of interventions.

In this chapter we distil key themes from the body of parental perceptions research and make space for the voices of families who have been subject to child protection interventions to be heard via verbatim quotations obtained from clinical and research case examples.

KEY THEMES FROM THE BODY OF PARENTAL PERCEPTIONS RESEARCH

The studies we draw from which elicit parents' perceptions of child protection interventions span the period 1991 to 2004:

- Howitt (1992) interviewed 17 families who had been involved with social workers over allegations of abuse. These families were recruited via parents' support/advocacy groups, and this group included several serious suspicious injury cases.
- Prosser (1992) interviewed 30 families via the parents' campaign group Parents Against Injustice (PAIN). In 29/30 cases, charges of abuse were eventually dropped against the parents, or courts found in their favour. This group included three serious suspicious injury cases.
- Ryburn (1994c) interviewed 12 families subject to compulsory adoption of children.
- Lindley (1994) interviewed members of 48 families whose children were the subject of care/supervision order applications in the courts. Families were recruited from within those who had contacted the Family Rights Group, and via local authorities involved with such families.
- Cleaver and Freeman (1995) surveyed 583 child protection conferences and undertook interviews with 30 families that were involved in the early stages of a child protection enquiry.
- Thoburn et al. (1995) reviewed 220 consecutive cases that were subject to child protection conferences across seven local authorities. The study included interviews with 30 families.
- Farmer and Owen (1995) interviewed members of 44 families where one child (or more) had been placed on the child protection register.
- Fernandez (1996) conducted a file analysis in Sydney, Australia, of 294 children entering care over a 4-year period (1980–4). In addition, 89 parents were interviewed.

- Buckley et al. (1997) interviewed 14 sets of parents subject to child protection interventions in the Republic of Ireland.
- In the USA, the Florida Legislature (1998) reported a survey of 204 families who had had involvement with child protection services.
- MacKinnon (1998) interviewed parents in 44 families in Australia who had experienced interventions from therapists and child protection services.
- Freeman and Hunt (1999) interviewed 34 parents in 25 families whose contact with child protection services had resulted in care proceedings on their children.
- Gleeson et al. (2001) utilised a questionnaire with 450 families in Victoria, Australia, to explore impressions of child protection interventions, including the question of whether their lives had got better or worse as a consequence of these interventions.
- Lindley et al. (2001) interviewed 43 parents in the context of examining the effectiveness of advocacy services for parents involved in child protection proceedings.
- Ferguson and O'Reilly (2001) interviewed 14 parents and 13 children who had been involved with child protection interventions in the Republic of Ireland in 1996.
- Corby et al. (2002) interviewed 34 sets of parents who had been assessed by social workers after the introduction (in the UK in 2000) of the Assessment Framework.
- The Scottish Executive (2002), as part of a major review of the Scottish child protection system, interviewed parents (exact number unclear) of 17 children who had been subject to child protection interventions.
- Spratt and Callan (2004) undertook semi-structured interviews with 12 families in Northern Ireland who had been subject to child protection interventions.
- Trotter (2004) interviewed 282 clients of child protection social workers in Victoria, Australia.
- Dale (2004) interviewed 27 members of 18 families in a central England local authority in 2002 about their experiences of child protection interventions. This study specifically identified positive client evaluations of child protection interventions (in addition to the familiar, previously well-reported criticisms).

This body of research covers a range of eras and cultures in child protection practice. In the UK, studies date from before the implementation of the Children Act 1989 (in 1991) to Assessment Framework practice from 2000 onward (especially Corby et al. 2002; Dale 2004). In most of the individual studies, the samples are small (as is typical of qualitative research); therefore, caution must be exercised in generalising from these views across all families who become involved in child protection services. This is particularly so as parents who agree to be interviewed for research tend to be those who feel most strongly about their experiences either positively or negatively. However, taken together, these studies include the views of well over 1000 families across England, Scotland, Northern Ireland, the Republic of Ireland, the USA and Australia regarding experiences of child protection interventions. Thus, the combined sample represents a powerful and quite consistent collective voice that needs to be heard.

One of the most disconcerting conclusions from parental perceptions research as a whole is the intense dissatisfaction, dismay and despair that remain a constant feature. With a few exceptions, feelings are very negative about the nature, style and outcomes of child protection interventions (see especially Cleaver & Freeman 1995; Freeman & Hunt 1999; Howitt 1992; Lindley 1994; Prosser 1992; Thoburn et al. 1995). What are the major concerns about how child protection services are provided? In essence, there are three main areas of complaint:

- the child protection system is arbitrary and opaque
- families feel they are treated unfairly
- families describe a negative interactional style of child protection practitioners.

We shall now consider these three areas in more detail.

ARBITRARY AND OPAQUE NATURE OF THE CHILD PROTECTION SYSTEM

> The thing is you don't know what they want from you, what they are looking for, what they expect. Nobody tells you anything; they just carry on. (A parent in Freeman & Hunt 1999, p. 25)

In unexpected traumatic circumstances, strangers from social services (and often the police) have suddenly intervened in their lives. Family members are shocked, disoriented, frightened and sometimes angry, as they cannot understand what is happening, and feel inherently disadvantaged because *they do not know how the system works*. They have little idea what the key processes are: what will be considered significant, what the next steps are, or how to influence the course of events:

> We didn't know what was happening when they turned up at the door; whether we had the right to refuse them entry and what would happen if we did. They said

they could have proceedings but no mention of my rights as the accused – never, ever all the way through. No-one explained my legal position or about the child if they were going to take her away from us. (A father in Thoburn et al. 1995, p. 55)

Specifically and repeatedly, parents report feeling powerless in the face of the child protection 'machine', and that they are not given information about their rights. Consequently, several studies have recommended that it is vital for parents to be given *written information* at the first point of child protection interventions to help orientate them as to what can be expected (e.g. Cleaver & Freeman 1995; Lindley 1994). More recently, Lindley et al. (2001) demonstrated the value for families of having a supporter or advocate involved at an early stage when child protection enquiries are commenced under Section 47 of the Children Act 1989. The Department of Health subsequently commissioned the development of a protocol on advice and advocacy for parents involved in child protection proceedings, with a view to national implementation (Lindley & Richards 2002).

However, recent studies and case examples highlight that the routine provision of appropriate information to parents, let alone the availability of independent advocacy, is still not occurring. Some families continue to be denied information about the nature of the child protection procedures and legal proceedings that they have become involved in. One couple, facing an allegation of historic abuse, were simply unable throughout the entire child protection process to get any written confirmation about what was alleged against them:

In the child protection meeting we were told that we couldn't have the information because that was privileged information to social services, and we weren't allowed access to this. We subsequently ended up having a row with the social worker on the telephone about this and said: 'We need to have it in writing' – and she said 'You can't'. And so we are left hanging. Presumably they have followed the correct procedures – we don't know! But, we are professional people, we can sort of deal with this – but what about other people who don't know what's going on – who haven't got the support around them? (Two parents in the study undertaken by Dale 2002c)

The lack of information about how the child protection system operates (and how it can be influenced) contributes to the impression some families have that they have become ensnared in a predetermined unstoppable process:

Throughout the process parents evidenced feelings of being powerless to resist an all-powerful agency and to avert a train of events which in retrospect was seen as somehow inevitable, even pre-planned. Many described being in a 'no-win' situation where the truth was distorted and used against them. (Freeman & Hunt 1999, p. 25)

For some families such interventions seem not far removed from the nightmare of Joseph K. in Franz Kafka's novel published in 1925, *The Trial*. The central theme of *The Trial* is of a citizen becoming ensnared in a bureaucratic web of confusion and ambiguity spun by the inscrutable agencies of an unfathomable court of law. In our context, why is it that some families experience the child protection system to be opaque, arbitrary and unfathomable, in an almost Kafkaesque way? What is it that can lead social services to refuse to make copies of their operational procedures available to families, outlining the processes and standards for interventions?

> They refused to give us copies of the procedures they were working to. I rang the Team Manager – she said point-blank: 'No, you can't have them.' (Siobhan, a grandmother: research interview undertaken in 2004)

This is difficult to understand by any standards of courtesy, respect, natural justice, human rights and fair process, given that in states of shock following discovery of the injuries and the resulting child protection interventions, it is difficult for family members to think clearly and retain information given verbally. On this basis, it is vital that user-friendly written information and (ideally) independent advocacy are provided for parents so that they can understand the workings of the system that they have become involved with and can better judge whether they are being treated fairly or not (Lindley & Richards 2002).

UNFAIR TREATMENT

Many parents and other family members feel that they have not been treated fairly by the child protection system. There is a view that the system itself is inherently unfair, and also that practitioners do not comply with the requirements of the system and behave capriciously. These issues can be distilled into two specific concerns regarding:

- arbitrary and inconsistent decisions and disproportionate judgments
- inherent negative assessment bias.

Arbitrary Case Management, Inconsistent Decisions and Disproportionate Judgments

Having undertaken independent child protection assessments, audits, reviews and research across many local authority areas over more than two decades, one of our strongest impressions is of the inconsistencies in the ways that essentially similar cases are handled. Even within the same local authority, the chance factor of which combination of professionals becomes involved with a family will result in different styles of professional intervention and case management plans.

Decisions to compulsorily separate babies and young children from the care of their parents and familiar extended family members should be among the most carefully considered in child protection practice. Several studies have indicated that many parents believe that such decisions are made casually, routinely, and without adequate consideration of alternative safety plans, and are then implemented in inhumane ways:

> How are you supposed to stop them? They just go ahead with their plans anyway, don't they? ... They are too powerful. (A parent in Freeman & Hunt 1999, p. 27)

Inconsistencies in case management can be startling and have the most profound consequences. For example, one young baby, having sustained serious suspicious injuries, was discharged from hospital according to an assessment and protection plan involving monitoring by extended family members:

> They said they were going to take him off me and put him in foster care – which I wasn't very happy about. So what happens then is the social worker had a word with my Mum and asked my Mum to get a month or two off work. So she got a month off work. I was living here but I couldn't be on my own with him – I had to be supervised. By the time my Mum had to go back to work I still had to be supervised – so then we had to bring my Grandma and Granddad into it! (Ms Durgan, a mother, in the study undertaken by Dale 2002c)

For another family in very similar circumstances, such arrangements were not permitted by social services. The family had no history with social services and little explanation was given. The mother and grandmother remained bewildered, distraught and outraged that on discharge from hospital their 8-week-old baby was placed with strangers – apparently on the grounds that the family was 'too close':

> She (social worker) came here – and you just couldn't win. You couldn't win. She said that I was too involved and that I was too supportive. ... We got in touch with another family who were treated very differently. The grandparents were quickly allowed to look after the grandchild on an EPO [Emergency Protection Order]. I asked 'Why not us? Who has deemed us to be a risk?' ... They made an awful lot of assumptions. We had no history with them at all. An awful lot of assumptions about our race, our culture; and they seemed to enjoy flexing their muscles. ... The fact that Rachel was seeing me every day – my sister sees our mother every day in Belfast – it's part of our culture! – But it was used against us. (Siobhan, a grandmother: research interview undertaken in 2004)

It is a common finding in family perceptions research that grandparents in particular feel snubbed and distraught when they are rejected by social services as alternative (temporary or permanent) carers:

> We had looked after the children and we were very concerned about them. . . . They didn't even come and see us properly. They could have talked to me more about it; there was a lack of communication. They didn't give us information as to why they were doing things. I still feel Social Services have too much power and give them a bit of power they abuse it. (A grandparent in Freeman & Hunt 1999, p. 28)

The Case of Simon

In a case known to the first author (we will call the father Simon), a 5-month-old baby had been in foster care since birth on the basis of concerns about an elder child who had died previously in mysterious circumstances in the mother's care. Simon had not met the mother at that time and had had no involvement in the sadly short life of her deceased baby. The mother acknowledged that she could not be considered as a carer for the new baby, who had been removed from her at birth. Since then the relationship between the parents had ended.

Simon was already the main carer of an elder child about whom no child protection concerns had ever been recorded, and he was demonstrably highly committed to his new baby son. The paternal grandparents were local and the centre of a stable and resourceful extended family. The kinship care proposal was that the grandparents and Simon would share the care of the baby in a mutually supportive way. However, social services (having rapidly identified adoptive parents via 'concurrent planning') refused to support the placement of the baby initially with parental grandparents despite having previously approved them as foster parents. In a judgment that praised the grandparents fittingly, the judge then endorsed the care plan of the local authority that the baby be compulsorily adopted. The bewildered and devastated family found this judgment to be incomprehensible but had insufficient financial resources to attempt any appeal.

A recurrent theme for families is the reluctance of social services to recognise the value of extended family/kinship resources alongside 'worst scenarios' regarding the level of risks, and lack of resources for more constructive reunification programmes (Dale 2004; Fernandez 1996; Howitt 1992; Prosser 1992; Ryburn 1994a; Thorpe & Thomson, 2003). In this context, explicit standards governing child protection interventions are needed. For example:

- How exactly is it decided whether or not it is essential for a child (and siblings) to be removed into foster care rather than being placed with grandparents/extended family?
- When an infant has been removed into care, how is it decided what levels of parental contact and involvement in caretaking tasks is appropriate?
- How is the nature of the restrictions to be imposed on the extended family determined regarding which relatives are allowed to maintain contact with the child?
- How is it decided that a case should be subject to care proceedings, or whether it can be managed on the basis of a 'voluntary' child protection agreement?

Some parents feel that the basis for such case management decisions is, at best, secret, often arbitrary, and, at the worst, disproportionate and punitive. Such decisions are also seen as being covertly pragmatic, often dressed in pseudo-professional rationalisations that families can experience as incomprehensible and patronising (and sometimes ridiculous). This particularly applies to the inconsistency of decisions to remove a child from parental care, to decisions to place (or not) within the extended family or with strangers, and to the wide variety of arrangements that are made for parental/family contact with the child in care. Parents require greater clarity, consistency and transparency in these areas of decision making to be better able to judge whether or not they are being subject to 'fair process'.

Standards of Proof

Parents also often express confusion and resentment about the differences in the nature of evidence and standards of proof between criminal and Family Court proceedings. In the former, at least 10 members of a jury of 12 people must be convinced 'beyond reasonable doubt' for parents to be convicted of a criminal offence against their child. In the latter, a single judge can make a 'finding of fact' regarding significant harm and 'free' an infant for adoption (dispensing with parental consent) on the basis of the 'balance of probabilities' standard of evidence.

The Case of Rachel

At the age of 8 weeks, a well-cared-for baby (Siercha) was found to have several fractures to her ribs and leg. Both parents were convicted of assault and sentenced to imprisonment, at which point their relationship ended (although both continued to maintain that neither of them had caused the injuries). The local authority refused to place Siercha within the extended family (none of whom had any past involvement with social services). She was placed with foster parents, and social services began actively searching for prospective adoptive parents (not difficult to find for a healthy baby of this age). After being in prison for over a year, both Rachel and her ex-partner were acquitted on appeal of all charges in relation to injuries to Siercha. However, by this time, the Family Court process had completed the stage of 'freeing for adoption', resulting in the compulsory irrevocable adoption of Siercha against her parents' wishes.

Given the significance of such Family Court decisions, parents often make the point that it is fundamentally unfair that decisions with such profound consequences should be taken by a single judge at the 'balance of probability' level – especially as, for many families (particularly those with inadequate resources), the decisions are largely non-appealable unless the judge has made an error in law (rather than a perverse judgment). It should be noted that some judges recognise that this view has some validity. For example, one senior Family Court judge commented that judges (like all professionals) are subject to *'bias, prejudice and an obstinate inability to shift'* (LJ Thorpe 2003, p. 309).

Inherent Negative Assessment Bias

> Social services is putting things down to try to paint as bad a picture as possible because they think ends justify the means. They will win their case no matter what and truth is the first thing to suffer. (A parent in Ryburn 1994b, p. 168)

> The ethos of the Children Act is that as far as possible, from the point of first contact, parents should be involved in decisions about their children. As far as the parents in this study were concerned these high ideals are just so much pie in the sky ... the majority considering that Social Services had already prejudged their case and made their minds up about how they were to proceed. (Freeman & Hunt 1999, p. 27)

Parents report that whatever feelings they show, or do not show, is negatively construed:

> If you didn't say anything you were passively aggressive – if you did say anything you were too emotional. (Siobhan, a grandmother: research interview undertaken in 2004)

The emotional responses of parents (such as expressions of frustration, irritation and sarcasm) to perceived negative styles of intervention may be seen as 'evidence' that the family is totally uncooperative and even inherently dangerous. Families describe a professional mentality that can appear almost paranoid: a fear that parents are so psychopathologically devious that they will 'fake good' in disingenuous dealings with professionals and at the first manipulated opportunity are likely to pounce in cold blood and murder their baby. While some parents undoubtedly do have murderous feelings toward their offspring, acting on this is extraordinarily rare. The widely overgeneralised fear of this happening may be a contaminated cultural residue of exhortations from proponents of Munchausen's syndrome by proxy (MSBP) for professionals to 'think dirty' (see further discussion on this in Chapter 7). Some families feel that too many professionals have been thinking too dirty, too often, and that this has caused them great harm.

Case examples such as those of Simon and Rachel illustrate an issue that provokes some of the strongest expressions of feeling in parents – the sense of unfairness that derives from professionals being perceived as having an inherently suspicious and pessimistic bias against natural families whereby almost every aspect of their personalities, relationships and lifestyle is negatively construed by social workers. On this theme, in a powerful critique of child protection practice in the USA, Crenshaw (2004) portrays child protection workers as being inherently biased by their emotional counter-transference reactions, and being attitudinally 'family-phobic'. In the same vein, some children's guardians and courts are seen as 'rubber-stamping' negatively biased core assessments and care plans presented by social services in care proceedings, resulting in disproportionate judgments based on idealistic views of compulsory adoption.

Parents believe that these draconian outcomes stem from routine assumptions of worst possible scenarios where child protection professionals have been encouraged to 'think dirty' in a family-phobic way. As we shall discuss in Chapter 10, 'concurrent planning' and 'parallel planning' (without appropriate assessment regarding the viability of reunification) can incline toward prejudgments in favour of compulsory adoption. This reflects *unreasonable* professional practice: absent, inadequate or biased assessments; disproportionate judgments; and, arguably, impingements of Articles 6 and 8 of the Human Rights Act 1998 (the right to a fair trial and respect for private and family life). This is strong language, but conveys the intensity of feeling of parents who have experienced the removal and compulsory adoption of one or more of their children:

Nobody ever asked down the road what sort of family we are. Nobody has ever considered the possibility of adoption in our extended families on both sides, and nobody has ever considered guardianship or something like that, because they just had their minds made up that it had to be adoption and that it had to be adoption arranged by them. (A parent in Ryburn 1994b, p. 166)

This is particularly so for parents in cases where there is intense dispute about the nature, validity and impact of medical evidence in relation to the causes of injuries. Although it is not possible to present the detail in this book, in the case of baby Siercha, new evidence subsequently obtained by the family raised significant questions of whether the injuries were in fact associated with an hereditary family medical condition. However, it was too late to prevent her compulsory adoption.

As is discussed in some detail in Chapter 7, the validity and reliability of expert medical evidence has become a very controversial issue a decade since the findings of Prosser:

> A considerable number of abuse cases we considered became problematic following the involvement of medical practitioners. . . . Parents accused of abuse believed that Social Workers and Police too often interpreted the medical practitioner phrase 'is consistent with abuse' as hard evidence that abuse had taken place. . . . In some cases we found the various diagnoses by experts and the certainty with which they contradicted one another to be bewildering . . . in a number of instances what was considered to be evidence of abuse was eventually identified as a 'natural' condition. (Prosser 1992, pp. 14–15)

Especially in cases that are subject to court proceedings (e.g. Freeman & Hunt 1999; Howitt 1992; Prosser 1992) parents feel caught in the Kafkaesque scenario where the burden of proof is reversed and *they are required to prove their innocence* or are offered inducements (e.g. leniency or their child being returned) to confess falsely:

> All parents in the sample described pressure, usually in the form of psychological threats, to admit guilt, brought by Social Workers. Social Services, claim parents, have considerable powers and they feel they are threatened with those powers in order to gain confessions. Parents believe the tactic of 'say you did it and you can have your child back' was deceitful, an improper use of power, and an unacceptable practice. (Prosser 1992, p. 7)

It is of concern that this practice appears to be continuing over 10 years later. Rachel described the attempts made by social services to get her to confess to injuring her baby:

> They tried to plea bargain: they said if we admitted to causing one fracture and neglect – knowing they were there and didn't do anything – then they were prepared to say that the other fractures were accidental. This was on the first day (of the care proceedings). But I wasn't going to admit it – I'm not prepared to say that I did it. . . . They kept saying that if we can't admit it then we can't be rehabilitated. They kept using that – if we admitted to doing it and to knowing, then we could get Siercha back . . .

They kept making false promises. They said a few times if you will admit to it, you can have your child back.... But if that's the case, that's frightening. I just thought: 'How can you say that? How can you do that to someone?' With the Guardian as well saying that she hopes she'll come back to us – they are just so cruel. I could never do that. It's someone's baby – you've taken someone's child – and you can just sit there and say such things. (Rachel, a mother, research interview undertaken in 2004)

This issue is at the core of many child protection interventions where there have been serious suspicious injuries to infants. Not infrequently, an impasse arises between the family insistence that the baby has not been abused, and professionals working within a culture that tends to view failure to confess as 'denial', which itself is construed as a high-risk factor (Lusk 1996).

It is in such situations that independent assessments can prove to be particularly valuable. In many cases (but by no means all) an independent, therapeutically oriented assessment intervention can provide a constructive way forward that is acceptable to all parties (and which often avoids the need for the high financial and emotional costs of contested Family/High Court hearings). Varied examples of such approaches in the UK have been provided (Asen et al. 1989; Bentovim et al. 1987; Dale et al. 1986; Dale 1991; Dale & Fellows 1999; Essex et al. 1995; Fitzpatrick 1995; Kennedy 1997; Robinson & Whitney 1999), as well as in Australia (Fitzgerald & McGregor 1995; Thorpe 2003; Thorpe & Thomson 2003). Assessing the thorny issue of 'denial' is a key focus of many of these approaches, as discussed further in Chapter 7.

NEGATIVE PROFESSIONAL STYLE

The worst thing? the threats, behaviour, the power they've got. The big words they used frightened me – really frightened me.... Arrogant, very arrogant. Ignorant as well. That person's approach: She didn't ask, she told.... At the time, in my mind I was thinking: 'If she's going to be funny, I'm going to be funny.' (Mr Taylor, a father, in Dale 2002c, p. 44)

Descriptions of a negative interpersonal style of professional action (and inactions) seep through many of the parental perception research reports. It is not only *what* is being done in the name of child protection, but also the *way* – the style – in which it is done that can feel so upsetting and provocative for many families. We shall cover this issue of negative professional style under two main headings:

● interactional style of child protection practitioners
● the emotional impact for families.

Nyack College Library

Interactional Style of Child Protection Practitioners

It is important to note that parents interviewed in research studies invariably accept that when reports are received about the welfare of children, professionals have a duty to make enquiries, and that in some cases urgent protective action is required. Parents also recognise that this is a difficult job, and that many professionals feel that they cannot win either way: they are criticised for inadequate or naive interventions that result in further abuse, or for intervening in disproportionately 'heavy' ways. What families do not understand, however, is why the attitudes and behaviour of child protection practitioners toward them sometimes are discourteous, unpleasant, hostile and cold:

> When the social worker came, he came in with the police and didn't identify himself. It was appalling, absolutely awful, he nigh on interrogated me. It was the questions he asked, and I wasn't in a fit state to talk to anyone. He was very much accusing. (A mother in Thoburn et al. 1995, p. 55)

> All along, social services seemed to be testing and pushing us. They wanted to see how far we would go. They were just waiting for us to snap. Waiting for us to make any little mistake. I don't think they really thought we were human then. (A father in Lindley 1994, p. 32)

> The two social workers say they are putting them up for adoption – they keep rubbing it in every time we see them. It doesn't matter how upset I am, they just go on, and on, and on.... We don't want them split up – it's not right is it?... I were adopted myself, that's why I don't want it with my children. (Mr and Mrs Harland in Dale 2002c, p. 39)

In a case of 'parallel planning', one mother recalled social services talking at a very early stage about the prospect of permanent separation from her baby:

> We went to a meeting and (social worker) said to me 'You've got a beautiful child – we've got plenty of people what would want her.' She then told me that they've got a family lined up – and that was before they'd even started looking into our family. (Rachel, a mother, research interview undertaken in 2004)

Another parent exclaimed:

> This is legalised kidnapping... there is a shortage of babies for adoption, so they take mine, and I can't do a thing about it. (Parent participant at parents' support group conference, 2003)

Beyond biases and negative professional style, some families make serious allegations of professional malpractice including threats, deception, manipulation, trickery, exaggeration, distortion – even falsifying and fabricating concerns (Freeman & Hunt 1999; Howitt 1992; Prosser 1992):

Accusations of fabrications, exaggerations and distortions ranged from inaccuracies in dates and names, to blaming the wrong partner for the abuse or labelling the parent as the result of past errors . . . Individual social workers came in for a barrage of invective, being variously accused of lying, distorting facts, judging things out of context, dragging up outdated or irrelevant information or making gross mistakes in their presentation of the evidence. Parents felt once again the focus was highly selective, social workers having 'only kept notes on the bad bits'. (Freeman & Hunt 1999, pp. 43–4)

In a case known recently to the first author, a local authority presented evidence to persuade a court that two siblings should be compulsorily adopted. It became clear that while the local authority had collated a voluminous bundle of evidence relating to historical parental inadequacy (but not abuse) of previous children, it had withheld all material relating to a recent social services assessment which, it transpired, had drawn positive conclusions about the parents' care of the current children. This practice echoes a comment by Murray Ryburn (a committed campaigner against compulsory adoption):

They [social services] had elected in this instance to suppress a vital piece of evidence which cast an entirely different complexion on their account of the mother's motivation and her links with her daughter. The process of the careful selection of evidence is one that accompanies the presentation of any case in contested proceedings. Sometimes the drive to win in the adversarial process leads to deliberate falsification of evidence. We can only assume here that professionals believe the end justifies the means. (Ryburn 1994a, pp. 189–90)

Emotional Impact for Families

When I had to hand her over it was the worse feeling ever. You just don't want to do it – you haven't got any choice – they say: 'You have to.' It was done on the ward, in front of everyone. The lady who was driving her just came up and – I was just telling Siercha how she had to be a good girl for Mummy and – (cries) – she was just smiling at me. And you just can't describe how that feels. It's soul-destroying. It breaks your heart. (Rachel, a mother: research interview undertaken in 2004)

Professionals, overburdened with abuse investigations or preoccupied with other problems, might easily lose sight of how violating the procedure could seem. (Cleaver & Freeman 1995, p. 163).

Thorpe (2003) described how professionals often fail to recognise the 'incredible loss' – and in some cases post-traumatic stress impact for parents – when their children enter care. In cases where infants have sustained serious suspicious injuries followed by urgent child protection investigations, the atmosphere for the family is doubly traumatic. First, there is the sequence of events within the family that led to the injuries (accidental or abuse) and their discovery. Whatever the cause, parents and extended family members will invariably be significantly shocked by knowledge that the baby is seriously harmed (at worse dead, or with life-threatening injuries and possible permanent disability).

Overlying the trauma of the injury events and context, is the additional shock precipitated by the emergency medical treatment and rapid police and social services involvement. There are some indications in the midst of such emotional turmoil and confusion, that the style of intervention by the police is often retrospectively seen as having been conducted in a professional and considerate manner:

> A positive feature from the cases in this sample was the general respect for the way the police handled enquiries they were involved in. Parents, with one exception, praised the police for being courteous, open-minded and fair. (Dale 2004, p. 144)

The key factor is an attitude of open-mindedness and basic courtesy alongside skills in relating to highly distressed (and sometimes very angry) family members in the context of major trauma. It is likely that many police officers have better training and greater experience in effectively managing acute traumatic enquiries that do most social workers. Social workers tend to score lower than police officers in the eyes of family members in relation to the sensitivity and fairness of their intervention at this stage. Families find the apparent lack of compassion from some child protection practitioners difficult to comprehend:

> Many parents feel judged as totally bad and, as a result, are treated with disrespect, and denied even basic courtesies of civil human interaction. (Thorpe & Thomson 2003, p. 3)

> In as many as 70 per cent of the families the investigation and case conference had a negative impact on the parental figures who frequently felt marginalised and badly treated. (Farmer & Owen 1995, p. 315)

> Parents cited instances in the meetings (child protection conferences) when they had not only been bewildered, angered or insulted by what was being said about them, but also felt harshly judged and unduly condemned. Some families complained of the cold and impersonal attitude of practitioners which left them feeling depersonalised by the experience. (Freeman & Hunt 1999, p. 29)

Is this reported 'dehumanisation' personal or political? Are increasingly hard-pressed professionals losing the capacity for empathy with parents and families in acute distress? Are social workers increasingly 'family-phobic'? (Crenshaw 2004). Has it now become the professional norm to hate the 'abuser' as well as the abuse (even when it is not proven)? Has a culture developed in which, increasingly, parents suspected of injuring babies are demonised as incorrigible recidivists who have forfeited rights to consideration and dignity? Is there any possible connection between the diminution of family support services, the emergence of 'hard-line' child protection interventions, and government targets for increasing the percentage of children that are adopted from care? To what extent is the stark analysis of child protection work in Australia applicable in the UK?

> Little serious thought has been given to the possibility that the means to protect children from one source of harm is in fact exposing them to another...far from promoting the best interests of children at risk in their own homes, Australian statutory child welfare systems seem unable to avoid adding insult to injury. (Thorpe in Fernandez 1996, p. xvi)

Complaints Procedures

Social services departments are obligated under the Children Act 1989 to operate formal complaints procedures in relation to their services. There is little published research about the rate, nature and outcomes of complaints that are made. Anecdotally, there is reason for concern that some families are as dissatisfied with the complaints procedures as they are with the child protection interventions. Returning to the case of Rachel, while she was in prison, the grandmother wrote a number of carefully composed, specific complaints about the behaviour and role of social services. Considered responses from social services responses to the complaints were not initially forthcoming:

> We didn't get anywhere – when we started fighting against them, they just fought harder. . . . We got responses but they didn't answer. They didn't answer first of all, and we had to take it to the next stage to say they hadn't responded. When I went to the complaint meeting I said: 'Your department won't answer any of my questions.'
>
> They said: 'Mrs 'A'– you've frightened our department so much, that they froze.' And I said: 'I've paralyzed the whole of social services – is that what you are bloody well saying to me?! The assistant manager and the area manager?' I said: 'I didn't know I wielded such power!' And I thought: 'You plonker!'
>
> She said to me: 'You've actually paralyzed our department.' And I said: 'For God's sake – it's actually five very simple questions – and because you couldn't answer them – I've paralyzed your department?!' (Siobhan, a grandmother: research interview undertaken in 2004)

Eventually, the validity of many of the complaints made in the handling of this case was conceded by social services, and a sum of compensation was paid to the family. Siercha remains compulsorily adopted.

Dale (2004) noted that dissatisfied families can be reluctant to use complaints procedures. Families were either unaware of such procedures or felt that invoking them would be a waste of time or counter-productive. Of particular concern was that at least two families had specifically decided *not* to complain formally, feeling that if they did so, social services would take (in their view) an even more punitive stance toward them.

In a recent independent assessment, the first author interviewed another mother and grandmother who were subject to social services rejecting the grandmother as a temporary carer of the children while pursuing parallel planning for adoption. There were aspects of social services' case management (especially the total absence of assessment in relation to potential reunification) that raised serious concerns. The mother was asked whether she had used the complaints procedure in relation to what she perceived to be significant lack of support and bias against her on the part of social services. She replied that she had discussed this with her solicitor, but had been advised against this step, as (in the words of her solicitor) it would 'Piss off the social worker' – and might further disadvantage her position in relation to social services.

This is not the first case in which the first author has heard that parents are discouraged by solicitors from making formal complaints against social services. Consequently, given the absence of routine evaluation of child protection interventions and the reluctance of some families to use complaints procedures, it is highly unlikely that Area Child Protection Committees, managers of agencies at all levels, and local elected representatives (who are ultimately responsible for services) will be aware of actual levels of dissatisfaction with the processes and outcomes of child protection services.

NEGATIVE PARENTAL PERCEPTIONS IN CONTEXT

This chapter has emphasised the reported experiences of some families (samples and individuals) who feel very negatively about the process and consequences of child protection intervention in their lives. As child protection systems do not routinely elicit the views of families who are subject to intervention, families have far too few opportunities to influence professional audiences. We hope that the emotional and rhetoric impact of these experiences will promote pause for reflection by practitioners, supervisors and managers involved in cases where infants have sustained serious suspicious injuries.

However, it is also important to recognise that these views of parents and extended family members have to be considered within a wider context. First, it would be naive not to recognise that some families will take the opportunity to join support groups and participate in research studies to espouse false protestations of innocence, and to rail about injustices of child protection systems when they (or at least one family member) are continuing to deny actual responsibility for abuse. Researchers, no more so than police officers, social workers, psychiatrist and judges, cannot reliably distinguish the 'distress of the innocent from the remorse of the guilty' (Cleaver & Freeman 1995). Consequently, research samples will inevitably include accounts of some families who are not being totally honest about the reasons for, and consequences of, child protection interventions.

Second, the body of 'risk research' (see Chapter 3) has highlighted that over-accommodation to the views and distress of adult family members can constrain practitioners from taking sufficient protective measures for injured infants. The fact that parents and family members are acutely distressed does not in itself signify in any reliable way that their infant is not at risk. To assume otherwise can and does result in tragic and sometimes fatal re-injuries to children, and, not infrequently, subsequent public criticism of child protection professionals for naivety and incompetence.

The third contextual point relating to the negative parental views expressed in this chapter is the need to emphasise that high-quality child protection practice *does* occur. Unknown numbers of families and children do benefit from and appreciate constructive child protection services. Unfortunately, this is largely unreported in research and especially in the popular media. Consequently, we shall conclude this chapter with a section derived from a study that elicited positive parental views about child protection practice.

Parental Perceptions of Positive Child Protection Practice

A small study undertaken in the Midlands (England) by the first author in 2002 involved interviews with 27 members of 18 families who had been subject to child protection interventions (Dale 2004). By no means all of this group felt positively, and we have already reported the views of some of those who were dissatisfied earlier in this chapter. Table 6.1 illustrates the spread of views of participants in that study.

Table 6.1 Participants' ratings of helpfulness of child protection services ($n = 18$)

Very helpful	Helpful to some extent	Uncertain	Did not really help	Made things worse/ was harmful
5 (28%)	4 (22%)	4 (22%)	1 (5.6%)	4 (22%)

Merging 'very helpful' and 'to some extent' gives an overall helpfulness-to-some-degree rate of 50%. Focusing on the satisfied group, it was apparent from descriptions given by families that there were many very skilled and committed child protection professionals working across agencies in the areas in which the interviews were conducted. These workers were portrayed as being friendly, interested, concerned and very keen to help in collaborative ways. A striking theme running through families' accounts of child protection interventions relates to the interactional style of professionals. This echoes the findings of an earlier study:

> Honesty, helpfulness, fairness and sensitivity were highly rated qualities. So too were the abilities to listen to and understand the family's viewpoint and to communicate in a down-to-earth way. Practical help and support together with minor but thoughtful kindness also conveyed care and understanding. (Freeman & Hunt 1999, p. 84)

The fact that some social work interventions had a therapeutic impact was greatly appreciated. In these cases, characteristics that were particularly valued included:

- being supportive
- listening carefully and effectively
- having skills in promoting cooperation
- being 'matter of fact'
- being 'human'.

The following quotations from Dale (2002c) convey parents' feelings about the positive style of social workers:

> Eye to eye contact – being able to talk to each other – say anything we want to each other. (Winnie) (p. 43)

> We get on really well with (social worker) – we have a laugh. Some of the social workers in London, they were right snotty. But down here they are not – they explain more to you than other social workers do. So we thought right, we'll get on with them – we like them. (Mr and Mrs Pendergrast) (p. 43)

> Whereas they can talk and jumble everything up and confuse you – she (current social worker) will explain what's going on and cut out the mumbo-jumbo – she gets to the point direct. (John Richardson)

> Dawn (mother): 'She were great – very pleased with her, she were right calm. She were fair – a very nice person. I could talk to her.'

> Louise (shy teenager): 'I could talk to her!!!' (Pearson family) (p. 41)

It was impressive to hear from at least two families who had been very unhappy with the child protection process that the positive qualities of particular social workers had gradually made an important difference to them:

> We've been very lucky – he's great. He's been very helpful, his mannerism – we've even looked forward to him coming. He's not treated us like criminals – not like how we felt treated at first. He's obviously taken everything in – seen the big picture. (Mr and Mrs Skye)

One father had become primary carer of a 3-year-old and a newborn baby after a life-threatening incident when the elder child had been alone with his mother. He was not initially impressed with social services involvement:

> To this day Social Services are 99% certain that (child's mother) tried to suffocate him. It couldn't be proved as she was in the flat on her own. . . . They know I was angry – I told them I couldn't understand what all this rubbish was about case conferences, child protection registers. I said to them 'He's not at risk! Why is he at risk? – I've packed my job in.'
>
> A few weeks went by, then the social worker would say 'We've got to assess you, Mr Taylor, as a parent.' I kept saying 'I don't need assessing as a parent – I've had five!' They said 'It's in your best interests as his name is on the child protection register. . . . They could put him into foster care!' As soon as I heard that it got to me. The words 'foster care' and 'assessment' I didn't like – so I set out to prove them wrong – and I passed with flying colours! (A father, Mr Taylor, in Dale 2002c)

This case demonstrated highly effective child protection work which required a skilled social worker to overcome initial parental hostility to a requirement to be assessed. Having effectively resolved the initial conflict, subsequent interagency interventions reflected excellent standards of child protection practice/resources with a corresponding high level of parental satisfaction:

> Social services were supportive to me – I knew I had back up and support – it were just someone to talk to basically, they were good listeners. They've liaised with me: case conferences, courts and children – it were little things like that that's meant big things to me. . . . They're very good listeners, very good at understanding – but they've got the power to over-rule you – which is a good thing I suppose. Because I've always said – put the child first. And it's things like that that made me cooperate and go through it with them. . . . They ring me up now and again saying 'Are you alright? Do you need anything?' (A father, Mr Taylor, in Dale 2002c, p. 41)

One mother (Ms Durgan referred to earlier on page 93) had described how, after an unexplained serious injury to her 6-month-old son, the social workers had encouraged her mother to take time off work to avoid the need for the baby to be taken into foster care while assessments were undertaken. It was apparent that the social worker had great skills and personal qualities to accept, contain and influence the intense feeling that were generated by the crisis of the injury and the child protection aftermath:

> At first it was not very good – I kept losing my temper – which is bound to happen when they are threatening to take your son off you.... As it's gone along, things have got better...we've got more friendly – we talk to each other – instead of shouting and bawling at each other (laughs)....She actually stayed quite calm – she tried to calm me down. I just couldn't hold my temper back – I had to let it out. She either just sat there and let me say what I had to say – or she'd sit there and talk to me and tell me to calm down. (Ms Durgan, a mother, in Dale 2002c, p. 43)

Further reflections included:

> At first when they said 'We're not here to take your son off you, we're here to help' – I didn't believe or trust them with that – I thought they were just saying that to calm me down. And now I've realised they're not here to take them off me – I've calmed down a lot....I accept that they had to think that –' cos we were both denying it – they weren't sure who did it. But now that they know that I didn't – it's a lot easier. They did what they had to – that's what they are there for. (Ms Durgan, a mother, in Dale 2002c, p. 43)

It is notable that these more positive views reflect those of parents who were initially traumatised by child protection interventions, who either managed to retain their child in the family, or, where the child, having been removed, was quickly returned to their care. It is unlikely that many parents who have been subject to lengthy separation from a child after a serious injury with disputed explanation, including compulsory adoption, would come to reflect so graciously on child protection practice.

Parents have strong feelings and views about the nature and outcomes of child protection interventions in their lives. Notwithstanding the huge public expenditure on child protection services, evaluation information from those directly affected is not routinely collected to assist continual review of service standards. Views of parents point to significant inconsistencies in the ways that similar situations are handled by the child protection system. There is a need for explicit national standards in child protection practice so that families can be clear at all stages what the criteria are of the process they find themselves in. There is also a need for transparency about the key factors that affect assessments and court judgments, especially those relating to removal of a child and factors that determine whether a child will be returned to his/her parents, can be cared for by extended family members, or requires permanent placement with strangers. In the last scenario, especially where this results in compulsory adoption without direct contact, much more explicit indicators are required to signal when such a draconian outcome is the only feasible alternative.

Given the profound impact on families of professional style, there is also an issue to be addressed about the disparity in family perceptions of the quality (and humaneness) of the style of child protection workers. What can be done to ensure that families in such traumatic circumstances receive a considerate and skilled response? One answer must lie in instituting more effective evaluation of the process and outcomes of child protection interventions. It is only on the basis of routinely gathered feedback that child protection agencies can develop systems for quality assurance regarding the style of practitioners. With such information, competency and professional development plans can be instituted through existing mechanisms of training, recruitment, supervision, appraisal, and promotion.

This chapter has presented typical critical views of families who become involved in child protection interventions. In general, they are perspectives that stem from a belief that the parents have been wrongly abused of abuse and that the families have been subject to gross injustice. Or, that while there may have been grounds for intervention, the ways in which this was carried out were unnecessarily unpleasant, and the actions taken disproportionate to the level of risk. Such families see themselves as behaving *reasonably* in the face of *unreasonable* child protection interventions. As we have emphasised, this is an important perspective and needs to be heard. However, as we shall discuss in Chapter 10, not all families behave *reasonably* in relation to child protection intervention (and by no means all child protection practice is *unreasonable*). This adds to the complexity of the task of providing effective, supportive and proportionate child protection services.

7

EXPLANATIONS FOR INJURIES AND THE THORNY ISSUE OF 'DENIAL'

> For innocent parents to have a child taken from them, or to be prosecuted and convicted of killing a child who actually died of natural causes, is the stuff of nightmares. It is right and desirable that there should be public indignation at the failures that lead to such terrible suffering....However, we must also acknowledge that in a small percentage of the cases where a baby dies, something unlawful will have taken place...some mothers, fathers and other carers do induce illness in their children and sometimes fatally harm them.
> (Baroness Helena Kennedy QC) (Kennedy 2004, p. 20)

In the first stage of care proceedings in England and Wales, judges hear evidence from expert medical witnesses regarding the nature of injuries and ways in which these may have been caused. Having heard such (often highly technical) evidence, the judge will rule, on the 'balance of probability', whether the infant has suffered 'significant harm'; and whether the injuries were non-accidental, who was most likely responsible, whether any person present 'failed to protect' the child, and/or whether (knowing the child was harmed) any adult failed to seek medical attention. These are the 'findings of fact' made at the 'causation' stage of care proceedings. In this book we are more concerned with wider family assessments that comprise the second stage of care proceedings trials – that of the 'disposal' or 'welfare' hearing, in which judges consider a wider range of evidence in determining what form of order (if any) the court should make to protect the infant (and, invariably, whether the infant will be returned to parents/carers, placed with other family members, or adopted).

In this chapter, however, we present an overview of some of the major diagnostic issues, dilemmas and controversies that arise at the causation stage of care proceedings hearings. We also discuss in some detail the thorny issue of 'denial' – that is to say, the possible reasons why parents/carers whose infants have been harmed continue to maintain that they were not responsible.

DIAGNOSTIC ISSUES, UNCERTAINTIES AND CONTROVERSIES

The focus on suspicious serious and fatal injuries reported in this book highlights the vulnerability of very young babies to physical harm in the first few weeks and months of their lives. Most homicides of children occur at the age of 0–12 months (Creighton 1995). The younger the child, the greater the likelihood that the force of an assault will result in serious injuries. Nine of the 17 deaths in the Part 8 Review group sample discussed in Chapter 5 were of infants aged less than 3 months. In the assessment (serious injury) sample, one-third of cases involved fractures to babies less than 3 months old; and at least the same proportion suffered serious permanent damage. The extent and severity of injuries in non-fatal cases seem broadly similar to those found in fatal case reviews where babies have died. Research on child abuse fatalities suggests that relatively few parents who are violent to their babies actually intend to kill (Falkov 1996; Resnick 1969; Stroud & Pritchard 2001; Wilczynski 1997). Factors of *chance* (Levine et al. 1994; Reder & Duncan 1999) play a major part in whether a serious assault proves fatal or not.

Accidents or Abuse?

One of the key complications in assessment and court hearings of these cases is that medical diagnosis of abuse or non-abuse can be uncertain and is sometimes conflictual. This is an area where the two key types of child protection error specifically occur: the false-positive (a diagnosis of abuse is made when the injuries are accidental); and the false-negative (a diagnosis of abuse is not made when this is the cause of the infant's condition). Research indicates that both types of diagnostic error occur, and both have profound consequences for children and families.

A US professor of paediatrics highlighted the challenge of diagnosing child abuse when a child has a medical condition such as demineralised bones or abnormal blood clotting. Are the fractures/bruising due to the underlying condition, abuse, or a combination of both? (Leventhal 2000). Leventhal stressed that unusual events do happen to children. He gave the example of a 5-month-old baby with two skull fractures indicative of two separate impacts. The baby's mother could explain only one incident – the baby falling from the settee. Child protection enquiries began, and later the elder sister revealed that she had dropped the baby – and had not said so before because she was not allowed to hold the baby. Consequently, Leventhal urged: 'Do not automatically disbelieve a history because it seems strange: the child's injuries may be consistent with this unusual history' (Leventhal 2000, p. 144).

Studies reveal that accidental injuries to babies and infants occur on a significant scale – and some research indicates that hospitals and doctors do not recognise that symptoms presented by a seriously ill baby may, in fact, be abuse related (Benger & Pearce 2002). A major epidemiological study of nearly 12 000 pre-mobile babies (0–6 months) reported that 22% had been involved in an accident since birth. The most frequent types were falls from beds or settees. The commonest site of injury sustained was to the head (97%), although serious injury (defined as concussion or fracture) occurred in less than 1% of cases. Consequently, the authors concluded that while falls involving infants are common, most such events result in no injury, and serious injuries were very rare (Warrington & Wright 2001).

Hospital studies have also explored the nature of accidental and non-accidental injuries. Reece and Sege (2000) estimated the accidents and abuse rates to be 81% and 19% respectively; and Rivara et al. (1988) reported that three-quarters of presenting injuries were unintentional (accidental) and one-quarter were the result of abuse. Accidental injuries were predominantly less serious, single injuries, and rarely resulted in permanent disability. Moreover, a feasible explanation was forthcoming in all cases of accidents. In contrast, the injuries that were considered to be the result of abuse tended to be multiple and much more serious, with a 25% rate of consequent permanent disability. No explanation was immediately forthcoming in 36% of these cases. The authors concluded that unintentional injuries to infants are common and also invariably minor. In contrast, closed head injuries, fractures to ribs and lower extremities, and abdominal injuries are suggestive of abuse (Rivara et al. 1988).

Brain Injuries

The most common injuries to the brain that occur in suspicious circumstances involve:

● damage to brain tissue through direct impact to the head or via rotational forces
● bleeding into the membrane layers (spaces) covering the brain caused by shearing injuries (subdural, subarachnoid and epidural haemorrhages)

- deprivation of oxygen and blood supply to the brain caused by apnoea (cessation of breathing)
- swelling of the brain tissue (cerebral oedema) as a consequence of any of the above.

(We are grateful to the consultant paediatrician Dr Peter Sidebotham (Sidebotham 2005, personal communication) for assistance with this categorisation.) Brain tissue is vulnerable to specific damage from direct impact, shearing injuries and blood/oxygen deprivation (hypoxic/ischaemic damage), and the short- and long-term consequences of these events depend on the severity of damage and the precise area of the brain that is affected. The shearing or swelling of connective nerve endings within the brain is known as diffuse axonal injury (DAI) and results from abnormal movement of the brain inside the skull as a consequence of rapid rotational acceleration and deceleration motion (such as shaking). David (1999) noted that DAI injuries are particularly significant, as they are probably responsible for immediate effects (unconsciousness) and long-term neurological damage in non-fatal cases. Diffuse swelling of brain tissue is also associated with poor outcomes (e.g. death or permanent disability) for affected infants (Kemp et al. 2003).

Subdural Haemorrhages

It has been suggested that subdural haemorrhages as a result of assault occur with an annual incidence in the UK of 21 per 100 000 infants (Jayawant et al. 1998; Kemp 2002). The consequences are grave: 12–30% prove fatal, and approximately two-thirds of victims suffer some degree of permanent brain damage. Important questions are asked of expert medical witnesses in cases where brain injury to an infant may be suggestive of assault (Jayawant et al. 1998; Karandikar et al. 2004).

Subdural haemorrhages in infants are not necessarily indicative of physical assault: there is a small, but non-trivial incidence of non-abuse or naturally occurring subdural haemorrhages (Hoskote et al. 2002; Howard et al. 1993; Jayawant et al. 1998; Johnson 2002; Sanders et al. 2003). Moreover, the size of the subdural haemorrhage itself does not correlate with the extent or severity of trauma (Johnson 2002). Establishing the cause (aetiology) of subdural haemorrhages is not simple: one professor of paediatrics in the UK recently outlined 70 different causes for subdural haematoma in the following 13 categories: trauma (e.g. road traffic accidents); medical surgical interventions; prenatal, perinatal and pregnancy-related conditions; birth trauma; metabolic disease; congenital malformation; genetic disease; malignancy;

autoimmune disorder; blood coagulation disorder; infectious disease; poisons/toxins/drug effects; and miscellaneous (David 2004b).

A medical research team in Sheffield that undertook a prospective study of 11 births discovered that nine of these babies were born with subdural haemorrhages. Three of these births were normal deliveries, five were forceps deliveries (after attempted ventouse delivery), and one was a traumatic ventouse delivery. One conclusion from the study is that subdural haemorrhages can be present immediately after birth, and that this is not necessarily indicative of birth trauma (Whitby et al. 2004). This is one of several diagnostic areas where, because of ethical constraints, research has limitations. For example, much research examining the forces required to cause degrees of brain injury has been undertaken by biomechanical experiments on monkeys (and results from these may not be directly transferable to the human infant). Consequently, uncertainty remains regarding how much force is required to cause subdural haemorrhages in human infants (Howard et al. 1993; Kemp et al. 2003; Lefanu & Edwards-Brown 2004). David (2004a) noted that in some cases it is very important and acceptable for expert medical witnesses to admit uncertainty about the cause of an injury: 'Regardless of pressure, never be afraid to say that one is simply not sure' (David 2004a, p. 803).

Lucid Intervals

There is a debate in the medical literature on the dating of brain injuries as to whether, after such an injury, an infant may have a 'lucid interval' (a period in which the infant appears to be well and behaving normally) before succumbing to the delayed effects of the injury. If lucid intervals occur after serious brain injuries, it is much more difficult to identify a specific time period within which the injury was caused. Research relating to confirmed accidental injuries has produced inconsistent findings on this question. One study of 95 children who died from such injuries found no evidence of lucid intervals – all of the children became noticeably ill immediately after the accident (Willman et al. 1997). In contrast, another study found that 12 out of 18 children who suffered accidental fatal head injuries did have (brief) lucid intervals before succumbing (Plunkett 2001).

From this research as a whole, it seems likely that any lucid interval following a brain injury is associated with the severity of the injury. For example, it is possible for an infant to have a shallow subdural haemorrhage without noticeable symptoms (Greenes & Schutzman 1998). Other infants may show symptoms, such as irritability, continual crying, and feeding poorly, which may be indistinguishable from common mild illnesses. At the severe end of the spectrum, the infant will suffer seizures or loss of consciousness rapidly from the injury. On this basis (although there are dissenting views), it is considered unlikely that a lucid interval of any significant period of time will occur in an infant who has sustained a severe brain injury (David 1999; Willman et al. 1997).

'Re-bleeds'

Another controversial issue relates to the significance of 're-bleeds' (Hymel et al. 2002). When computerised tomography (CT) and magnetic resonance imaging (MRI) brain scans reveal that an infant has two or more subdural haemorrhages of different ages, the question arises whether this is necessarily indicative of assault (shaking or impact injury) on the same number of occasions? Or to what extent is it possible that further bleeding, perhaps provoked by normal activity, may spontaneously recur at the site of the original injury? Re-bleeding is believed to occur frequently in resolving subdural haemorrhages, but the amount of bleeding is seldom large. There is no evidence that re-bleeding causes brain damage (David 2004a). Clearly, it is vital that 're-bleeds' are not construed necessarily as evidence of multiple assaults (Johnson 2002).

Retinal Haemorrhages

Retinal haemorrhages involve bleeding that occurs in front of, beneath or within the layers of the retina. There are a large number of possible medical causes for retinal haemorrhages. It is also common for babies to be born with retinal haemorrhages, and while most have disappeared by 8 days, in some cases they persist for up to 3 months (Baum & Bulpitt 1970; David 1999). Retinal haemorrhages can also result from blood coagulation disorder and attempts at resuscitation. Studies have consistently shown that it is unusual for retinal haemorrhages to be a consequence of accidental severe head injuries (although there are some recorded exceptions to this). However, retinal haemorrhages are commonly found in infants who have subdural haematoma from impact injuries, and this raises the suspicion that shaking associated with the head injury causes the retinal haemorrhages. However, the exact biomechanical force needed to cause retinal haemorrhages in babies (and indeed other force-related injuries) remains unknown.

Fractures

While not common, bone fractures can occur as a result of accidents to children of all ages (although accidental fractures in babies and infants are rare). This area has been well researched in attempts to differentiate reliably between accidental and non-accidental fractures (e.g. Chadwick et al. 1991; Hobbs 1984; Hoskote et al. 2003; Reece 2000). Some uncertainty remains about the nature of fractures that are likely to result from different impact events such as falls from differing heights onto different surfaces. One study concluded that in 25% of cases the fractures sustained by infants had a non-accidental cause (Hoskote et al. 2003). While inconsistent explanations and delayed help seeking are often indicators of maltreatment, Hoskote et al. also noted that these features can be present in cases of genuine accidental injuries.

Hobbs (1984) reviewed a sample of 89 infants who had suffered skull fractures. It was concluded that non-accidental skull fractures were likely to involve multiple or complex fractures, a fracture that was depressed or particularly wide, fractures of more than one bone and fractures other than the parietal bone. In this study, no fracture considered to be non-accidental was less than 1 mm wide; in contrast, two-thirds of the accidental skull fractures were 1 mm (or less) wide. From the research as a whole, it is generally concluded that skull fractures may be caused by simple falls, but that this is not common. When this does occur, the fracture is usually a simple linear one. In contrast, skull fractures that are multiple or bilateral, or cross suture lines are more likely to be non-accidental. In addition, skull fractures coexisting with other injuries (e.g. retinal haemorrhages, other fractures of different ages, extensive bruising) significantly raise the level of suspicion about maltreatment.

Rib fractures often are a feature of cases of suspicious serious injury to infants. To what extent is the presence of fractures to the ribs of a baby an indicator of maltreatment? Infants may be born with fractured ribs, and such fractures also are known to occur during attempts at resuscitation. However, resuscitation-induced rib fractures tend to be anterior rather than posterior – the latter being more indicative of maltreatment (Sidebotham 2005, personal communication). Abuse-related rib fractures tend to be inflicted by a squeezing force, and in some cases there are fingerprint bruising patterns on the infant's torso that give some indication how the infant was held while this occurred. Alternatively, rib fractures may occur by blunt force such as the infant being stamped on. The age of fractures of ribs can be estimated radiologically by observation of the extent of the formation of callus during the healing process (but this is not totally precise). In this way it is sometimes determined that infants have sustained multiple fractures that must have occurred from assaults on different occasions.

Burns, Bites and Bruising

Tragically, on occasion, babies and infants sustain serious burns from unfortunate accidents. This may reflect a unpredictable and non-preventable incident (such as a parent being momentarily distracted), or it may occur in a context of chronic neglect and domestic chaos. In cases of accidental serious burns, explanations are usually forthcoming. One study of 50 children treated at a London burns unit noted that in 49 of these cases parents (usually highly distressed and guilt-ridden) were able to give immediate and accurate accounts of what had happened (Martin 1970). Absence of an immediately forthcoming and cogent explanation for a serious burn to an infant inevitably raises acute questions of maltreatment. Deliberate burning of an infant by a parent/carer raises the spectre of sadistic intent and parental personality disorder. Some parents deliberately burn children with cigarettes. Caution must be exercised in the diagnosis of such 'burns', however, as infants with impetigo have been misdiagnosed as having cigarette burns.

Serious bite marks to babies and infants are an uncommon form of injury. The question that arises in such circumstances is usually not so much whether this was an accidental or inadvertent injury as who was responsible for what is likely to have been an intentional (if impulsive) act with some element of motive to cause pain. Specialist dentists (forensic odontologists) will be called upon to help identify the perpetrator of the bite marks. Sometimes, in such cases, it emerges that an older sibling (or some other child) must have bitten the infant. It is easier for forensic odontologists to determine this on the basis of the size of the bite mark, that is, whether it corresponds to the general size range of adult mouths in comparison to those of children of different ages. It can be more difficult to distinguish between different adults as potential perpetrators (as when two parents blame each other). The characteristics of the arrangement of teeth may result in forensic odontologists being able to agree to exclude a suspect. In other cases, the judge ultimately has to decide between the differing opinions of expert forensic odontologists as to which parent was responsible. There is very little published research on the ageing of bruising caused by bite marks to children.

In general, bruising is the escape of blood from ruptured blood vessels caused by a blunt force damaging the blood vessels. The blood escapes into the subcutaneous tissue and the skin. The appearance of a bruise is affected by, among other things, the volume of blood leaked (which may cause swelling), the site of the impact, the degree of force applied to the skin and the age of the child. A recent systematic literature review has compared research knowledge about patterns of bruising that are likely to be accidental with those that are likely to be the result of maltreatment (Maguire et al. 2005). One conclusion was that non-abusive bruising in pre-mobile babies is very uncommon.

Dating of Injuries

Technological advances have enabled medical specialists to date the occurrence of various types of injury with increased precision. For example, subdural haemorrhages can be dated with some degree of accuracy by CT and MRI, which can distinguish acute bleeding and help date older haemorrhages. However, this is never totally precise, as there are natural variations in the rate of blood breakdown, and the colour of blood will also depend on the precise MRI sequence that is used (Johnson 2002). The age of bone fractures can be estimated in relation to repeated radiographs showing the degree of callus formed as bones heal. However, skull fractures cannot be dated in this manner, as the skull does not form callus in the same way as other bones.

The accurate dating of bruising is less precise. While the colour of bruises evolves over time, allowing some general estimates to be made about the timing of the injury, paediatricians have become more tentative in estimates, as it is increasingly recognised that there is a greater general variation in bruising patterns and colour changes than was once believed to be the case:

> Textbooks have provided schedules of colour changes of bruises over time. However, these schedules are unreliable, and should not be used . . . attempts to age bruises based on their colour is fraught with difficulties. . . . The only established fact is that the presence of a yellow colour within a bruise indicates that it is at least 18 hours old. (David 2004a, p. 901)

Degree of Force

There are disagreements between medical experts as to the severity of force required to cause fractures and subdural/retinal haemorrhages. It has been common for some experts to state that the force required for a particular injury to occur must be of the level of a road traffic accident, or a fall from a height of several storeys. However, these are rough approximations that do not take into account the role of unknown and idiosyncratic factors:

> One is well advised to exercise caution and avoid dogmatic statements about how flexible are the bones of babies and how enormous the force must have been ... the only really solid ground is that in an infant with healthy bones, normal handling and normal activities do not produce fractures, and domestic accidents (such as short falls) rarely produce significant injury. It is self evident that significant force must be needed to break a bone, but in the absence of any reliable and hard scientific data it is wise to avoid overstating the amount of force that is likely to be involved. (David 2004a, p. 802)

The degree of force necessary to produce features of brain injuries similarly remains uncertain and cannot be specifically quantified. However, subdural and retinal haemorrhages rarely (if at all) appear after common domestic accidents or rough play (however, these would be detected only if the infant became ill enough for medical help to be sought and appropriate investigations were undertaken). It seems likely that the force required to cause subdural haemorrhages varies with the age of the infant, with younger babies being susceptible to significant injuries from smaller forces given their relatively large heads in comparison to body weight and underdeveloped musculature.

Experience of Pain

Another contentious issue can arise in court cases when parents state that they did not know that their infant was injured, and therefore should not be blamed for not having sought help sooner than they did. To what extent can medical experts give confident opinions about the degree of pain that an infant will experience and express in different types of injury? This can be a crucial question in cases where part of the suspicion about a non-accidental cause of a serious injury is derived from the parents/carers apparently failing to seek medical help for their infant, who would have been in demonstrable and unusual pain. Failing to seek medical help for an injured infant can result in criminal conviction for neglect, and may result in a judicial finding in care proceedings of 'failure to protect'.

According to an eminent UK professor of paediatrics, the question of pain levels for infants following serious injuries is an area that is seriously under-researched (David 2004, personal communication). Consequently, there is a poor evidence base regarding the normal range of pain that infants experience and express in relation to serious injuries:

Fractures cause two kinds of pain. One is acute pain resulting from the forces applied to the bone and the pain resulting from the bone breaking. The other is ongoing pain in the days and weeks after a fracture has occurred. The immense variability means that over-confident assertions are worth avoiding. While the occurrence of the fracture itself is certain to cause significant immediate pain, the way that this pain is communicated to carers or parents can vary between different children and at different ages... in infancy, rib fractures and meta-physeal limb fractures often produce no detectable ongoing pain at all... the point is that caution is required before concluding that a reasonable carer should have known that something was seriously amiss in a child with rib of metaphyseal limb fractures. (David 2004a, p. 802)

Consequently, there are limits to which medical experts can state with confidence that an infant would have been in demonstrable pain that a reasonable parent would not have failed to notice, or that the parent/carer must have ignored it, thus failing to seek necessary medical attention.

Coexisting Injuries

International reviews (e.g. American Academy of Pediatrics 1993; Carty & Ratcliffe 1995; David 1999; Wilkins 1997) identify specific brain injuries and combinations of injuries that are highly indicative of abuse. Fatal injuries to infants from maltreatment commonly involve brain damage resulting from impact injuries to the head, shaking or both. There may be no external observable signs of injury (Krugman 1985). The combination of injuries that is often stated to be a definitive marker of abuse is subdural haemorrhages, retinal haemorrhages and fracture of skull, ribs or limbs. Such combinations of injuries provide stronger evidence of maltreatment, as these patterns of injuries are not notable after forms of accidental trauma, as in road accidents, or resuscitation attempts, nor as a consequence of rough handling. There is greater diagnostic uncertainty regarding specific injuries such as subdural haemorrhages, retinal haemorrhages, or fractures of the skull or ribs. When they occur in isolation, there is less clarity about the force required for such injuries, and whether the causative action was accidental, inadvertent or intentional.

'Shaken Baby Syndrome'

In the early 1970s, reports were published of infants with subdural and retinal haemorrhages who did not appear to have apparent external head injuries (Caffey 1972; Guthkelch 1971). Caffey coined the term 'whiplash shaken infant syndrome' to describe a pattern of injuries resulting from shaking-type events that could be either accidental or abusive. The term 'shaken baby syndrome' (SBS) has become commonplace, but (as we shall discuss later) this is a phenomenon of considerable professional dispute. The SBS diagnosis involves a classic triad of injuries, including subdural haematoma, DAI and retinal haemorrhage, resulting from an impact to the head and shaking (especially where there are associated grip-type injuries, such as a fractured long limb used as a 'handle' and fingertip bruising) (American Academy of Pediatrics 1993; Carty & Ratcliffe 1995).

SBS most often affects babies under 6 months of age. It has been noted that babies' crying can be particularly problematic during the 6-week to 4-month age bracket (Barr 1990), and that this is also the peak incidence of SBS (Reece 2000). An incessantly crying baby may be shaken by an exasperated parent until the crying stops – as a result of cessation of breathing (apnoea). After a shaking incident, parents may put their baby to bed, hoping that he/she will recover. However, some babies slip into unconsciousness rather than sleep, and are later found dead. Otherwise, as brain damage intensifies (due to haemorrhaging and swelling), emergency help is finally sought when the baby is convulsing or comatose.

Signs and symptoms of SBS are neurological and present on a spectrum from minor to immediate death. Minor symptoms include irritability, poor feeding, lethargy and vomiting. With no external signs of injury, these subtle symptoms can easily be misinterpreted on medical examination as infant colic or mild viral illnesses (David 1999). The outlook for SBS infants is poor, especially when medical attention is delayed. Approximately 60% of babies who are critically ill in this way at the time of medical attention being sought die or are left with permanent profound disabilities (American Academy of Pediatrics 1993).

As we have mentioned, the nature and existence of SBS have given rise to considerable controversy, and we shall return to this later in this chapter.

Munchausen's Syndrome by Proxy (MSBP) – Now Known as 'Fabricated or Induced Illness'

The term 'Munchausen's syndrome by proxy' (MSBP) was coined by the paediatrician Professor Roy Meadow in 1977 to describe a form of child abuse in which a parent (almost always the mother) presents a false history to medical staff about a child's illness which is either fabricated (the child is not ill) or induced (the parent has deliberately caused the child to be ill, for example by salt poisoning). In the case of fabricated illness, the child is subject to unnecessary medical investigation and procedures. In the case of induced illness, the mother may sabotage necessary medical treatment (for example by contaminating drips).

When this perplexing condition occurs, children can be placed in acute danger and death can result. One UK professor of paediatrics established a hospital-based 'covert video surveillance' system to monitor mothers suspected of secretly causing deliberate harm to their infants (Southall et al. 1997). This programme was halted by ethical and legal challenges. However, some of the video recordings (shown at professional conferences) leave little doubt in some of the cases that the mothers could suddenly behave very violently toward their infants while otherwise maintaining a plausible stance of being caring and concerned.

Unfortunately, in the 1990s, MSBP became another child-abuse 'fad'. Proponents of the MSBP diagnosis advised professionals to 'think dirty', resulting in unknown numbers of over-anxious mothers being perceived as potential MSBP abusers. As discussed in Chapter 2, overdogmatic expert evidence given in criminal trials resulted in a number of high-profile miscarriages of justice (as in the cases of Sally Clark and Angela Cannings). In July 2005, Professor Roy Meadow was struck off the medical register having been found guilty by the General Medical Council of serious professional misconduct by giving erroneous and misleading expert evidence at the criminal trial of Sally Clark. In the wake of such miscarriages of justice, greater caution has emerged about false-positive identifications of MSBP that might arise from observations of highly anxious parents. The increasingly disputed condition of MSPB was renamed 'fabricated and induced illness'.

NON-ABUSE EXPLANATIONS

Given the complexities and uncertainties regarding diagnoses of child abuse, it is not surprising that some injuries thought to be a result of abuse can turn out to have non-abuse explanations. One factor that arises from time to time is that doctors with a specific determination to uncover child abuse can unwittingly become subject to biases that profoundly affect their perceptions and judgments. In the UK, one of the most notable examples of this was the removal of 121 children from families in Cleveland in 1987, because of overconfidence by a team of paediatricians in an unvalidated diagnostic technique for sexual abuse known as anal dilatation (DHSS 1988). In the child protection culture of that time in Cleveland, the consequent denials by the parents of abusing their children was taken as confirmation of abuse (the Kafkaesque scenario described by parents in Chapter 6).

A medical team in Brighton reported on three infants presenting with possible physical abuse injuries who in fact had a form of rare organic disease (Male et al. 2000). Care proceedings on the grounds of suspected abuse had been initiated on a 3-month-old baby with an 'unexplained' transverse fracture of his right fibula. Investigation subsequently revealed that this was due to a benign tumour arising from surrounding tissue. Abuse was also initially suspected in a 3-year-old girl who had 'fingerprint' type bruising, until a type of leukaemia was eventually confirmed. In the third case, abuse was suspected with a 2-year-old girl who had a 2-week history of bruising under her eye, a swollen cheekbone and reluctance to walk. Sadly, the real cause was confirmed as terminal cancer (Male et al. 2000). The anguish for parents of being wrongly accused of child abuse through being unable to explain injuries in these circumstances is difficult to comprehend.

Birth-Related Injuries

Birth can be one of life's greatest traumas. A range of injuries, including subdural haemorrhages, retinal haemorrhages and rib fractures, can occur during the birth process, especially when there is a need for assistance such as forceps or ventouse extraction. Consequently, it is not uncommon for babies to be born with injuries which (if they were discovered only in the first weeks of life) could mimic signs of serious abuse, especially SBS. It is not known how many babies suffer birth-related subdural and retinal haemorrhages and are discharged home without these being detected, where they gradually resolve without further complication.

Accidents

Emergency medical services frequently treat babies and infants who have sustained serious injuries from genuine accidents that were observed by others, and no questions about abuse arise. Unusual, improbable and freak accidents occur to babies and infants (Leventhal 2000). Despite being generally very attentive, sometimes parents/carers may not always be aware of what happened. Unusual events and lack of explanation often raise suspicions of abuse or neglect.

The distance an infant has to fall to sustain injuries of particular severity generates controversy. The dominant view is that 'short falls' do not result in serious injuries (e.g. skull fractures and subdural haemorrhages). Proponents of this view often give expert evidence that such injuries require the impact of forces equivalent to falling from the second or third floor of a building; or being unrestrained in a car crashing at a speed of 35 miles per hour. In contrast other experts report that *unusually*, serious injuries can result from short falls involving considerable less force than a fall from a building or a car crash (Plunkett 2001). While this book was being written, two very sad items appeared in a national newspaper:

> Funfair inquest: a 7-year-old child died after tripping on a helter-skelter mat at the wonderland Pleasure Park...and banging her head on concrete at the base of the slide...the (inquest) jury returned a verdict of accidental death. (*The Times*, 4/12/04)
>
> A three-year-old infant has died in hospital a month after falling as he climbed steps at school and hitting his head. (*The Times*, 14/8/2004)

If these events (the falls) and their *highly improbable* tragic outcomes (the deaths) had occurred at home on the stairs, it is quite likely that parental explanations would not have been considered adequate to account for the severity and consequences of injury, and that child protection enquiries would have resulted. To minimise false-positive abuse interventions, it is vital that investigators keep an open mind about improbable events and unlikely consequences. In an aptly titled paper – 'Head Injury: Abuse or Accident?' one reviewer concluded:

> Small infants rarely sustain serious injury from accidents in the home and any brain injury with subdural and retinal haemorrhage should raise suspicions of abuse. Babies can, however, be dropped accidentally or fall from changing tables and sustain linear fractures and epidural haemorrhages.... In the absence of clear signs of abuse we cannot jump to the conclusion that injury is non-accidental just because there is brain injury or subdural haemorrhage....There are too many variables and unknowns to allow a categoric statement that a certain fall did or did not injure a child....Evidence given in court must be unbiased and factual; we must not allow our rightful abhorrence of abuse in all its forms to blind us to the precept that a person is innocent until proven guilty. (Wilkins 1997, pp. 393–7)

Sudden Infant Death Syndrome (SIDS)

This syndrome, often also referred to as 'cot death', describes the sudden and unexpected death of an apparently healthy baby, typically affecting sleeping infants between 2 weeks and 6 months of age (Fleming et al. 2000). SIDS is the leading cause of death of infants under 1 year of age in the USA. The diagnosis of SIDS arises from post-mortem examinations, death scene investigations and detailed reviews of the history of the child and family. It is a diagnosis of exclusion: no illness or event to cause sudden death is established by such enquiries. While SIDS generally cannot be predicted or prevented, certain infants are more susceptible. These include infants with a sibling who died of SIDS; babies whose mothers used heroin, methadone or cocaine during pregnancy; low-birth-weight infants; infants with an abnormal breathing pattern (apnoea alarms can be used to monitor breathing); and babies who sleep on their stomachs.

Controversies have arisen about the diagnosis of SIDS (Matthews 2005), with arguments that it is both overdiagnosed, when real abuse is not recognised (as in parents who smother their children not being discovered), and under-diagnosed, when there is failure to recognise natural causes (as in parents who experience two or more cot deaths being subject to criminal charges and child protection proceedings). Professor Roy Meadow coined a now discredited formula ('Meadow's law) that 'one cot death is a tragedy, two is suspicious, and three is murder unless proven otherwise' (Meadow 1997). As we noted in Chapter 2, Professor Meadow's erroneous statistical evidence that the chance of two SIDS deaths in the same family is one in 73 million was instrumental in the original conviction and subsequent acquittal on appeal of Sally Clark for the deaths of two of her baby sons.

To place this statistical error in context, a recent extensive study reported on families where new infants (6373) were born after the death of a previous baby (deaths ascertained as SIDS). Fifty-seven of these infants died within 12 months of birth. Nine of these deaths were expected due to serious identified medical conditions. Of the remaining 48, seven were classified as probable homicides. Consequently, 41 were classified as sudden unexpected deaths in infancy (SUDI). The researchers noted that 'second (cot) deaths in families are not rare and that the majority (80–90%) are natural' (Carpenter et al. 2005, p. 34).

Brittle Bone Disease

Brittle bone disease (osteogenita imperfecta), a rare, serious condition affecting around 6000 people in the UK, causes regular fractures of bones. It has other characteristic signs that in most cases make diagnosis fairly straightforward (by specific medical investigation). However, as the case of 'baby B' discussed in Chapter 2 illustrates, there are families whose lives have been blighted by misdiagnoses and consequent child protection interventions and court judg-ments of abuse when their infant, in fact, has an unusual (and improbable) susceptibility to fractures. The Brittle Bone Society (www.brittlebone.org) has a support group for parents who have found themselves in this position, and members give harrowing accounts of false-positive 'abuse' identifications.

'Temporary Brittle Bone Disease'

More controversial is the postulated diagnosis of temporary brittle bone disease (TBBD). This is described as a condition where some infants have increased susceptibility to fractures in the first year of life, resulting in multiple unexplained fractures without evidence of other internal or external injury. As the child grows, the condition resolves and such spontaneous fractures cease. In the USA, Miller (1999) reviewed 26 cases of infants with multiple unexplained fractures that fit the criteria of TBBD and studied nine of them with either CT or radiographic bone density measurements. Miller (1999) concluded that TBBD is a real entity and that historical information related to decreased fetal movement or intrauterine confinement and the use of bone density measurements can be helpful in making this diagnosis. Many other medical experts have expressed doubt about the existence of TBBD (Hobbs & Wynne 1996).

Dr Colin Paterson (a UK consultant in biochemical medicine) reported on a clinical sample of 128 children referred with fractures over a 21-year period. Of the 65 he diagnosed with TBBD, 48 were returned to their parents (two subsequently died in circumstances that he did not associate with child abuse). For 43 of the remaining 46 children, Paterson states that his follow-up information revealed no evidence of any subsequent non-accidental injury (Paterson 1997). Methodologically, many questions can be asked about this analysis. For example, it is not clear how systematically the follow-up data were gathered. If this was largely on the basis of Dr Paterson's remaining in contact with parents he had championed in contested court hearings, then the self-reports of these parents regarding no further child abuse concerns may be unreliable in the absence of independent verification.

Dr Paterson frequently gave evidence over many years in care proceedings in the UK (and equivalent proceedings overseas) in cases of babies who had sustained seemingly non-accidental injuries that these were in fact caused by TBBD. However, on three separate occasions, his evidence was publicly criticised by judges, the final occasion being in the High Court in March 2001, when Mr Justice Singer described Dr Paterson as having 'tunnel vision' and his evidence in the proceedings as being 'woeful'. Following this, a formal complaint was made to the General Medical Council by Dame Elizabeth Butler-Sloss (president of the Family Division of the English High Court). The complaint was that Dr Paterson had misrepresented medical evidence while acting as an expert witness in child protection cases. On 4 March 2004, Dr Paterson was struck off the medical register when the complaints against his practice in court cases were found to be substantiated by the General Medical Council.

Mistaken Diagnosis of shaken baby syndrome (SBS)?

The condition referred to as SBS has generated significant controversy. Vigorous campaigns in the USA and Australia argue that catastrophic reaction to vaccines in some cases is the real cause of brain swelling and bleeding that are indistinguishable from injuries, and that adverse reactions to vaccination (and associated medical mismanagement) are misdiagnosed as SBS child abuse (Buttram & Yazbak 2000; Scheibner 1998, 2001). Others point to the impact of vitamins C and K deficiency (Innis 2004; Kalokerinos 1981), coagulation disorder (Innis 2004; Oudesluys-Murphy 2004), capillary fragility (Clemetson 2002), and forms of epilepsy such as Lennox–Gastaut syndrome (Adams & Victor 1989).

In the UK a voluntary organisation adopted the name 'the Five Percenters' based on the prevailing medical belief that 95% of SBS cases are proven (resulting in false-positive injustice in at least 5% of cases). Access to the 'Five Percenters' is via their website: www.sbs5.dircom.co.uk. Another helpful source to access the views of SBS sceptics is the US website www.sbsdefense.com.

Specific unresolved medical disputes focus on whether shaking of an infant (without other trauma) is sufficient to cause the 'classic triad' of injuries (subdural haematoma, DAI and retinal haemorrhage) that is generally (but not universally) held to be firmly diagnostic of SBS. Opinion is divided whether these characteristic injuries require an impact (as well as shaking), or whether they can be caused by shaking alone (Duhaine et al. 1998; Harding et al. 2004).

Opinion is also divided as to what degree of shaking force is required to cause such injuries (if they do result from shaking alone without impact). It has been common for expert evidence to be given in court hearings that the degree of shaking would need to be extensive and quite ferocious. However, research on brain tissue of deceased infants has recently suggested that brain haemorrhages may develop after incidents involving much less force (but still greater than in the normal course of events) than previously commonly assumed (Geddes et al. 2001). These researchers concluded that the damage arose from lack of oxygen (hypoxia) due to apnoea (cessation of breathing) caused by specific damage to the neck (craniocervical junction) around the brainstem. The craniocervical junction is uniquely vulnerable in babies because of the disproportionate weight of the head in relation to under-developed neck muscles.

In 2004, a fierce debate on this topic took place in the *British Medical Journal*. Critics of misdiagnoses (and miscarriages of justice) based on misconceptions of SBS concluded, 'We need to reconsider the diagnostic criteria, if not the existence, of shaken baby syndrome' (Geddes & Plunkett 2004, p. 720). The defence of SBS was equally robustly led by Harding et al. (2004), and Reece (2004). The subsequent on-line rapid-response correspondence illustrates the emotive intensity of this dispute: (www.bmj.com – search for 'shaken baby').

This debate is one of extreme importance in cases (most susceptible to false-positive errors) where there are no other injuries suggestive of maltreatment (in a context of previous good parenting and child development). As we have discussed, in many cases of serious suspicious injuries to infants, diagnoses can be uncertain, and eminent experts may disagree. Judges have to make 'findings of fact' at the legal level of 'balance of probabilities'. In this context, as parents often point out, a 'finding of fact' is a misnomer, as this level of proof can reflect a judgment that is only 51% certain about the cause of an injury and who was responsible. Less probable – indeed improbable – events do occur – as acknowledged by a senior Family Court judge: 'We all know that improbable events occur' (LJ Thorpe 2003, p. 304).

However, cases that are improbable are generally deemed to be child abuse (Howitt 1992). This raises a social and legal policy question regarding the most appropriate level of proof for decisions that will affect the entire life of a child (for example, compulsory adoption). The lower level of 'balance of probability' generates increased risk of false-positive errors (infants not being returned home who could safely have been returned). The 'beyond reasonable doubt' criminal standard increases the false-negative risk (where infants are returned home, only to be subject to further significant harm).

SIGNIFICANCE OF 'DENIAL'

The reasons why some parents do not provide medically coherent explanations for serious suspicious injuries to infants are a cause of confusion and concern in child protection assessments, case management and court proceedings. What are the conceivable reasons whereby parents may be inhibited in acknowledging responsibility in those cases where they were responsible?

The issue of 'denial' is a thorny and complicated one because there is no reliable way to distinguish accurately the behaviour of a parent who genuinely denies responsibility when wrongly suspected from that of a parent who denies in an attempt to avoid detection of actual culpability. Guilty people can convincingly fake innocence, and innocent people can appear to be very guilty (in a stereotypic way). Innocent people can also fake guilt via false confessions, and some may even genuinely (but erroneously) believe themselves to be guilty. This complexity is exacerbated, as we have seen, in that there can be genuine (but improbable) accidental and unusual medical explanations for injuries that appear strongly to be abuse related. In such cases, before this has been established (if, indeed, it is), child protection professionals, juries and judges have often viewed parents' protestations of ignorance and innocence with deep suspicion.

Acute Stress and Post-traumatic Responses

The discovery that an infant has sustained serious injury invariably constitutes a traumatic experience for parents/carers. This is so where the injury is unquestionably accidental, whether or not the parent witnessed and was involved in the accident. When it is parents' own behaviour that has resulted in a serious injury to their infant, there is also likely to be a shock reaction which compounds the emotional intensity prevailing when the parent reacted violently toward the child. The impact of shock can have a major influence on the behaviour and attitudes of parents/carers at the time of the injury incident, the immediate aftermath of medical emergency and accusations of abuse, and the post-traumatic chronic anxiety induced by the protracted uncertainties and profound consequences of care proceedings (and possibly a criminal trial).

In states of shock following traumatic experiences, people often do not think in rational and consistent ways, and can behave emotionally in a manner that appears not to be congruent with the reality of the situation. There is a large research and clinical literature on post-traumatic stress responses, much of it relating to natural disasters, warfare, accidents and the effects of crime. From this, two reactive conditions to severe stress have been recognised. First (largely based on research with US veterans of the Vietnam War), the formal psychiatric classification of 'post-traumatic stress syndrome' was included in the third edition of the *DSM* (*Diagnostic and Statistical Manual of Mental Disorders*) in 1980, and revised as 'post-traumatic stress disorder' (PTSD) in *DSM-IV* in 1994 (APA 1994). Second, is the condition of 'acute stress disorder' (ASD) (which was introduced in the *DSM-IV*) to describe initial reactions to trauma that might predict the subsequent onset of PTSD (Harvey & Bryant 2002).

PTSD involves three sets of symptoms that may follow events which involve a threat to life or physical integrity, and which invoke a subjective response of fear, helplessness or horror:

- persistent re-experiencing of the traumatic event
- persistent avoidance of stimuli associated with the event
- persistent symptoms of increased arousal.

ASD involves the experience at least three of the following criteria:

- a subjective sense of numbing or detachment
- reduced awareness of one's surroundings
- derealisation (sense of detachment from surrounding social and physical environment)

- depersonalisation (sense of detachment from one's physical or psychological being)
- dissociative amnesia: 'dissociative amnesia is characterized by an inability to recall personal information, usually of a traumatic or stressful nature, that is too extensive to be explained by ordinary forgetfulness' (APA 1994, p. 477).

Following a serious suspicious injury to an infant, it is the second criterion of PTSD (persistent avoidance of stimuli associated with the event) and all of the criteria of ASD (but especially dissociative amnesia) that may be relevant to the way that some parents/carers behave in the aftermath of the occurrence and discovery of the injury. There is also the possibility of some degree of impairment of memory for the injury event.

Memory Impairment Scenarios

It is common that people who are accused of committing a wide range of crimes claim that they cannot remember doing so (Kopelman 1997). Estimates of claimed amnesia for committing offences vary greatly between research studies; for example, 22% (Parwatikar et al. 1985), 23% (Cima et al. 2004), 26% (Taylor & Kopelman 1984), 40% (O'Connell 1960) and 60% (Bradford & Smith 1979). These studies were mostly in relation to suspects accused of adult murders.

To convict a person of a crime requires a distinction to be established between deliberate and accidental conduct. In addition to proving that the criminal act occurred (*actus reus*), it is necessary to prove an element of criminal intent (*mens rea*) – that is to say, that the actions were conscious and voluntary. On this basis, murder trials often consider expert evidence relating to the defendant's mental state, such as capacity to understand the charges and to instruct counsel (fitness to plead), and questions of diminished responsibility by virtue of varied forms of mental impairment. In this context, when a defendant claims amnesia for the crime, consideration must be given to the likely genuine causes of this – or the degree to which this may be simulated by the defendant.

Researchers are generally agreed that in a proportion of cases of adult murders the offender genuinely does not recall committing the offence. The following are postulated mechanisms for this:

- personality factors
- repression, suppression and denial
- dissociative amnesia
- automatism

- state-dependent memory
- intoxication
- psychotic and neurological conditions.

We shall discuss these briefly in turn.

Personality Factors

Psychological studies of offenders' personality types suggest that hysterical/histrionic personalities (dramatic, attention-seeking, exaggerated and childish, with superficial expression of emotions) may be inclined to genuine amnesia, as hysteria is associated with the ability to put unwanted thoughts out of the mind (Swihart et al. 1999). People with psychopathic personality disorders are particularly prone to fake amnesia: 'memory loss, amnesia, blackouts, multiple personality, and temporary insanity crop up constantly in interrogations of psychopaths' (Hare 1993, p. 43). It also seems likely that people with psychopathic personality disorders are particularly prone to remember violent offences. This is because the personality attribute of shallow emotion does not trigger intense emotional arousal which is believed to be a mechanism for failure to encode a memory.

Repression, Suppression and Denial

Repression and suppression are psychoanalytic concepts of defence mechanisms that protect the personality from unbearable impulses and distressing experiences. The main theoretical difference between the notions of repression and suppression is that the former is held to be an unconscious act independent of ordinary forgetting, whereas suppression involves some deliberate activity on the part of the individual to put specific thoughts 'out of mind'. The notion of repression of traumatic memories and the 'recovery' of repressed memories became controversial in the 1990s (Read & Lindsay 1997). The psychoanalytic assumption that a traumatic memory can be repressed and recovered (via psychoanalysis, hypnosis or other forms of therapy) does not accord with current scientific research that identifies memory processes as being essentially reconstructive (that is, continually evolving rather than being preserved in an unadulterated form).

In the psychoanalytic sense, repression, suppression, dissociation and denial are all *mechanisms of defence* that promote cognitive avoidance which reduces stress, and reflect attempts to ward off the horror that would arise from recognition that one has committed a reprehensible act (McLeod et al.

2004). Recent research has suggested that denial has a valuable function as a mechanism to protect from psychological effects following trauma (Mayou et al. 2000). From this perspective, forms of 'denial' are not necessarily psychopathological or indicative of levels of subsequent risk.

Dissociative Amnesia

The notion of dissociation, which dates back to the nineteenth century, describes a process of mental splitting (dual consciousness) which shields the personality from intense distress (Janet 1889). This theory holds that traumatic events which threaten to overwhelm the personality cause the mind to divide, resulting in one 'part' holding the memory, which is not accessible to the other 'part'.

There is extensive research (and fascinating controversies) about the existence and nature of dissociation as a traumatic and post-traumatic stress response, and with regard to dissociative amnesia as an explanation for the genuine failure of victims and perpetrators to remember violent events (McSherry 1998, 2003; Porter et al. 2001). The first author has discussed this controversy in relation to the phenomenon of 'survivors' of sexual abuse having 'recovered memories' of their childhood abuse (Dale 1999).

Modern theories of dissociation describe the biological impact of extreme stress resulting in a failure for the memory to be encoded – that is to say, the amnesia is connected with a memory not being formed in a normal way (rather than a failure to retrieve a formed memory). One group of violence researchers described the case of man who lost contact with his wife at a party for about 15 minutes and presumed that she had disappeared to have sex with a male colleague. In fact, she was on a balcony talking with two women. Later at home, he brutally attacked her while she was sleeping. Under interrogation, he described 'drowning in a red tide' and called such incidents 'red-outs' (Dutton 1995). This phenomenon has been reviewed by Swihart et al., who noted:

> Apparently an individual can get so angry with his/her intimate partner that s/he can severely beat or kill that partner and then not remember doing so: that is, they can experience a red-out resulting in circumscribed dissociative amnesia. (1999, p. 200)

This description accords with the psychiatric category of 'Intermittent explosive disorder' as outlined in *DSM-IV*:

> Several discrete episodes of failure to resist aggressive impulses that result in serious assaultive acts or destruction of property. The degree of aggressiveness

expressed during the episodes is grossly out of proportion to any precipitating psychosocial stresses . . . the individual may describe the aggressive episodes as 'spells' or 'attacks' in which the explosive behaviour is preceded by a sense of frustration or arousal and is followed immediately by a sense of relief. Later the individual may feel upset, remorseful, regretful, or embarrassed about the aggressive behaviour. (APA 1994, p. 610)

Automatism

'Automatism' has been defined as:

an involuntary piece of behavior over which the individual has no control. The behavior is usually inappropriate to the circumstances and may be out of character for the individual. Afterward the individual may have no recollection . . . of his actions. (Fenwick 1990, p. 2)

Post-traumatic automatism implies the presence of a head injury and subsequent amnesia of the automatic events that follow. Causes of automatism are multifactorial, including psychological and physiological processes such as epilepsy and hyperglycaemia. Sleepwalking is a well-known, relatively common form of automatism, and actions committed by people sleepwalking are not considered to be within their conscious knowledge and control. This is clearly relevant to questions of criminal responsibility if a person commits a serious offence while sleepwalking. Automatism is a complex medical and psychiatric phenomenon which provokes complicated legal dilemmas (McSherry 2003). However, from the body of psychiatric and legal literature, there is little doubt that automatism can result in people committing offences that they have no conscious knowledge of.

State-Dependent Memory

Memory is generally conceptualised as involving three processes: *encoding/recording* memories, *storing* memories, and *retrieving* memories. Problems can arise for various reasons at each stage. One theory is that memory impairment may occur when there is a mismatch between the prevailing physical and emotional conditions at encoding and these conditions at attempted retrieval. On this basis, a person may be better able to remember an event when in a similar emotional state to when the event occurred and the memory was encoded. This may be particularly relevant to memory processes for violent actions that occur in a state of intense emotional arousal, such as 'red-outs' (Porter et al. 2001; Swihart et al. 1999).

Intoxication

It is common knowledge that memory is compromised by varying levels of intoxication. Taylor and Kopelman (1984) reported from a sample of 203 homicide and other offenders that a large proportion had committed the offences in the context of heavy alcohol intoxication, usually with prolonged histories of alcohol abuse. The term 'alcoholic blackout' has long been used for this specific type of memory impairment. The characteristics of a substance-induced 'blackout' are distinguishable from an intense emotion-induced 'red-out' in the following ways:

> Alcohol or substance induced amnesia is more likely to involve a blackout: an inability to recall anything that occurred once a certain level of intoxication has occurred. The red-out is more likely to involve the following: amnesia for the most violent part of the crime with some memory for events both before and after the violent event. (Swihart et al. 1999, p. 207)

Psychotic and Neurological Conditions

Many psychiatric and neurological disorders affect the ability of people to control and remember their behaviour. For example, forms of psychosis, such as paranoid delusions, can result in tragic misperceptions of reality – the person delusionally believes s/he is protecting the family from the devil; in reality, a child is stabbed. Temporal lobe epilepsy in which brain and cognitive functioning is disrupted can generate symptoms such as memory disruption, disorientation, angry outbursts and automatism. A history of head injury can result in disinhibited aggressive behaviour and memory impairment.

This knowledge is derived predominantly from research into violent offences by adults against adults. It reveals that there is substantial evidence in certain cases that violent acts can take place that the offender genuinely does not remember committing. As we have seen, there are varied and cogent theoretical explanations for this. However, 'not remembering' does not, in itself, indicate risk of recurrence. It is also important to recognise that some offenders may be highly motivated to fake amnesia (Cima et al. 2004). As McSherry noted, amnesia 'is easily simulated and difficult to disprove, it can be very problematic for clinicians to diagnose this condition accurately' (McSherry 1998, p. 168).

Memory Impairment in Cases of Fatal and Serious Suspicious Injuries to Infants

In the context of this discussion of adult–adult violence, the question arises, to what extent do cases occur where one parent *has* caused the serious injuries to the infant and *genuinely* has no memory of doing so? This possibility is significantly under-researched in the child abuse literature. Given that it is well established that this phenomenon occurs in relation to adult–adult violence, there is no reason to assume that it would not have a similar prevalence in adult–child violence.

False-Positive Not Guilty Scenarios

Some parents, despite 'findings of fact' (on the balance of probabilities), continue *truthfully* to deny responsibility for causing the injuries to their child. The case of baby 'M' reported in Chapter 2 is a judicially determined example of this, where ultimately an initially undiagnosed medical condition (brittle bone disorder) was identified as being the cause of the serious injuries. Parents in such situations sometimes describe professional pressures exerted upon them to confess falsely as the only way of possibly having their child returned. Miscarriages of justice and unnecessary compulsory adoptions occur in these situations.

Secret Guilty Scenarios

Situations also arise where both parents/carers deny knowledge/responsibility for injuries but where one (without the knowledge of the other) was secretly responsible. Some parents genuinely believe the plausible but false assurances of their partner that he/she was not to blame. The innocent parent does not know this and is therefore truthful in continuing to deny responsibility and to look for other explanations. This stance is reinforced by dynamics in the relationship where the parent cannot conceive of their partner being responsible. In other situations, there may be abuse explanations that are genuinely unknown to the primary caretakers – such as a sibling, other relative, carer, babysitter, nanny, or friend having accidentally or maliciously caused harm to the infant.

Alternatively, in other cases, both parents/carers adamantly deny knowledge of responsibility for injuries, but both are aware that one of them (or both) was responsible. Keeping this explanation secret is reinforced by the major likely consequences of confession (criminal charges, likely removal of all children, social/family ostracism, loss of employment and lifestyle, etc.). In the absence of diversion of prosecution schemes (where individual and family therapy is provided as an alternative to prosecution or non-reunification of the infant), there are very few positive incentives to accept responsibility in such circumstances.

Approaches to Denial – 'Force-Field' Analysis

In the organisational theory of force-field analysis, change is characterised as a state of imbalance between driving forces and restraining forces (Lewin 1951). Forces promote change, and forces resist change. This perspective can be useful with regard to understanding (or at least hypothesising) about the response of parents/carers whose infants have sustained serious suspicious injuries. If a parent was responsible, what are the forces that might promote and resist confession of this to the other parent? If a parent does so confess, what are the forces that that might lead both parents to reveal or conceal this from the authorities?

Cases arise where a parent almost immediately acknowledges responsibility for an action that has caused serious harm to their child. Little is known about the psychosocial characteristics of parents who immediately acknowledge responsibility in contrast to those who do not. In the cases we are specifically concerned about in this book, it can be hypothesised that the collection of forces promoting 'denial' are more compelling. Remaining silent initially may be a shock reaction, but it also provides immediate space for consideration of the best way forward that may minimise the major repercussions that stem from accusations of serious child abuse. These include:

- criminal repercussions
- child protection repercussions
- personal and family repercussions
- social and community repercussions.

Criminal Repercussions

A parent who does confess to causing serious harm to an infant is almost certain to be charged with a criminal offence. We noted in one small sample (Dale et al. 2002) that it tended to be young, single mothers with limited intellectual resources who seemed most likely to confess (and subsequently to be convicted of an offence). However, for many parents, fear of prosecution and conviction is a powerful force acting against confession of responsibility.

In many cases, while it may not be a conscious strategy, parents who maintain that they have no idea how the injuries occurred (and who do not incriminate each other) have a greater chance of avoiding being charged with an offence or being convicted. It is not known what advice solicitors give to parents in this regard. (However, it would be surprising if solicitors did not advise parents not to incriminate themselves.) Being charged with an offence of causing serious harm to an infant (and particularly being convicted) has immense negative consequences for many parents and families. This often includes loss of job, income, and sometimes their home.

The dilemma for some parents of being involved simultaneously in criminal and care proceedings has been described:

> Herein lies a paradox, for persistent denial in the criminal court renders it more likely that responsibility cannot be proven beyond a reasonable doubt and so the parent is advised that they should not incriminate themself. However, at the same time, within the civil court context, for a parent not to accept responsibility may mean that the child is less likely to be returned to their care. Caught in such a bind, the self-protective instinct may well be a factor which maintains denial. (Bentovim 2003, p. 253)

Child Protection Repercussions

On discovery of a serious suspicious injury to an infant, social services will routinely be alerted by the hospital and will begin making enquiries into the family background. Urgent decisions will be made about the safety of other children in the household, and, not infrequently, siblings are removed into foster care (or the care of relatives). We discussed in considerable detail in Chapter 6 the various ways (mostly negative) that parents experience such interventions. Many parents and extended family members experience a high degree of threat and fear in relation to social services, and such feelings invariably act as a strong force for denial. Parents cannot discern (even if they are thinking clearly enough) whether 'confessing' is more or less likely to result in their child's being returned to their care. Parents not infrequently report being told by social workers that a 'confession' is the only chance they have of having their child returned home. Notwithstanding this, parents generally continue to maintain their innocence.

Personal and Family Repercussions

Self-image and self-esteem are likely to be significantly affected by awareness that one has committed a reprehensible act, especially if this is out of character and has a high factor of social stigma (such as child abuse). We discussed earlier the postulated psychological defence mechanisms that operate (by means of acute-stress and post-traumatic responses and memory impairment) to protect the integrity of the personality from being overwhelmed by shame and guilt.

A parent who has assaulted an infant may have more hope that his/her family will remain intact if members unite in supporting the alleged offender in his/her consistent denial of responsibility. Responding in unison to contest such allegations and the 'unfairness' of professional and legal practice can be a powerful unifying force for some families. In contrast, accepting responsibility for seriously harming an infant will invariably raise fears for the future of the entire family (e.g. forced separations, relationship breakdown and major conflicts within the extended family).

Social and Community Repercussions

Strong forces exist to maintain a stance of denial of responsibility, as to confess for many parents invariably would have a major negative impact in many areas, including social status, reputation, employment, standard of living and friendship networks. News about 'child-abusers' spreads rapidly through communities, particularly if there is local press coverage of a case. Some communities ostracise parents accused of child abuse; others may actively persecute them, delivering local varieties of 'rough justice'.

CONCLUSION

In the history of modern child protection literature, clinical reports and reviews have highlighted entrenched parent/carer 'denial' of responsibility for serious suspicious injuries to infants as being a significant high-risk factor in relation to the likelihood of recurrence. Professional practice should have now left behind the era and culture of child protection work whereby 'denial' is construed as confirmation of guilt (Lusk 1996). More recently, it has been recognised that a context of 'denial' needs much better understanding, and that there are cases where reunification can be successful even though responsibility for causing the injuries has not been accepted (e.g. Asen et al. 1989; Dale & Fellows 1999; Dale et al. 2002a; Essex et al. 1995; Essex & Gumbleton 1999; Robinson & Whitney 1999; Turnell & Edwards 1999).

In the not-too-distant-past, in sexual abuse investigations, the terminology of 'disclosure interviews' was biased toward the assumption that abuse had occurred. In a similar way, the concept of 'denial' in investigations and assessments of serious suspicious physical injuries to infants is biased toward an assumption that parents are deliberately concealing conscious awareness of maltreatment, and that their refusal to confess is confirmatory evidence of this. While such cases do occur, other scenarios that are conceptually included within the term 'denial' are in fact very varied. Consequently, in our view, the time has come to abandon the use of the term 'denial' in professional discussions and legal proceedings concerned with cases of serious suspicious injuries to infants.

8

CHILD PROTECTION ASSESSMENT CONTEXTS

When dealing with children, the court needs all the help it can get. (Butler-Sloss 1996, p. 205)

In this chapter we outline some of the different contexts within which specialist assessments are undertaken to assist courts in making crucial decisions about infants who have sustained serious suspicious injuries. We note the limitations of the Assessment Framework (Department of Health 2000) in this respect, and consider the contributions of psychiatrists, psychologists and independent social workers acting in the role of expert witness at the 'disposal' or 'welfare' stage of care proceedings.

ASSESSMENT FRAMEWORK

As was discussed in Chapter 4, the government-commissioned collection of research studies of the 1990s into the processes and outcomes of referrals to child welfare systems (Department of Health 1995) had a significant impact on child protection policy and practice developments. In England and Wales, this included the introduction of new government policy and practice guidance relating to assessments – the *Framework for the Assessment of Children in Need and their Families* (Department of Health 2000). The Assessment Framework provides an ecological model to be followed in multidisciplinary assessments of children in need. Many readers will be familiar with the triangular concept central to the Assessment Framework utilising the three assessment domains of (1) child's developmental needs, (2) parenting capacity and (3) family and environmental factors. We endorse the underlying principle that 'the combination of evidence-based practice grounded in knowledge with finely balanced professional judgements is the foundation for effective practice with children and families' (Department of Health 2000, p. 16).

Unfortunately, the body of research which focuses on inadequate child protection system performance in child abuse fatalities (discussed in Chapter 4) is not integrated into the Assessment Framework. In fact, the Assessment Framework and its companion text *The Child's World* (Horwath 2000) contain very few specific references to serious physical injuries to babies and infants. There is no 'domain' relating to exploring and understanding the circumstances of serious events – the injury incident. Nor does the Assessment Framework recognise the dangers of false-positive child protection errors and the impact of inappropriate, disproportionate and unreasonable professional practice, as has been revealed in parental perceptions research (Chapter 6). In sum, the Assessment Framework does not adequately address the technical, ethical, legal and human rights issues involved in the assessment of suspicious serious injury cases to minimise the likelihood of both false-positive and false-negative identifications. For these reasons, in view of the complexity and contentiousness of the cases, specialist independent assessments will be required. We shall now discuss various aspects of specialist assessment that are often utilised in addition to Assessment Framework core assessments undertaken by social services.

SPECIALIST ASSESSMENTS

Specialist assessments from a range of professionals may be commissioned to provide specific understanding about an aspect of the child's development, parental strengths and difficulties or the family's functioning. (Department of Health 2000, p. 42)

Some of the main forms of 'specialist' or 'independent' (we use these two terms interchangeably in this context) assessments that are regularly commissioned in child protection practice include:

● psychiatric assessments
● psychological assessments
● residential assessments
● community-based family-centre assessments
● independent social work assessments.

Psychiatric Assessments

The role of psychiatry in child protection risk assessments has two separate aspects and profiles, reflecting the professional division between psychiatrists who are trained to work with adult patients (adult psychiatrists) and those who are trained to work with children and families (child psychiatrists). Both arms of psychiatry play a significant role in cases that are subject to care proceedings. For example, one sample of 557 court cases recorded that expert reports from child psychiatrists were obtained in 41% of cases, and from adult psychiatrists in 33% of cases (Brophy 2001).

Brophy's research provides a fascinating insight into the role, experiences and views of psychiatric (child) expert witnesses in care proceedings. Only a self-selected proportion of psychiatrists engage in medicolegal assessment practice, and a range of factors are increasingly discouraging psychiatrists (and experts of other specialities) from undertaking work for courts in cases concerning children. One of these is the growing sense of personal and professional risk involved in providing expert opinions in contested cases (for example, having to face increased numbers of formal complaints being made by aggrieved or vexatious parents to professional bodies). Another is unpleasant experiences in courts (not only reserved for psychiatrists), including the use by barristers of aggressive and manipulative techniques in attempts to undermine the confidence and credibility of the expert giving evidence (King & Trowell 1992), an issue which the judiciary is actively addressing (Gillen 2002; Wall 2000).

For psychiatrists who do engage in court work, there is a demarcation (which at times can be a little unclear) between the roles of adult and child psychiatrists in child protection assessments. Brophy (2001) explored the views of 17 child psychiatrists on this issue. Illustrative of some demarcation tensions that can arise, one child psychiatrist in the study commented:

> I feel very strongly that some adult psychiatrists aren't trained to assist children in their needs ... it's extremely important that instructions to adult psychiatrists are very focused on diagnosis, treatment required, prognosis, likely effects of the illness on their parenting availability, but not actually on them as a parent. Whereas adult psychiatrists often stray a bit into commenting more generally and they're often asked to, and I feel they would do themselves a better service if they stuck more tightly to the issues. (Brophy 2001, pp. 37–8)

While (according to Brophy's study) adult psychiatrists may have involvement in one-third of cases concerning suspected child abuse in care proceedings, it has been consistently noted that they have a minimal involvement with (non-court-related) child protection risk assessments. Adult psychiatrists (with some exceptions) traditionally have tended not to focus on the family context and children of their adult patients. This is evidenced by their well-established reluctance to become involved in interagency child protection work in general and child protection conferences in particular (Falkov 1996). This is a long-standing matter of concern, as research consistently indicates a significant rate of mental health problems and (diagnosed and undiagnosed) psychiatric disorders (including personality disorders) affecting parents whose children are abused (Adshead 2003; Cordess 2003; Falkov 1996; Stroud & Pritchard 2001).

The contribution of adult psychiatrists to risk assessments is valuable in several areas where there are concerns about risks to children, including:

- impact on a child of parental major psychiatric disorder (especially forms of psychosis and drug addiction)
- assessment of 'dangerousness' that stems from specific forms of psychiatric disorder
- issues of 'treatability' in relation to specific psychiatric disorders: what is the best treatment for the parent, and what is the likely prognosis if the parent complies or does not comply with treatment?
- assessment of the positive effects and undesired consequences of medications prescribed for psychiatric disorders.

One of the reasons given for the low level of involvement of adult psychiatrists in interagency child protection assessment and case management is that a specific conflict of interest can arise between their primary responsibility to their (adult) patient and the welfare of the patient's children (especially in situations where the patient does not accept the nature or degree of these concerns). This issue led two psychiatrists (one adult, one child) to conclude: 'The adult psychiatrist needs to combine treatment of the parent and advocacy of the parent's rights with recognition of the child welfare issues' (Cassell & Coleman 1995).

Child psychiatrists, often working in multidisciplinary teams, have traditionally been more willing to have a greater role in child protection risk assessments, to adopt a whole-family perspective, and to become involved in interagency child protection work (Reder & Lucey 1995; Sheldrick 1998). Unfortunately, such services are increasingly scarce nationwide, and this has adversely affected the ability and willingness of child psychiatrists to become involved in child protection assessments.

Methodology of Psychiatric Assessments

Brophy (2001) noted the number of sessions child psychiatrists had with families in order to conduct an expert-witness child protection risk assessment.

Of six child psychiatrists working nationally, four conducted assessments in complex child protection cases in only one session. The other two took between one and three sessions. Child psychiatrists working locally tended to utilise several sessions, over half of this group having six or more appointments per assessment. There are few comparable data for assessments undertaken by adult psychiatrists, but there is no reason to believe that their approach is significantly different. While brief psychiatric assessments can be valuable (particularly in very urgent circumstances), they can also suffer from the negative bias inherent in 'snapshot' assessments:

> There are many 'flying experts' in the disciplines of psychology and psychiatry who are happy to see a patient/client on one, or perhaps two at the most, occasions and then provide a report.... 'Flying experts' may be quick and cheap but all too often their involvement results in ill-founded generalisations and partial assessments. (Stevenson 2002, p. 111)

Vetere (2002) also expressed concern about the class bias that can arise in relation to middle-class professionals undertaking rapid assessment of working-class parents:

> The worse excess, for me, is when the expert witness assessment does not take account properly of the impact on parenting of wider social processes such as poverty, violence, ill health, migration, and poor housing, and how these processes get inside people's heads, so to speak, and impact directly on their competence, well-being and sense of self-worth. In my experience most parenting assessments are carried out by middle class professionals on working class parents. This is the way of the world, but I would like to see some reflection on these class and cultural divides in the expert reports, that thoughtfully considers where different opportunities and standards might operate in people's lives, in a class-based way. (Vetere 2002, p. 108)

On this important theme (which is not specific to psychiatrists), one of us (PD) vividly remembers a rapid clinical judgment expressed by a consultant adult psychiatrist after a joint domiciliary visit to a depressed young mother, living on an Oldham council estate, who was fearful that she might harm her baby: 'These slimy Limeside scrubbers are all the same.'

A senior member of the Northern Ireland judiciary also drew attention to snapshot and class-based biases in some assessment practice:

> We must recognise the danger that parenting assessments are being carried out by middle-class professionals on working class parents.... We must meet together and reflect on class and cultural divides in the expert reports and ensure that opportunities and standards that operate in people's lives are not being assessed in a class-based way. The assessment of parenting abilities and the potential for change needs to be carried out in a way that allows the proper exploration of the ability to change. Is it right that one or two meetings with the

parents, accompanied by one observation of a contact meeting should provide a sufficient basis to allow a systematic exploration of the instructions in the face of the inherent problems in the assessment process? Are we sacrificing quality for quantity? Should we have fewer experts but ensure those that are employed need to develop a working alliance with the parents over a longer period to assess whether they can work in cooperation with professions so as to enable a full assessment of therapeutic potential.... Are we making too many snapshot assessments due to the pressure of time and the exigencies of the court pressures? (Gillen 2002, p. 303)

We have many times encountered parents who felt aggrieved that, in their view, insufficient efforts had been made by brusque psychiatrists (and psychologists) to put them at their ease. Parents also report that single assessment interviews (sometimes after they had travelled long distances) did not give them sufficient opportunity to convey information about themselves, their lives and their situation, in ways that they felt were properly understood and taken into account. A forensic psychiatrist emphasised the futility of such an approach with many parents:

There is no point in aggressive confrontation which is likely to increase the defensive denial...a psychotherapeutic approach...which seeks to understand the subjective experience of the 'failing' parent, can be effective in establishing an initial therapeutic alliance. (Cordess 2003, pp. 173–4)

This issue of professional style (which, of course, does not apply just to psychiatrists) contributing to bias in assessment practice is a very important one that we have discussed in Chapter 6.

Psychological Assessments

Assessments of parents and their parenting skills/style are commonly requested from clinical or forensic psychologists in Family Court proceedings regarding infants who have sustained suspicious serious injuries. Clinical psychologists undergo a rigorous postgraduate training and certification process with a firm emphasis on scientific procedures and research methodology. In addition to interviewing and making observations of behaviour (approaches which are common to all professional disciplines), one particular characteristic of psychological assessments is the use of a range of standardised psychometric intelligence and personality tests.

Psychologists may administer tests such as the Wechsler Adult Intelligence Scale, Eysenck Personality Inventory or Minnesota Multiphasic Personality Inventory to identify levels of intelligence and indicate personality characteristics. Information and opinion derived from such tests can be a valuable overall contribution to an assessment, and also have important influence on how assessments are conducted. This is particularly so in cases where parents may have some form of learning difficulty, and may disadvantage themselves by pretending that they understand the concerns and interventions of professionals, when in fact they do not comprehend what is being communicated to them. We know of sad cases where parents have 'failed' assessments on the basis of being 'uncooperative' or 'non-compliant', whereas, because of hidden intellectual disabilities, they had not understood (or retained) what was expected of them. Psychometric testing before or at the early stages of an assessment can produce specific recommendations to guide the approaches and expectations of professionals, and reduce the potential for parents to be disadvantaged in such ways.

While psychometric tests can be informative, it is always vital to bear in mind that such tests were not developed specifically in relation to the challenge of identifying (validly and reliably) characteristics of high-risk parenting and child abuse. Identification of psychopathology (by such tests) does not have a specific and clear association with the quality and safety of parenting (Crenshaw 2004).

Other tests sometimes used by psychologists in child protection assessments include projective exercises aimed at identifying family relationships (e.g. the Bene–Anthony Family Relations Test and Thematic Apperception Test) and attachment patterns (e.g. variations on Ainsworth's Strange Situation Test and story-stem completion tasks (Green et al. 2000)). Projective testing is highly subjective, and responses are undoubtedly influenced by idiosyncratic factors that may be unknown to the tester. Consequently, the validity of conclusions drawn from projective tests is debatable and controversial – one psychologist commenting that they 'may reveal as much about the examiner as the subject' Crenshaw (2004, p. 178). At best, the value of projective testing is in raising questions and generating hypotheses for further exploration. In our view, major decisions about the lives of children should not be significantly influenced by conclusions drawn from psychometric or projective psychological tests.

Residential Assessments

Residential assessment facilities for parents with infants and babies are scarce. Far too often, cases arise where serious concerns are felt about the safety of a baby and where lack of alternative resources results in the 'removal' of the child to foster care. Of most concern are cases where babies are separated from their mothers at birth (usually on the basis of serious concerns regarding care of previous children) and placed with foster parents, thus inhibiting the development of an optimal parent–child attachment and relationship.

'Removal at birth' is a chilling phrase that is often uttered too casually in professional child protection discussions, as if staff, bombarded with work, become dissociated from the draconian nature, impact and consequences of what they are proposing. We have known cases of removal of babies at birth from mothers (and, of course, fathers) in circumstances where residential or community assessment and supportive services would have been an appropriate and feasible alternative. The measure *is* necessary in certain cases where a parent presents an immediate acute risk to a newborn baby, for example as a consequence of psychotic illness, an 'out-of-control' lifestyle involving drug addiction, violent adult relationships, other high-risk lifestyle or sadistic abuse of previous children.

However, recent rulings in the European Court of Human Rights (ECHR) have made clear that 'removal at birth' must, in practice, be an exceptional measure. The judgment, in the case of *K and T v Finland* [2000] 2 FLR 79, noted that 'removal of a newborn baby from a mother who was in good mental health at the time, whatever the mother's previous history, without a consultation with the family was arbitrary and unjustified' – and constituted a breach of Article 8 of the European Convention of Human Rights: the right to family life. Two other judgments (in the UK and the Netherlands in 2002 and 2003, respectively), both concerning suspicions of the controversial condition of Munchausen's syndrome by proxy, have reinforced this position (Tolson 2004). This development has significant implications for child protection assessment practice, not least that it highlights the increased need for a range of residential assessment facilities. Residential assessments are provided in two main contexts, as we shall now consider.

Institutional Residential Assessment Facilities

There are a small number of specialist units in the public (NHS and local authority) and private sectors providing residential child protection assessments. They are expensive resources and there is very little published evaluation of either their clinical or cost-effectiveness. One of the best known is the Cassel Hospital in London, which provides specialist assessment and treatment for families, adolescents and adults with severe personality and emotional difficulties. The Cassel is a national resource, and many local authorities have opted (or have been ordered by courts) to pay for the admission of families for extended periods of assessment. The role and style of the Cassel elicits strong views. One reviewer of a book on the work of the Cassel written by its director criticised the polemical style of the book (Kennedy 1997) as being illustrative of the approach of the Cassel:

The main problem with the book, however, is the way Kennedy uses it, on the one hand, to eulogise about the efficacy of the work of the Unit and how much money it can save the taxpayer; and, on the other, to take swipes at 'social workers who are either basically antagonistic... to rehabilitation, or who cannot bear to examine... their own emotional reactions' (Stainton Rogers 1998, p. 212)

This response hints at the conflicts that have arisen between local authorities and the Cassel in relation to the role, style, length, conclusions and costs of this undoubtedly expensive residential hospital assessment service. Unfortunately, there is no published research which provides an account of the views of families involved in residential child protection assessments (voluntarily or involuntarily), and this perspective would be invaluable in clarifying whether the expense of any particular resource is justifiable.

Community Residential Assessment Facilities

Community-based residential assessments are provided in two main forms. A small number of family centres have residential facilities undertaking child protection assessments, and several local authorities are actively recruiting foster placements able to take mothers with babies. This requires foster parents with special skills and qualities. For example, their observations are likely to have a key role in decisions in some cases to separate some mothers and babies permanently; and such foster parents must be prepared to face cross-examination in court in relation to their observations.

An underdeveloped potential for residential assessment is to use resources within extended families. In some cases, there is no reason why a residential assessment facility could not be created within the family's own home, or the homes of extended family members. Combinations of relatives and peripatetic professional staff can fulfil the assessment observations, interventions, supervisory and support tasks. Such a model, which fits philosophically with principles of kinship care and the practice of family group conferences, is currently underutilised in child protection assessment in the UK.

In other situations, innovative and pragmatic placement opportunities can be created for residential assessment as a particular need arises. In one successful case with which we are familiar, a local authority (reluctant to incur the cost of a distant institutional residential assessment and the separation from community support for the family that this would entail) utilised a staff flat in an existing residential establishment for the family to move into for the duration of the assessment. With the use of a rota of peripatetic supervising staff, this arrangement worked particularly well and had the added benefit of allowing the key social worker (responsible for the overall assessment to the court) and the guardian *ad litem* to make their own regular observations.

Many more local residential assessment facilities are needed to provide carefully considered alternatives to parent–child separations in situations where there are serious concerns about parenting, but also where there may be real potential-for-change opportunities with a network of local monitoring, supportive and therapeutic services. However, it is also important to be realistic about the nature of families that local residential resources can appropriately cope with. Community residential assessment resources are not likely to have staff with the levels of training, experience and support to be able to cope appropriately with parents who have significant psychiatric problems, major personality disorders and serious substance dependencies. Such cases (if residential assessment is indicated) do require residential unit facilities (such as the Cassel) where there is 24-hour nursing cover with appropriate protection, containment and security measures.

Cautions About Residential Child Protection Assessments

Although we support the need for residential assessment facilities, it is important to note that this intervention can have certain significant limitations. While a staffed residential-unit structure provides the security for 24-hour observation of families where the parent(s) is considered to present an acute risk to the child, there are no data showing the sorts of observations that would be made about 'ordinary' families under 24-hour surveillance in such abnormal surroundings. To what extent would many of the critical observations that are often contained in residential assessment reports also be made in respect of ordinary families in such circumstances where risk of abuse is not a factor?

This highlights one of the main potential biases of some residential assessments in that they tend to accumulate and magnify negative observations (sometimes of very trivial factors) and lose sight of the wide variations in normal behaviour and social context. We have seen a number of residential assessment reports that comprise extensive documentation of observations of deficits in parenting actions (and inactions), but where little feedback, advice, coaching and encouragement have been provided to the parents to assist them to improve their motivation, consistency and skills as parents.

Confusion can also arise when parents feel compelled to be resident, do not comply fully with the rules and regulations, express dissatisfaction and challenge the residential regime. One notable residential assessment report reflected the instant staff dislike and disapproval of two parents at the beginning of an assessment, as they transgressed the 'politically correct' expectations of the residential centre:

> On the first day after Mr T moved into [Residential Assessment Centre], he wore a T-shirt with an unsuitable and offensive slogan. It read 'Warning – Trainee Gynaecologist'. He was asked by staff not to wear this and why it might be seen as offensive, particularly in a place such as [Centre]. Mrs T expressed surprise about the staff view of its unsuitability, saying that she had bought it for him and a different one, which was worse. She seemed unaware of its unsuitability and how demeaning it was to herself.

To respond with 'challenges' to such behaviour (rather than actually working in assessment mode to explore and understand its significance and meaning) is the antithesis of an effective, neutral, hypothesis-testing assessment approach. In this case, the confrontational style set the tone for the whole assessment, and the parents' protests about trivial rules and regulations were subsequently continually interpreted as confirmation of their inherent uncooperativeness and incapability as parents.

During the many weeks (and sometimes months) families are away in residential assessment placements, they become divorced from the local social and community supports that often are vital for successful reunification. This results in assessments focusing on the minutiae of parents' behaviour and relationships in very artificial environments that are decontextualised from their wider family and social circumstances. To what extent are observations formed of parents and families over many months in a residential centre such as the Cassel validly predictive of how the family would cope back within their own communities? Is it possible that the length of separation from local family and social supports actually disadvantages some families in making the changes that are sought by social services and the courts? These questions raise concerns of a lack of ecological validity in residential assessments when they take place long distances from the family's home, extended family and local support networks.

A final issue about residential assessment facilities arises in relation to significant inconsistencies in their use. We are aware of many situations where residential assessment has been provided for some families, but not for others in very similar circumstances. Representing the perspective of Cassel Hospital as a national service provider over many years, its director commented:

> Unfortunately, it is my experience that the outcome for a family following an assessment is often a bit of a lottery, depending upon the attitude and, indeed, finances of a particular social services department, the quality of legal representation, and the attitudes of the judge hearing the case.... While one family

living in one area of the country may end up keeping their children, another family from a different area with very similar problems, and even less severe problems, may end up losing their children. (Kennedy 2002, p. 847)

What determines whether a family is 'worthy' of a residential assessment rather than a community-based assessment? What determines whether a family is given the chance of an independent assessment or, indeed, a residential assessment before the draconian step of compulsory adoption is taken? Too often, it is chance and funding factors relating to the particular combinations and idiosyncrasies of the group of professionals who find themselves involved in a case.

Sometimes, in care proceedings, solicitors for parents and guardians *ad litem* promote the need for residential assessment, and it is not uncommon that the local authority opposes such application. A key House of Lords (2002) ruling in 1996 (Re C (A minor)) established that courts can order local authorities to resource residential assessments of families where a child is subject to an Interim Care Order (prior to the final hearing of the case). In this case, a 5-month-old baby had suffered serious unexplained injuries, and paediatric opinion considered these to be non-accidental. An assessment was undertaken by social workers of the local authority, who recommended to the court that further residential assessment was required. This view was supported by a separate psychological assessment and by the guardian *ad litem*. However, the senior management of the local authority involved concluded otherwise, on the basis that the cost of the proposed residential assessment could not be justified in view of the limited prospects of the parents being able to care for the baby appropriately in the future. The local authority argued that the court did not have the power to order it to resource residential family assessments. The House of Lords (2002) ultimately ruled that the courts did in fact have such powers under Section 38(6), Children Act 1989.

With this decision in 1996 in the House of Lords, the new interpretation of Section 38(6) was that courts could order local authorities to resource family *assessments* (not necessarily residential); they did not have the power to order *therapeutic* interventions (during the course of Interim Care Orders). In this context, the question has subsequently often arisen, to what extent is the proposed residential placement for *assessment* purposes as opposed to *therapeutic* purposes? As many commentators have pointed out (Dale & Fellows 1999; Kennedy 1997; King & Trowell 1992), the distinction between assessment and therapy is, in practice, often unclear, especially given the imperative to assess *potential for change*.

A further key judgment in January 2003. (Re G (A Child) Interim Care Order: Residential Assessment) removed this rather artificial distinction in interpretation of Section 38(6). By this judgment, courts clearly had the power to order assessments that explicitly include a therapeutic component. The case arose from a residential assessment of a family being undertaken at the Cassel Hospital. After 3 months, in view of the progress being made by the mother, the hospital recommended to the court that the stay of the family at the Cassel should be extended. The local authority objected, proposing that the placement should be ended, the baby placed with a grandparent, and that therapeutic work with the mother could continue on a non-residential basis. At the hearing, the judge upheld the position of the local authority, ruling that he had no power to order that the residential assessment be continued, on the basis that it had become therapy rather than assessment. On appeal, this view was rejected. The appeal judges stated that when considering applications under Section 38(6):

> The essential question was whether what was being sought could be broadly classified as an assessment to enable the court to obtain the information necessary for its own decision. The court should not seek to draw a distinction between assessment and therapy, since permissible assessments enabling the court to obtain such information could well contain the provision of a variety of services, supports and treatments, with or without accommodation. (In Re G (A Child) (Interim Care Order: Residential Assessment) [2004] EWCA Civ 24)

While wholly beneficial from the point of view of natural justice and the human rights of parents and children, this judgment will have implications for local authority budgets. The judgment in the same case also made clear that local authorities have to be explicit at the outset about the extent to which resource issues lie behind their opposition to applications for (or to extend) assessment. Not to do so will in future be interpreted as a breach of the parent's human rights. This is important, as in many cases in the past, it has been quite clear to all parties in court that local authority objections to further assessments, while couched in somewhat spurious professional terms, were in fact based on an inability or unwillingness to pay for the services that were required.

Community-Based, Family-Centre Assessments

Many local authorities in the UK provide or have access to family centres that, as part of their work, can provide family assessment and support programmes. Such work is of immense value in assisting and facilitating vulnerable, disadvantaged and often socially isolated young families in the development of consistent parenting skills and the establishment of peer support networks. Some family centres include child protection assessment activities as part of their programmes, and will undertake observations and assessments of families where infants have been removed into care and questions arise about the viability and appropriateness of reunification. Family-centre assessments take many forms, but are typically structured around programmes which involve combinations of home- and centre-based contacts focusing on parenting skills development.

While we argue in this book that specialist risk assessments are required in cases where infants have sustained serious suspicious injuries, such assessments are often helpfully informed by family-centre involvement focusing intensively on parental attitudes toward the children in the family, and providing coaching in parenting skills (if required). If such input can be provided effectively throughout the many months that cases take to reach the final hearing in care proceedings, the court (and experts who are reporting) will have clear and recent indications regarding parents' level of motivation, attachment issues, commitment, parenting skills deficits and improvements. When this work is not undertaken by a family centre during the course of care proceedings, the quality of evidence available to the expert witnesses and the judge is often far from satisfactory and ultimately disadvantageous to parents and their children.

Independent Social Work Assessments

In many parts of the country, experienced social workers provide independent risk assessments on a private basis. In some areas, independent social workers may be commissioned by local authorities (sometimes to cover staff shortages) and undertake *initial* or *core* assessments on behalf of social services. Other independent social workers provide expert-witness risk assessments for court proceedings. Such assessments may be commissioned by the local authority, by a solicitor representing the *children's guardian*, or by solicitors acting for parents (and commonly by combinations of these parties).

The role of independent social workers in child protection risk assessment has grown significantly in recent times. There are several reasons for this, including:

- decline in the quality of assessment skills, experience and practice in social services departments
- decline in the resources of social services departments, including high vacancy rates and increased use of agency social workers
- withdrawal of voluntary agencies (e.g. NSPCC) from undertaking direct child protection assessments
- increased need for 'second opinions' in relation to basic social services assessments to satisfy requirements of the European Convention on Human Rights (especially Article 6: right to a fair trial).

The marked decline in the ability of social services departments to undertake assessments of a necessary standard was remarked upon in the review commissioned in 2000 by the Lord Chancellor's department into concerns about the length of time civil court cases (under the Children Act 1989) involving children were taking. One finding of this review was the extent to which expert witnesses were increasingly being commissioned to compensate for staff shortages elsewhere, and 'the problems caused by an apparent lack of trust in social services assessment procedures, often exacerbated by the turnover and inexperience of some staff and the overloading of those staff remaining' (Finlay 2002, p. 6). This is a problem that seems set to deteriorate further, as (notwithstanding recently raised standards in basic training for social workers to a 3-year degree level) social workers in statutory agencies have fewer and fewer opportunities to develop and sustain the levels of knowledge and skills to undertake complex child protection assessments.

Independent social work risk assessments take many forms as determined by the specific questions in the letter of instructions, timescales and the level of available resources. While in very urgent situations a single interview may have to be relied upon for an interim view of a situation, it is far more common for independent social work assessments to utilise multiple sessions in different combinations with relevant family members. Such sessions would focus on:

- perspectives on the nature of the original harm
- individual parent/carer factors
- parent/carers' relationship
- parent–child(ren) relationships
- extended family (kin and friendship) relationships, influences and resources
- social/community influences and resources
- the nature of interactions between the family and professionals.

Recommendations for or against reunification in cases of serious suspicious injuries to infants from independent social work risk assessments require a balancing act of the significance of risk factors, the degree to which risk factors can be ameliorated, the identification of family strengths, and the availability of appropriate resources for a specific risk-management strategy. Generally, acceptance of full responsibility and provision of a convincing explanation for injuries provide a firmer basis for risk prediction than circumstances in which acceptance of responsibility is absent or partial, and understanding of the dynamics of the incidents of concern remains incomplete. Assessments of the likelihood of further harm can be made more confidently (but never with 100% accuracy) in the former than the latter scenario.

Multidisciplinary Nature of Child Protection Assessment

In this chapter we have described how a range of professional disciplines have a central role in undertaking child protection assessments. This has been the case since the 'rediscovery' of physical abuse in the early 1960s, and decades of subsequent research has highlighted the multifactorial causes of abuse and the interdisciplinary nature of effective prevention, treatment and protective interventions. Consequently, no *profession* is in a position to claim primary status or authority in child protection assessments to which others should defer. The significant issue relates to specific assessment knowledge, skills and levels of experience that are possessed to varying degrees across professional boundaries. Such key skills include:

- research knowledge (awareness of relevant research and methodological limitations in applying research findings in individual cases)
- skills in engagement with family members (who are likely to be anxious, defensive, angry, etc.)
- skills in history taking (being able to create a constructive environment to obtain relevant information from family members in a systematic way)
- observational skills (especially regarding parent–child interactions)
- interviewing skills (listening, communicating understanding, giving feedback, exploring responses to feedback, probing, etc.)
- skills in regulating the emotional intensity of interviews (given that family members invariably have strong feelings about their situation)
- thinking and analytic skills (synthesising complex information and developing and exploring hypotheses from a neutral perspective)
- monitoring counter-transferential responses to a family, and other potential sources of assessment bias
- knowledge and skills in assessing potential for change in view of identified personal and family problems
- writing skills (assessment reports need to be cogent, authoritative, clear and balanced documents).

As we have argued, these are collections of skills that are not the preserve of any one profession, and all disciplines involved in child protection assessments need to be wary of the potential for assessment bias as a consequence of undeveloped skills and insufficient experience in all of these key areas.

ASSESSMENT OF ATTACHMENT

Finally in this chapter, we address the specific issue of assessment of attachment. This is presented separately, as it is a key area increasingly drawn upon by professionals undertaking parenting and risk assessment (e.g. psychiatrists, psychologists, social workers, family-centre workers). We are concerned that the utilisation of attachment theory via observations of attachment patterns can be susceptible to significant misinterpretation and misapplication that can result in errors and injustice in child protection practice.

Attachment theory has become predominant in child protection and child care practice in the USA and the UK since the 1990s. From an evolutionary perspective (to promote survival), the theory describes and categorises styles of human relating across the whole lifespan. Consequently, babies exhibit attachment-promoting behaviour and responses (e.g. smiling, cooing, crying) toward their parents/carers and significant others. How these behaviours and responses are interpreted and attended to contributes to the growing child's sense of identity, behaviour in relationships and sense of the world. Psychological 'templates' (internalised models for understanding self and others) are thereby created, continually developed and reinforced, becoming a significant part of the person's lifelong relational style – e.g. trusting, suspicious, dependent, anxious, avoidant (Shaver & Mikulincer 2002).

In a process of reciprocal influencing, characteristics of parents/carers interact dynamically with the infant's attachment-promoting behaviour and responses. Infants whose needs are anticipated, accepted and responded to lovingly by consistent, attuned significant others are likely to form *secure attachments*. Secure attachments provide a developmental context of safety for exploration, sanctuary from environmental anxieties, assuagement of distress and positive self-esteem. All other things being equal, secure attachments imply the likelihood of optimal emotional development and positive mental health. In contrast, children whose needs are not recognised, are ignored or are responded to inconsistently, or who are regularly maltreated are likely to develop *insecure attachments* (ambivalent, avoidant or disorganised). Such children often (but not necessarily) become increasingly difficult and less rewarding to parent (which in turn may provoke further parental hostility and rejection), and are less likely to develop their full potential (intellectually, emotionally and socially). They may experience recurring problems in making and sustaining effective relationships throughout life (including eventually as parents themselves), and be susceptible to a range of mental health problems.

The notion of attachment arose in the work of John Bowlby, James Robertson, Mary Ainsworth and colleagues in the 1950s and 1960s. Bowlby's seminal paper for the World Health Organisation, published in 1951, was based on observations of children in post-war Europe who were orphaned or homeless, mostly living in institutions (Bowlby 1951). This highly influential work was followed by further research on parenting and substitute parenting reported in a series of three books: *Attachment* (1969), *Separation, Anxiety and Anger* (1973) and *Loss, Sadness and Depression* (1980). These books reported the effects of separation and loss on mother–child relationships, and Robertson identified typical reactions in hospitalised young children of the stages of protest, despair and detachment. (Robertson 1970). Ainsworth et al. (1978) developed an empirical procedure (the Strange Situation Test) to distinguish responses to separation between infants who were securely attached and those who demonstrated insecure attachments. Main and Solomon (1986) extended this typology to include the notion of disorganised attachment.

A major contribution to the development and refinement of attachment theory was provided by the research of Rutter (1981, 1995), who distinguished between the impact of the separation itself, and the disruptions and disturbances in family relationships that proceed many separations. Rutter also noted that infants have a propensity to form multiple attachments, amending Bowlby's earlier view that it was the mother–infant bond that was crucial for positive mental health development. Attachment distortions became a formal psychiatric concept with the inclusion in the American Psychiatric Association (APA) classification system of psychiatric disorders in 1994 of the diagnosis of 'reactive attachment disorder' – in which children display marked inhibited or disinhibited behaviour specifically related to 'grossly pathological' parenting (APA 1994). Useful sources for understanding the nature and development of attachment theory in much more detail include Green (2004), Holmes (1993), Howe (1996) and Howe et al. (1999).

Cautions Regarding Forensic Application of Attachment Theory

The development of attachment theory stems from substantial intellectual and rigorous empirical foundations. However, like many popular theories of human development and behaviour, attachment theory has the potential to be misunderstood and misapplied in relation to specific forensic (court) situations where questions arise about parental capacity to care appropriately for children (and as a way of understanding disturbed behaviour of infants). Concerns fall into two main areas:

- the validity of the research base of attachment theory
- clinical interpretations of attachment made from observations of parent–child interactions.

The Validity of the Research Base of Attachment Theory

Initial research work on identification of attachment types was primarily based on the study of small samples of middle-class white families in the USA in the 1960s and 1970s (LeVine & Miller 1990; Takahashi 1990). Subsequent research has indicated that there are significant class and cultural variations in 'normal' patterns of parent–child attachments. For example, in later cross-cultural studies, so-called insecure 'avoidant' and 'resistant' attachment patterns were shown to be quite typical of normal family relationships in Germany, Japan and Israel (van Ijzendoorn & Kroonenberg 1988). Although the research is lacking, it is likely that similar variations in 'normal' attachments patterns also occur in relation to ethnicity and social class. In general, across cultures, approximately 45% of children and adults demonstrate 'insecure' attachment patterns (Howe et al. 1999). Consequently, assessors relying on attachment theory perspectives and techniques must take great care that they are not making judgments about families in relation to a cultural template of family relationships that is derived from specific and anachronistic, Caucasian-American, middle-class parenting practices.

There are also methodological concerns about the body of attachment theory research which require cautions that some practitioners undertaking court-related assessments either seem to be unaware of, or choose to ignore. In particular (like much social science research), the clinical (and legal) applicability of research conclusions is limited by definitional difficulties, imprecise and inconsistent measures, observational bias, small sample sizes in studies, weak statistical relationships between measured variables, and contradictory findings in different studies.

All of these factors create limitations to the generalisability of findings and their applicability to specific clinical/forensic cases. Moreover, notwithstanding the work of Crittenden (e.g. 1992, 2000), there is very limited research comparing the range of attachment behaviour between families where abuse is known to have occurred and those where it has not. In this context, an academic child psychiatrist noted that being subject to forcible separation will affect the nature of the subsequent attachment (Green 2004). However, very little (if any) of the research underpinning attachment theory has been carried out with this very important specific group of children (Baker 2003). In all, these methodological factors affect the degree of confidence that can be placed in the clinical and legal application of attachment theory based observational assessments in individual cases. Such limitations should always be taken into account and explicitly acknowledged in reports provided in court proceedings.

Clinical Interpretations of Attachment Made from Observations of Parent–Child Interactions

The second area of concern relates to the context in which observations and interpretations of parent–child attachments are made. Child psychiatrists and clinical psychologists (in particular) often use predetermined scenarios to observe the type, quality and quantity of interactions (such as approach and avoidance) between a child and a parent. Social workers tend to make equivalent observations more informally – often on many occasions and in different contexts.

The best-known example of a predetermined scenario is the *Strange Situation Test*, as developed by Ainsworth and colleagues in the USA in the 1970s. This research tool was designed to create, measure and categorise attachment stress in infants by observing a series of contrived separations and reunifications (including the departure of the mother and the arrival of a stranger) between attachment figures and infants (Ainsworth et al. 1978). Infants who responded with certain sets of behaviour were considered to be *securely attached*; other ranges of response were taken to be indicative of insecure (abnormal) attachments. From this research, the application of attachment theory to child protection work became operationalised by many practitioners on the assumption that the clinical/forensic significance of parent–child attachments could be identified from brief observations based on informal adaptation of the *Strange Situation* Test. On this basis, observations suggesting apparent absent, insecure, ambivalent, avoidant, disorganised or other pathological attachments are seen by some as valid indicators of inadequate, neglectful or abusing parenting, and thereby of future levels of risk.

However, there are important limitations to child protection assessments based on contrived and limited observations of apparent attachments. For example, it is not easy to distinguish between the impact of a child's *temperament* (as opposed to attachment) when observing parent–child interactions (Rutter 1995). Moreover, assessment practitioners relying on observations of parent–child separations and reunifications may fail to take sufficiently into account the significance of *contextual factors* that may influence the behaviours that are observed. Unlike the controlled laboratory conditions of Ainsworth's research into the *strange situation*, some assessment practitioners make their observations in highly variable and pragmatic circumstances (and often do not consider the potential impact on the behaviour of parents and child of their own presence).

We have known cases where parents and children (separately) have had to make long journeys to clinics to be observed being introduced, separated, reintroduced and separated again, ostensibly to identify types of attachment. We are concerned that sometimes the unusual circumstances and stressful nature of such decontextualised encounters are not sufficiently taken into account in the opinions that are formed (often critical of parents) from such observations. Young children have arrived for such assessments tired, irritable and hungry from travelling. Parents can be highly stressed by these journeys, and very anxious about the appointments. In such circumstances, how valid can observations be about attachment behaviour – particularly when there is no normative research (that is, information on how a range of non-abusing families would behave in such circumstances) for comparison?

A significant problem can also arise in attachment theory-based assessments when these appear to pay insufficient regard to one of the fundamental premises in the origins of attachment theory itself – that of the significance of *separation* and *loss*. As we have emphasised, many snapshot assessments of 'attachment' are undertaken in situations where infants have been removed from the care of their parents (and where permitted contact is often quite minimal). Consequently, in child protection assessments (unlike the families in much of the research upon which models of attachment have been based), parents are being observed in contact (including greetings and partings) with their children who are not currently living with them. As with the factor of temperament, this issue can be crucial in assessments concerning the potential for reunification of a child, and in relation to contested adoptions:

> It is important to make a clear distinction between difficulties in forming attachment and difficulties resulting from separation anxiety. Often in contested adoptions the evidence of the local authority focuses to some degree, as a reason for ending contact and considering adoption, on the child's reactions to contact with parents. What is in fact a normal behavioural display of separation anxiety is often misinterpreted by social services as a display of outright rejection by the child of the parents. (Banks 1994, p. 110).

Several decades ago, Robertson (1953, 1970) highlighted the emotional distress and damage caused to hospitalised children by regimes that allowed very minimal parental visits (so that children would 'settle'). These studies resulted in a complete change in hospital visiting policy to the open access arrangements which are now commonplace. The lessons of these historical hospital separation studies appear to have been forgotten in current child protection practice, where infants in foster homes during child protection proceedings are sometimes allowed only very minimal contact with their parents.

In 1986, it was being stressed from research that it can be difficult to determine to what extent the behaviour of children in care is due to inadequate attachments – or to the separation from parents and the circumstances surrounding this. These researchers emphasised that assessments of attachment ('love tests') should not be relied upon in unusual situations – as when children have been taken compulsorily into care (Milham et al. 1986; Ryburn 1994a). On this basis, in current child protection practice, some observations of parent–infant interactions that highlight 'insecure attachments' as an inherent deficit in parenting quality and commitment fail to adequately appreciate the situational influences that stem from the experience and emotional consequences of loss inherent in compulsory parent–child separation.

Reviewers are warning that evidence for attachment theory remains uncertain, and that the limitations of the theory in assessment practice are insufficiently recognised (Baker 2003; Bolen 2000; Byrne et al. 2005; Green 2004; Gullestad 2001; Rutter 1995). Green (2004) concluded:

> It becomes crucial to consider a child's attachment status in the context of other wider aspects of development and careful assessment needs to unpick the relative balance of nature versus nurture in a particular child's developmental presentation...errors can be made by ascribing every problem of social functioning in children to problems in child rearing or parenting. It can be particularly important to be alert to this in situations of parenting failure coming to the judicial system, since it is just here that uncritical assumptions may be made about the origin of difficulties based on probability or overgeneralization rather than from careful assessment and consideration of the individual child in their context. (Green 2004, pp. 16–17)

In this context, a US social work researcher recently expressed concern that misapplication of attachment theory may 'become a vehicle for transmitting political and ideological agendas', and asked: 'Are we rushing headlong into another controversy?' (Bolen 2002, p. 95). On the basis of such concerns, it is vital that courts are vigilant about the potential for unrecognised bias that may result from decontextualised assessments of 'attachment' – particularly when these are undertaken on a snapshot basis.

9

POTENTIAL FOR CHANGE

The assessment of parenting abilities and the potential for change needs to be carried out in a way that allows the proper exploration of the ability to change. Is it right that one or two meetings with the parents, accompanied by one observation of a contact meeting should provide sufficient basis to...enable a full assessment with full therapeutic potential...? Are we sacrificing quality for quantity? [Mr Justice Gillen, Lord Chief Justice's Office, Northern Ireland] (Gillen 2002, p. 303)

We repeat part of the quotation from Mr Justice Gillen (above), as it is fundamental to the focus of this chapter: to what extent do assessments focus on the potential for change regarding identified difficulties and, crucially, what timescale is it reasonable for courts to allow parents to demonstrate that they can make required changes?

Reports from independent specialist assessment services consistently highlight the importance of an interactional (rather than 'checklist') process of assessments, and also the importance of including a specific focus on *potential for change* in the families being assessed (e.g. Bentovim & Tranter 1984; Dale et al. 1986; Dale & Fellows 1999; Essex & Gumbleton 1999; Kennedy 1997). This has been accepted by the government in that the Assessment Framework (Department of Health 2000) at several points endorses this principle:

- The process of assessment should be therapeutic in itself (Para 1.56).
- For some families, the process of assessment is in itself a therapeutic intervention (Para 4.3).
- In most situations, meeting children's needs will almost always involve responding also to the needs of family members. The two are closely connected and it is rarely possible to promote the welfare of children without promoting the welfare of significant adults in their lives (Para 4.5).
- Most parents are capable of change, and following appropriate interventions, [are] able to provide a safe family context for their child (Para 4.27).

Notwithstanding such encouragement, there is nothing in the Assessment Framework that provides guidance for practitioners regarding the context, skills and approaches required to assess and promote potential for change in parents in a fair and competent way. Although the practicalities are often challenging, few would disagree with the principle that assessing and promoting potential for change should be a core component of effective child protection practice. However, it is often neglected. Consequently, many assessments are disproportionately deficit focused – collating dossiers of parental inadequacy, disturbance, and apparent reluctance or refusal to cooperate with agencies. Moreover, in attempting to assess family problems, social workers are often told that it is they themselves and the child protection 'system' that the parents construe as being their major problem. It can be very difficult for local authority social workers to be seen to be undertaking fair assessments when at the same time they are accumulating evidence for court proceedings about parental failings, and perhaps also 'concurrently planning' the compulsory adoption of the infant in question. This is not a good basis for the development of the 'therapeutic alliance' that is needed to provide a therapeutic opportunity within an assessment process.

In this context, two significant questions arise. First, to what extent are identified family problems that are commonly (but not always) associated with serious suspicious injuries to infants amenable to change? Second, what approaches, skills and services can help facilitate such changes? In this chapter we compare and contrast a range of theories underpinning the notion of therapeutic change (theories of change), highlight key 'problem' domains (what needs to change?), specify factors regarding change potential in these areas (what can change?), and outline a variety of professional skills that are important in the assessment of change potential (how does change occur?).

THEORIES OF THERAPEUTIC CHANGE

The psychiatric, psychotherapy and counselling research/practice literature is replete with theories as to why people develop personality and relationship problems. Established models for promoting therapeutic change include the following major approaches:

● psychiatric
● psychodynamic
● humanistic
● cognitive-behavioural
● psychosocial

- systemic
- feminist
- solution-focused.

Imagine the situation of a young married couple, Mr and Mrs Problem, aged in their 20s with three young children (including a new baby), who have been living as a family in a socially stressful environment for several years. Mr Problem is becoming regularly involved in angry disputes with work colleagues, neighbours and family members. Mrs Problem is frequently listless, withdrawn and incommunicably tearful. Both parents are finding the demands of their children increasingly stressful. In what ways is it possible to understand the meaning and significance of such behaviours, and how can each person best be encouraged and assisted to change? An immediate question arises as to what extent either Mr or Mrs Problem considers their situation to be in need of assistance or change – or to what extent it is *others*, such as relatives or professionals, who are concerned? The degree to which problems are recognised and accepted, and change desired, will be a key factor in relation to the success of any therapeutic intervention, and many approaches include a focus on promoting this transition. We will briefly outline several common models for understanding behaviour and promoting therapeutic change in relation to Mr and Mrs Problem and their family.

A *psychiatric approach* would utilise the traditional and directive 'medical sickness model' to diagnose and treat any formal mental disorder. With responsibilities under the Mental Health Act 1983, a psychiatrist will also consider whether patients present a serious danger to themselves or others. Does Mr Problem have any psychiatric or neurological condition that promotes aggression and reduces impulse control? (There are a range of psychiatric conditions that can have this effect.) Is Mrs Problem seriously (post-natally) depressed and perhaps suicidal? Does this present a risk to the children? Should either or both parents be referred for counselling and, if so, what type? Is alcohol and drug usage a significant contributory factor for either or both parents? Is the prescription (or review) of anxiolytic or antidepressant medication indicated? Is the prescription of medication itself part of the problem? For example, there is increasing concern about the reported disinhibiting effects (and out-of-character violent outbursts) in some people who have been prescribed selective serotonin re-uptake inhibitor antidepressants (Crompton 2004).

A *psychodynamic approach* would be interested in the early childhood experiences of the parents. What early frustrations, deprivations, losses and anxieties are being reenacted in the aggressive and withdrawn behaviour of Mr and Mrs Problem? To what extent are they replicating their own early experiences and attachment patterns in the parenting of their own children? The psychodynamic therapeutic response inclines toward non-directive and interpretive long-term (some would say interminable) insight-promoting therapy sessions with a focus on exploring historical (especially childhood) experiences and the developmental challenge to contain or 'resolve' unconscious destructive, aggressive and sexual instincts. More modern, 'object-relations' psychodynamic approaches would reduce the Freudian (conflictual instinct approach) by an emphasis on attachment difficulties in interpersonal relationships (Hobson 1985; Lomas 1994).

Humanistic approaches are many and varied, and share an underlying optimistic view of the potential growth and self-healing potential of human beings. They generally reject medical (expert) 'diagnosis-treatment' processes. Instead, the philosophy of change is essentially horticultural in that therapy provides *core conditions* of empathy, acceptance, attention, warmth and positive regard to promote positive emotional growth in self-image, the development of personal meaning and responsibility, and the ability to communicate and relate authentically. From this perspective, humanistic/existential therapists would be inclined to explore the key emotions and unmet needs underlying Mr Problem's temper and Mrs Problem's withdrawal, emphasising the nature of individual choice in relation to these responses, with a view to facilitating alternative constructions of meaning, and less destructive expression of such feelings (Rogers 1957; van Deurzen-Smith 1988).

Cognitive-behavioural approaches stem from the long history of applying principles of learning theory to specific, observable human problems. The approach is twofold. First, it strives to identify the habitual maladaptive thinking patterns that trigger undesired behaviours, and to introduce and rehearse alternative cognitions (thinking patterns) about common situations. Negative affect, such as depression, is seen as the consequence of faulty cognitions and consequent misperception of self, others and the environment. Therefore, the therapeutic focus aims to 'restructure' thinking patterns to prevent experience from being routinely construed negatively, thus avoiding the self-reinforcing adverse effects on mood and self-image that Mrs Problem may be experiencing (Beck 1976). The second approach is to develop a programme of coaching or motivational interviewing aimed at graded behavioural change. For example, Mr Problem may continually misperceive the motives of people around him and respond habitually in an aggressive, self-defensive way that 'gets retaliation in first'. He would be encouraged to practise interpreting encounters from a neutral cognitive perspective – rather than a psychological default position of mistrust. Mrs Problem may have given up initiating interactions through acquired beliefs (cognitions) that these will be unrewarding (or worse). She would be encouraged and coached in a graded sequence of activities to rebuild her self-confidence in initiating and responding to social interactions. See Jehu (1988) for a description and evaluation of this approach in a therapeutic service for adults who were abused as children.

Psychosocial approaches are at the core of the history of clinical social work practice (e.g. Hollis 1965). The approach incorporates theories of human behaviour and social systems focused on problem solving in human relationships, utilising an eclectic mix of individual, family and group interventions (which may be quite directive). The predominant approach is to enhance the biopsychosocial functioning of people interacting with their environment (where efforts may be made to make changes in both). An approach from this perspective with Mr and Mrs Problem would be to undertake an initial psychosocial assessment that would take full account of the environmental stresses contributing to undesired behaviours. As well as encouraging both partners to become more resilient in respect of such environmental stresses, intervention may also focus, in a practical way, on attempting to reduce the stressors themselves (perhaps by supporting an application for rehousing) and galvanising extended family support and community resources (such as HomeStart).

Systemic approaches understand behaviour from the perspective of the dynamics of the relationships between the people involved. They became influential particularly throughout the 1980s (e.g. Asen et al. 1989; Bentovim 1992; Dale et al. 1986; Giarretto 1982; Minuchin 1977). This perspective focuses upon dynamics such as care and control, approach and avoidance, and dependence and independence, enacted through the varying roles and interactions of family members which generate, sustain and intensify patterns in relationships that are seen as problematic. A systemic therapist would be likely to see Mr and Mrs Problem together in conjoint sessions. To what extent is Mr Problem's aggressive behaviour linked to exasperation at his wife's withdrawal from more responsive and fulfilling roles? Or, to what extent does Mrs Problem's withdrawal minimise the extent to which she will be the focus of her husband's unpredictable aggression? What will happen to the relationship if the couple develop more authentic communication and explain to each other what their behaviour really means? Is it ultimately less risky to tolerate the problems and maintain the status quo – a form of equilibrium? If change begins to occur, what will be the effect of this on the other members of the family? If Mr Problem learns to relate more effectively to people in the outside world, what will the impact of this be for Mrs Problem? If Mrs Problem becomes less withdrawn, what will be the implications for Mr Problem and their relationship? Does the prospect of giving up the 'problem' secretly create fear for the future? Is the 'problem' the most comfortable compromise? Systemic approaches also intervene in the dynamics that arise between families and statutory agencies (Dale et al. 1986; Crenshaw 2004).

Feminist approaches would construe our scenario of Ms and Mr Problem in terms of socially determined power differentials between men and women

(Chaplin 1988; Dominelli & McLeod 1989). This perspective attained significant influence in the 1980s partly as a challenge to perceived 'mother-blaming' aspects of systemic approaches. Gender-based power inequalities are seen to stem from the vested interests of patriarchal family and social systems which provide men (seen constitutionally as potential abusers) with the opportunity for socially sanctioned dominance and exploitation of women and children. Therapeutic responses aim to 'empower' women directly (often to escape from such relationships that are construed as domestic violence), and to 'challenge' and regulate the behaviour of men by legal sanctions (e.g. non-molestation orders). Ms Problem would be encouraged to join local women's aid groups to gain new perspectives and increased self-confidence from the peer support, encouragement and modelling of other women who have escaped from domestic violence and established new independent, confident lives. Mr Problem, hopefully, would learn some important lessons about himself from this family breakdown and would gradually be able to establish an effective shared-parenting relationship with his ex-wife and children. At worse, Mr Problem would be reflecting upon the inability of family courts to enforce orders for contact between separated fathers and their children in intractable contact disputes (Piercy 2004).

Solution-focused approaches stem from the observation that it is not necessary to understand, or even explore, the nature of the problem to be able to assist people toward more satisfying lives. A solution-focused practitioner would be more interested in asking Mr and Mrs Potential-Solution questions that generate a vivid picture of where they want to get to (future without the problems), rather than exploring what they want to get away from. An assumption of the approach is that there will already be developments in their lives that are helping toward this end. The solution-focused practitioner will be keen to identify these, and thereby draw the couple's attention to them. It is often in the detail of the vision of the desired future and what is already happening that is helping (exceptions to the problem) that the seeds of the solution are to be found. A solution-focused approach is essentially pragmatic, focusing on what works and seeking to build on this. The success of this approach is dependent on practitioners having an attitude of respectful curiosity and genuinely believing that they need to learn from their 'customers' how to be most helpful to them (De Jong & Berg 2002).

We stress that these examples are oversimplified caricatures (that will undoubtedly irritate adherents and purists) of different ways of theoretically construing common problems that arise within families, and associated ways of promoting therapeutic change. (In practice, most experienced and effective counsellors/therapists draw on aspects of several different approaches.) The key point is that there is a wide variety of very different, but internally coherent, approaches that practitioners may call upon to guide their formulation of the 'problem' and the focus and style of their interventions. While this can be seen to provide a rich plurality of possibilities, it can also contribute to a confused and rivalrous context in which practitioners justifiably may draw very different conclusions about therapeutic potential (and the necessary timescales for change) in the same and similar situations. If, for example, Mr and Mrs Problem's youngest baby sustains a serious suspicious injury (for which both parents deny responsibility), very different opinions may be formed regarding risk and potential for change among practitioners utilising the range of different theoretical perspectives outlined above. This is especially so with regard to estimated timescales for significant change. The availability of contrasting therapeutic models (many of which have a minimal evidence base of effectiveness) contributes to the problem of chance-related inconsistencies in child protection assessment and case management, and this has a major effect on outcomes.

The Dodo Bird

Which of these approaches is most likely to be beneficial for Mr and Mrs Problem individually, for their relationship and for their children? Not surprisingly, adherents of particular therapeutic models tend to believe that their own approach is most appropriate. The history of psychotherapy research has explored the question of whether certain forms or models of therapy are more effective than others (see Lambert 2003, for a comprehensive review). In this very complex methodological area, it is generally accepted that the view of the Dodo Bird in *Alice in Wonderland* still prevails: 'Everyone has won and all must have prizes' (Luborsky et al. 1975). Pursuing this, an eminent psychotherapy researcher concluded:

> The most recent analyses of approaches by theoretical 'schools' do support the Dodo bird. On the whole, all theoretical approaches produce about equally positive results, although some approaches do emerge as superior for certain problem types. (Gelso 1979, p. 16)

This conclusion promoted developments in therapeutic approaches that are *integrative*, in that the practitioner is trained and experienced in the utilisation of different theoretical approaches according to circumstances and client preference (e.g. Erskine & Moursund 1988). Although Dale & Fellows (1999) undertook a preliminary review of a large clinical assessment sample in relation to identifiable therapeutic benefits from participation in an independent service, it is important to note that very little psychotherapy/counselling research has been undertaken in relation to potential for change of parents who are involved in child protection assessments. In the absence of such research, the Dodo Bird's conclusion is significant regarding child protection assessments, in that a range of therapeutic models can legitimately be called upon to understand and promote change in complex family situations.

In our view, an integrative approach is most suited to assessing and promoting potential for change in families where serious suspicious injuries to infants have occurred. Courts can be confused by credible professional witnesses who offer contrasting opinions about the potential and timescales for change. In the absence of research which establishes the greater validity of any therapeutic approach as superior to others in potential for change assessments, varying opinions in individual cases are to be expected and cannot be dismissed as theoretically wrong. However, in such a context, it is vital that assessors are explicit about the theoretical perspectives that inform their opinions about parental potential for change. There is no doubt, from several assessment reports we have seen presented to courts, that in many cases this would make very interesting (albeit in some cases, very brief) reading.

WHAT NEEDS TO CHANGE?

As outlined in Chapter 8, independent social work assessments focus upon several key areas: the nature of the original harm, individual parent/carer factors, parent/carers relationships, parent–child(ren) relationships, extended family and social/community influences and resources, and the nature of interactions between the family and professionals. These are all key areas for the specific assessment focus on potential for change.

The Nature of the Original Harm

One important question relates to what can reasonably be expected in assessments regarding changes in parents'/carers' explanations about how the suspicious injuries were caused. In Chapter 7, we discussed the 'force-field analysis' concept of the interplay of pressures that inhibit 'confessions'. Often the context is one where police enquiries are continuing and criminal prosecution remains a distinct possibility. In such situations, most solicitors advise parents to consider very carefully what personal information they are willing to share with professionals. It is important to recognise that such caution (very understandable in the legal context) can have a significantly antitherapeutic effect (in that the crisis cannot be discussed openly – as would be the case, for example, with a traumatic, sudden accidental death).

From the force-field analysis perspective, the predominant force bears upon keeping silent, and such contextual pressures promote and reinforce psychological 'denial'.

Individual Parent/Carer Factors

When parents encounter professionals immediately after the discovery of the serious injury to their infant, the parents are likely to be in a highly aroused (if not abnormal) emotional state. There is the sudden impact of realising that their infant is seriously harmed (perhaps in a life-threatening way); the cumulative impact of the symptoms, tests, diagnosis and accusation of abuse; and the growing fear and disorientation from the medical, police and social work enquiries. In the midst of this acute crisis, parents/carers are often deeply shocked and increasingly depressed.

In such traumatic circumstances, the way in which people react is not necessarily characteristic of their normal attitudes, feelings and actions. In particular, professionals may observe emotional overreactions (including loss of control), emotional underreactions (apparent lack of feelings/responsiveness), and sometimes an incongruous emotional oscillation (lability) between the two states. In particular, parents may experience symptoms such as numbness, narrowed field of attention, emotional flatness, despair/hopelessness, hyperarousal, projected anger (blaming others), disorientation, cognitive avoidance (of the event) or even dissociative amnesia.

In Chapter 6, we quoted one mother as saying that any emotional responses may be negatively construed by professionals: 'If you cry, you are an emotional wreck. If you don't, you've got no feelings.' A common assessment error involves conclusions that parental behaviour in the midst of such crises (e.g. not being totally truthful, being avoidant, being emotionally labile, being withdrawn, being hostile) is necessarily a sign of parental unreliability and lack of cooperation with professionals (which is then construed as inherently high risk). There is a consequent risk of negative bias in assessments if such initial responses of parents/carers are taken to be a reflection of inherent personality characteristics.

The same point applies in the weeks and indeed months following the injury event. In all likelihood, parents/carers will have had to face the compulsory removal of their infant into foster care. Adjustment to such loss and separation has to take place in the very unusual circumstances of whatever level of contact is determined by social services to be appropriate. At the same time, the parents are likely to be involved in continuing police enquiries regarding the injuries, and the local authority almost certainly will have commenced care proceedings with a view to obtaining a care order on the infant.

Family solicitors will be delicately warning parents that the powers of the local authority extend to ultimately recommending to the court that their child be compulsorily adopted. In the midst of this, parents/carers will have become immersed in the complex world of child protection procedures, review meetings, core assessments, specialist assessments by expert witnesses, and regular court hearings, which are usually adjourned. This period of uncertainty can last for many months. Typically contested cases are completed in just under 1 year, but some drag on even longer. This constitutes a prolonged period of post-traumatic chronic anxiety regarding one of the most fundamental fears that parents can face: that their child will be not be returned to their care and may be placed compulsorily with stranger adopters and never seen again.

The point of reiterating this description of parental experiences of the traumatic injury event and its chronic anxiety aftermath is to emphasise that parental responses after the separation from their child may not be typical of their attitudes and behaviour in normal circumstances. Consequently, if professionals record concerns about parents' attitudes and behaviour during this phase, it is vital that this is carefully assessed in the context of the impact of the crisis and post-traumatic chronic anxiety as described. As many parents in such circumstances are prescribed antidepressant medication by their doctors, it is also important to clarify that aspects of parent's behaviour which cause concern to professionals at this stage (which may be misconstrued as ambivalent attachment or emotional unresponsiveness to their child) are not a clouding ('woozy') side effect of prescribed medication.

In this respect, the potential-for-change issues are similar to those in general counselling/psychotherapy regarding treatment for post-traumatic stress disorder (except that for parents in these cases the trauma and fearful uncertainty is ongoing). There is a need to explore the potential for mood stabilisation, desensitisation, reality testing, cognitive distortions and environmental misperceptions, and general coping strategies. Therapeutically, there is a need for a great deal of support. Strengths need to be identified and mobilised: what psychological and emotional resources can the parents draw upon and develop to respond to this crisis in the most mature, constructive and child-centred way?

Another important factor regarding potential for change relates to individual parent/carer levels of personality *maturity* or *immaturity*. In many cases, prominent features of a general parental immaturity are evidenced in descriptions of self-centredness, attention-seeking, impulsivity, overdramatic responses, untruthfulness and aggressive self-justification. The potential-for-change question in such circumstances is to what extent the traumatic injury events and frightening child protection repercussions have provoked a crisis response of rapid acceleration of psychological/emotional maturation. And to what extent can independent, therapeutically oriented assessments add to this momentum? In some cases (but by no means all), the trauma of the injuries and the child protection repercussions (including the separation from and threat of permanent loss of the child) can provide a strong stimulus for a process of rapid emotional maturation. However, because of the potential for 'faking good', this needs to be tested over a period of time with evidence from different sources and perspectives.

NSPCC research (discussed in Chapter 5) has noted that, in approximately three-quarters of families where serious suspicious injuries to infants had occurred, one or both parents had current major mental health concerns (not necessarily formal psychiatric conditions) and/or substance addiction of a degree that impaired daily functioning (such as orientation, self-care, alertness, and ability to perceive accurately and respond constructively to the environment and others). Assessments need to understand the behavioural implications of these problems, and to establish to what extent parents are motivated to comply with appropriate therapeutic and (drug/alcohol) treatment regimes. Hair-strand and regular urine testing are important aids in such assessments (as self-reported cessation of addictive behaviour is notably unreliable).

The types of fatal cases illustrated in earlier chapters of this book provide graphic cautions regarding impulse-control failures related to immaturity, habitual temper dyscontrol, personality disorders (antisocial and psychopathic) and alcohol/substance intoxication/addiction. In such situations, parents may present in assessments with extreme self-centredness and total externalisation of blame and responsibility for every problem (not only the injuries), may display a strong preoccupation with their own needs, and may be completely unable to empathise with others, including their own child. A consistent inability to reflect on feedback regarding such attitudes and behaviour with any self-critical perspective is a poor indicator for therapeutic change.

This is not to say that in such cases reunification should automatically be excluded on a 'checklist' basis. However, it is vital that specific feedback is given to such parents so that they are left in no doubt about the nature of the changes that must be made in a relatively short period of time. We have known cases where a parent has been able to respond positively to such feedback and engage constructively in focused, therapeutic assessment work (Dale et al. 1986; Dale & Fellows 1999), yet many other parents have been unable to extract themselves from the mire of such entrenched problems. Any reunification of an infant with serious suspicious injuries to parents with acute mental health problems, personality disorders, disabling/disinhibiting substance addictions and (sustained/serial) domestic violence requires a particularly compelling standard of evidence of genuine and sustained change.

Parental Relationship

It is quite common for infants who sustain serious suspicious injuries to have been conceived very early in a relationship that was impulsively intimate. This is often a sign of significant emotional immaturity. Young women with low self-esteem who are immature and emotionally deprived find themselves unexpectedly pregnant in such circumstances, the father of the baby often being someone that they barely know. If an injured infant is to be reunified to a mother who has such a history, it is vital that therapeutic change has occurred so that future intimate adult relationships do not continue to follow this pattern. This requires the development of insight into recognition of the pattern, and reduced impulsivity so that any prospective, new relationship can be explored and developed in a more cautious way. It also requires an improved ability to assess the character of a potential new partner so that a tendency to form impulsive unsuitable intimate relationships can be reduced.

Violent relationships between parents (domestic violence) are commonly (but by no means invariably) a feature of households where infants sustain suspicious serious injuries. The assessment focus on the parental relationship will inevitably also consider the complex dynamics regarding 'failure to protect' the infant from the anger and aggression of the other parent. Where there has been significant 'failure to protect', assessments need to explore and clarify the degree to which the parents can develop insight and achieve change in the relevant dynamics of their relationship. To what extent can parents (if they remain together after the injury) engage constructively in assessments to understand the particular pattern of violence (including mutual provocation and retaliation) within their relationship, and work toward developing more productive and mature ways of resolving tensions and conflicts? If parents have separated after the injury incident and its repercussions, to what extent can they each similarly recognise their own contribution to this problem – and be clear how this pattern can be avoided in future relationships?

In this context, assessments can usefully focus on testing the ability of the parent(s) to develop relationship skills: listening/understanding/empathy, supporting/influencing, negotiating/compromising, balancing dependence and independence, managing issues of difference, possessiveness/jealousy, etc. Even relatively brief assessments can identify the potential (or lack of it) for cognitive and behaviour change and development in these key relational areas. Also in a therapeutically oriented assessment, the dynamic of the relationship that develops between the assessor and the parent is one practical indicator of this.

Parent–Child(ren) Relationships

Serious suspicious injuries to infants can occur in families where there are existing concerns about parenting style and skills, as well as in families where parenting is of a consistently good and competent standard. In most cases, the injured infant (and sometimes siblings) are placed in foster care during the course of care proceedings, resulting in parent–child separation. Where parenting skills have been questionable, the separation may mean that parents lose even more confidence and competence. Where skills were good, they may suffer also due to the separation. Consequently, a vital component of assessment of potential for change is observation of parenting skills 'in action' together with a specific focused coaching input to assist in identified areas of difficulty. Family centres can play a crucial role in coaching parenting skills and positive change in this area, and can have therapeutically beneficial effects in other areas (such as parental confidence and self-esteem).

Assessments focusing on potential for change should always include exploration of parents' responses to feedback that is given about parenting skills from observations of contact. To what extent can the parents accept the feedback given and respond to coaching to improve the quality and consistency of parenting skills? Or to what extent, notwithstanding such input, do inconsistencies and difficulties remain, and in what ways might these be related to factors such as intellectual impairment, continuing psychiatric/personality disorders, substance intoxication/addiction, or an underlying ambivalence or emotional rejection of the child? In addition to interviewing parents about self-reported parenting skills, observations and discussion of feedback is vital to obtain the fullest possible picture of difficulties in this area, and potential for change.

To achieve this, contact between parents and their child needs to be frequent and meaningful. In our experience, social services are very inconsistent in arrangements for parents to have contact with their infants in foster care. In similar cases, we have known this to range from 30 hours over 7 days a week to 2 hours per week on a single occasion. The frequency, length and venue make an enormous difference to the quality of parent–child interactions during contact. The fact that parents are invariably being observed at all times during contact is also an important factor to take into account. What is the impact of being observed? To what extent do parents behave 'naturally' in such circumstances of observed contact? Is it possible that anxiety from being observed interferes with the consistency, quality and confidence of the parents' interactions with their child (creating a negative impression bias)? To what extent, when being observed, do parents 'fake good' and 'put on a show' of quality parent–child interactions that is not reflective of their normal behaviour (positive impression bias)?

If difficulty or distress is apparent between parent and child during contact, it is also important to consider carefully whether this is due to inadequate parenting skills or commitment, poor attachment or underlying parental emotional ambivalence toward or rejection of the child, or whether this is a manifestation of distress at forced and prolonged parent–child separation. Is the child fearful and wary of contact? Or distressed and anxious from the separation (and disoriented by the frequent arrivals and departures of parents)? As we commented in Chapter 8, snapshot assessments of attachment seem particularly vulnerable to pessimistic bias in this area.

Kin and Friendship Influences and Resources

Assessments identify to what extent parents themselves had adverse experiences in childhood, and in what ways the circumstances of their upbringing continue to involve problematic relationships with key extended family members – especially ex-partners, parents, stepparents and siblings. Extended family relationships may range on a spectrum from the significantly over-involved (enmeshment), through the highly ambivalent (continual rows and reconciliations), to total estrangement. Assessments will need to establish to what extent the extended family is a major part of the problem, or an untapped resource that (with facilitation during the assessment process) can be identified as a more consistent support. Given the likelihood of some difficulties in the family history (few families are exempt from this), a focus on potential for change will explore to what extent it is possible to develop more cooperative and supportive relationships between the various relatives.

In assessments with this focus, interviews are held with key extended family members, and between parents and these significant others. It is important to assess the extent to which the extended family may be relied upon to be a significant and consistent part of any support and monitoring reunification plan if the infant were to be returned to parental care. Also to be assessed is whether the extended family could be relied upon to take protective action if, after reunification, signs began to appear that past problems are recurring (such as unstable lifestyle, decline in home conditions, recurrence of mental health problems, or new impulsive relationship). Or, to what extent might they be fearful of doing so, or collude with the parent? Alternatively, if the parents have to be excluded as future primary carers, it is vital to assess properly extended family members regarding their motivation, commitment and ability to be permanent substitute or shared carers.

Social/Community Influences and Resources

In some cases, one of the contextual features of serious unexplained injuries occurring to infants is when (often depressed) parents become psychologically and emotionally overwhelmed by significant social stresses and/or isolation. Due to family breakdown, distance or estrangement, there may be no local supportive family figures. Low personal self-esteem and poverty may prevent parents (especially mothers, and particularly single mothers) from participating in local community support activities. The step from such social isolation toward active participation in local community supports can be profoundly life changing. Again, the work of family centres can be particularly valuable in facilitating peer contact and support between lonely, isolated and stressed parents. Community supports such as playgroups and schemes such as HomeStart also play a vital role in engaging parents in activities and relationships that bolster self-esteem. The potential-for-change aspect of assessments will need to consider the benefits which might accrue from such activities, and the extent to which parents can be motivated to participate effectively.

Nature of Interactions Between Family and Professionals

The issue of potential for change is also pertinent to family relationships and interactions with professionals and agencies. Some families are construed as being high risk by social services by virtue of their uncooperativeness, hostility and avoidance of contact with social workers. We noted in Chapter 4 that this can, indeed, signal significant concern. Yet, it is not necessarily so. As we have argued earlier in this chapter, the impact on the family of the crisis of the injury incident, and the post-traumatic chronic anxiety stemming from the child protection intervention process must also be taken into account. As we shall discuss further in Chapter 10, the *reasonableness* of the child protection intervention itself must also be considered in understanding the nature of parents' responses to professional interventions.

It is not uncommon that, when care proceedings are initiated after the discovery of a serious suspicious injury to an infant, it can take 6 months or more before the court makes a judgment whether the injuries, on the balance of probability, were due to abuse or not. Throughout this time, the infant will most likely be in foster care, with the parents experiencing degrees of post-traumatic chronic anxiety, as described above. During this period of half-a-year or more, what services are offered to parents? Child protection practice by social services varies enormously in this respect. We have known of cases where social services have coordinated excellent interdisciplinary 'packages' of assessment and support, including skilled and sensitive social work assessment, attendance at a family centre and individual counselling for both parents. We have known of other cases where no supportive services whatsoever were provided, and where the social work contact was minimal, focused predominantly on gathering, by telephone, information required to progress 'parallel/twin-track planning' for possible compulsory adoption.

This begs the crucial assessment question of whether parents are unreasonably uncooperative with or hostile toward social services, or to what extent their behaviour is reactive to the unsupportive way in which social services have approached their task. Consequently, when there is an antagonistic or uncooperative atmosphere between the family and the child protection system, it is very important that the reasons for this are independently assessed, and the prospects for improvement gauged.

WHAT CAN CHANGE?

We have described a number of therapeutic issues and indicators that are significant in assessing potential for change from a child protection perspective. The independent assessment service provided by the NSPCC between 1986 and 2000 indicated that positive change in this direction was often possible when it was addressed as a specific assessment issue. A review of a large sample of families who were involved with this service (in the context of serious allegations of child abuse) indicated that nearly 60% derived some therapeutic benefit from the experience (Dale & Fellows 1999). These benefits were discernible in relation to the following issues:

- Some degree of amelioration of the continuing negative impact of parents' own childhood abuse.
- Development of greater responsibility for the maltreatment/neglect context by parents or other carers.
- Increased parental emotional and psychological maturity.
- Improvement in parents' mood and greater self-control.
- Increased parental self-awareness, self-esteem and self-confidence.
- Increased parental understanding, empathy and appropriate responsiveness to children's behaviour and needs.
- Enhanced parental consistency and confidence in parenting abilities.
- Improved family communication processes and relationships with extended family members.

- Improved relationship between family and agencies (especially social services).
- Reduced likelihood of a contested final court hearing being necessary (for example, independent assessment was able to make recommendations that were acceptable to all parties in court proceedings).

These were key positive outcomes from family engagement in the provision of a therapeutic assessment opportunity. During such assessments, what are the indicators of the potential for such change and the lack of it?

Indicators of Potential for Change

Specific behavioural indicators of therapeutic potential are as follows:

- Ability and willingness to attend appointments consistently. A change in atmosphere, with parents attending sessions because they 'want to', rather than because they 'have to'.
- Parents are able to overcome initial fearful/suspicious/hostile feelings and to engage in conversations that focus on the concerns on record that professionals have about them (without necessarily agreeing with all of these).
- Parents demonstrate some abilities of 'psychological mindedness' – that is to say, within their intellectual capabilities, they are able (or show signs of becoming able) to reflect upon their own thinking processes, emotional responses and behaviour from an observer perspective.
- Parents become more able to accept the usefulness of reflecting on their own contributions to complex situations (rather than blaming others for everything).
- Information and 'themes' are retained and linked between sessions. Parents show evidence of continuing to reflect upon the key issues between sessions. Sessions do not start from 'square one' – repetitively going over the same material.
- There is indication of greater insight and awareness: 'If I knew then what I know now' reactions. There is increased recognition of need for change in relation to key concerns (e.g. controlling behaviour, stress management, thinking skills, use of substances, etc.).
- Parents become willing to participate constructively in joint sessions with each other, and with significant others (such as key extended family members). These sessions generate open and constructive discussion about the central issues.

- There are increasing signs that parents can receive and consider feedback given in good faith about their attitudes and behaviour, and give serious thought to such observations.
- There are demonstrable reductions in the impact of psychosocial stressors and associated signs of increased stability of lifestyle.
- There is a responsiveness to an integrative assessment approach to potential for change. Parents become cooperative in conversations focused on understanding the effects of psychosocial history and the nature of current psychosocial stressors (including relationships), and develop positive but realistic future aspirations. This includes attending constructively to the question: 'What can you do to convince the court that reunification would not place your child at unacceptable risk?'
- There is an engaging response to discussion of further therapeutic need and a focus on relapse prevention, including an acceptance that even if significant change is made, the dangers of relapse must be anticipated and planned for. Signs of ability to identify 'early warning signs' and to have preprepared safety-first responses, including the utilisation of identified support systems.

Indicators of Lack of Change Potential

It is equally important to recognise that some parents cannot, or will not, make constructive use of independent assessment opportunities. Some parents will not attend at all despite flexibility in appointment arrangements. Some parents attend inconsistently, indicating that they have paid little attention to the focus of previous sessions. The following points are indicative of situations where it is likely to be concluded that there is little sign or prospect of significant potential for change:

- Demeanour in sessions: persistent and unrelenting aggression, hostility, agitation, sarcasm that does not diminish in the course of interviews notwithstanding calm feedback that this is likely to detract from the possibility of a positive evaluation.
- Signs or reports of continual serious substance misuse. Parent(s) being in an intoxicated/sedated state in assessment sessions (or agitated by intense substance craving) is not a positive sign.
- Significant lack of truthfulness in discussing psychosocial history and current circumstances. This is a matter of degree – very few therapy patients are totally truthful with their counsellors/therapists, even when the setting is (almost) confidential. In assessments, practitioners will have access to external sources of information to confirm or disconfirm parents' accounts.

The reason for discrepancies needs to be carefully explored before conclusions are drawn. However, parents who habitually lie about significant events are likely to reflect less positive therapeutic potential.

- Continuing discrepancies between stated positive intentions in sessions, and contradictory observations and reports from others.

These indicators, tested over several sessions, provide important evidence that a significant, therapeutic assessment opportunity has been provided, yet the conclusion has to be drawn that there is little prospect of sufficient change and increased maturity for the foreseeable future. Some families are indeed 'untreatable' (Jones 1987) or 'hopeless' (Bentovim et al. 1987). However, there is no formula or checklist that can identify the untreatable and hopeless family, and this should always be specifically tested independently in each case (especially where there is conflict between the family and the statutory agencies). Potential for change should also be assessed in relation to explicit theoretical perspectives, and the reasons to conclude that change potential is low or minimal should be specifically stated so that they can be subject to professional (peer) and judicial review.

Cases with Few Identified Psychosocial Factors of Concern

In the NSPCC SIDE research (Chapter 5), 25% of families in which there were serious suspicious injuries to infants had few apparent psychosocial problems. Such families:

- have no history of involvement with social services
- have apparently intact and supportive parental and extended family relationships
- have not caused any concern by their health visitor or family doctor about their care of the baby (indeed reports are often very positive)
- are often professionally successful and socially respected within their communities.

That babies come to sustain serious suspicious injuries in such families is particularly perplexing. In care proceedings where it is found on the balance of probability that the injuries were caused by maltreatment, how can *potential for change* be assessed when there are so few apparent problems? If there are no apparent problems, what is the relevance of assessing potential for change? Two views are commonly formed about such families. First, as there are no identifiable problems to resolve, the unknown risk factors, by definition, remain untreated and unaltered. Therefore, change (from the circumstances that produced the injury) is not possible, and, consequently, there must be a high risk of recurrence of the injury-promoting circumstances. The second view is that because there is an absence of the major factors commonly associated with serious child abuse (domestic violence, parental mental problems, substance misuse, and family or social pressures), the risk of re-injury must be lower than for families who have significant, identifiable contextual concerns.

Whether in any individual case such parents are falsely denying actual responsibility, or genuinely contesting an erroneous allegation and court judgment, it is clear that two sudden major traumas have been experienced. First, their infant has suffered an unexpected, unexplained serious injury that may be fatal, life-threatening or the cause of permanent disability. Second, the injury has been treated as suspicious and the parents experience the child protection system invading every aspect of their lives.

Our experience is that many families in such circumstances eventually appreciate the opportunity for independent assessment sessions to be able to discuss the impact of these traumatic events – so long as they have confidence in the neutrality, skills and integrity of the professionals providing the service. In this sense, many families demonstrate therapeutic potential when this is construed as the need to understand the nature and impact of the traumatic events that they have found themselves the centre of. It is particularly important in such a context that 'denial' is not 'confronted', but that the parents are facilitated in the search for their own best understanding of events and their aftermath. The services described by Dale & Fellows (1999) and Essex & Gumbleton (1999) in the UK, and Turnell & Edwards (1999) in western Australia are examples of such an approach.

SKILLS IN ASSESSING AND PROMOTING THERAPEUTIC CHANGE

As noted in Chapter 8, assessment practice requires certain knowledge, skills and experience; and assessing indicators of potential for change requires change-promoting knowledge and skills that have been acquired in the context of working therapeutically with people who have the same sorts of difficulties as the parents being assessed. The assessor and the parents need to remain clear that this is not a therapeutic relationship. Therapeutic relationships are characterised by confidentiality (with certain exceptions) and commitment to the client's own best interests.

Assessing potential for change in the context of child protection legal proceedings is far from confidential, and the client's interests are secondary to the best interests of the children concerned. (This is why some very experienced and highly qualified counsellors and therapists can experience difficulties if they are not familiar with child protection contexts.) Nevertheless, the assessor will wish to create a context that approaches a therapeutic environment as far as is possible, and will utilise specific therapeutic skills and approaches such as the following:

- Providing a convenient, comfortable, private and respectful *environment* for the assessment sessions (this does not exclude assessments sessions taking place in the family home if necessary and appropriate). It is important to bear in mind the stresses that may occur if parents have to undertake long or difficult journeys to assessment sessions.
- The ability to create an appropriate *working relationship*, utilising skills to engage parents who are likely to have mixed feelings of anxiety, fear, confusion, mistrust, suspicion and hostility. A working relationship may take a number of sessions to develop. As emphasised in Chapter 6, in this respect parents are significantly influenced (in both positive and negative ways) by the *style* of practitioners.
- The maintenance of a *stance of 'respectful uncertainty'*. It is important to avoid dual traps of providing inappropriate reassurance or premature negative opinion.
- The ability to listen fully to, and communicate understanding of (without endorsing) the precise *subjective experiencing* of the parents. This sounds simple, but it is not. Counsellors and therapists in training practise this skill extensively, monitoring transference and counter-transference dynamics and responses.
- Competent use of *microskills*, such as clarifying, probing, circular questioning, paraphrasing, summarising, identifying and exploring exceptions.
- Giving *feedback* in a respectful, clear and constructive manner (which may sometimes be quite challenging) and exploring responses to feedback that is given.
- Exploring *multiple hypotheses* (e.g. regarding circumstances of the injury incident) and *'what if?'* hypothetical scenarios (e.g. regarding possible outcomes).
- Exploring and clarifying the *significance of personal or family history*, recent events, current situation and future aspirations. What are the important past, present and future issues from a psychosocial perspective?
- Carefully *observing* the behaviour of the parents in the assessment interviews (including contact sessions with children) and noting factors such as intellectual capacity, concentration, emotional experiencing or expression, mood, communication styles, parenting skills and attachment.
- Identifying *what use has been made of previous help* utilised or offered? What has been helpful and unhelpful in previous agency or professional

interventions? What form of help should have been provided or requested?

- Exploring what *strengths*/resources/strategies the parents identify within themselves, their extended family and the community to help them move toward identified future aspirations.
- Identifying what professional services and therapeutic/support interventions are indicated to enhance and further develop change potential. What is the current best *assessment of therapeutic needs* and what are the parents' views about this?
- Ability to deal constructively with *transference and counter-transference dynamics* – being able to use immediacy skills to explore to what extent parents' responses are reality or transference based, and to self-monitor effectively personal emotional reactions to the family.
- Skills to engage *systemically* but neutrally with complex sets of relationships, including the parents' relationship and extended family relationships.

It is regrettable that contemporary social work training has few therapeutic components. In contrast, practitioners with training in counselling or psychotherapy will have studied theories of change, methods of interventions, and factors relating to clients, therapists and the therapeutic relationship that promote or hinder progress. They will have participated in skills development workshops, and received regular clinical supervision of their practice. In addition, they will have learnt to monitor their own psychological and emotional responses to the behaviour and situations of clients, including experience in detecting and responding appropriately to transference and counter-transference dynamics. Few social workers today have the benefit of such training, and (as discussed in Chapter 6) this can be reflected in styles of practice which clients sometimes report as being unhelpful, patronising, unprofessional and occasionally hostile and punitive.

10

FINE JUDGMENTS

Exceptionally important cases. Cases, we remind ourselves, where invariably a decision is being taken as to the long-term/permanent removal of children from their natural parents. (What other area of forensic activity, since the abolition of the death penalty, empowers the state to intervene so drastically in the family life of the private individual?) (Coleridge 2003, p. 799)

This comment by a High Court family judge firmly focuses our attention on the gravity of the issues at stake in assessments of cases of serious suspicious injuries to infants. It leads us to reiterate and reinforce that the main concern of this book is the need for reductions in the incidence of *both* major types of child protection error:

● cases where infants do not receive effective protection from sources of real risk (the false-negative error)
● cases where child protection systems intervene in families in unnecessary, inappropriate, disproportionate and damaging ways (the false-positive error).

We have illustrated and discussed the nature and impact of both types of error throughout this book. To recapitulate: some infants are sadistically killed, injured and re-injured (if given the chance) by parents who are so damaged/disturbed that there is no prospect of sufficient change for them to become adequate and safe parents. On the other hand, seriously injured infants (and non-injured siblings) have been subjected to compulsory adoption when it is likely that with appropriate services they could have been returned safely to their natural family/kinship environments. Moreover, unknown numbers of infants have been separated from their parents/families on the basis of erroneous diagnoses of abuse and mistaken court judgments that injuries were caused by abuse. The low evidential standard in care proceedings of 'balance of probability' (rather than 'beyond reasonable doubt') inclines toward false-positive errors, as less probable non-abuse hypotheses invariably are dismissed in favour of presumed abuse explanations (Howitt 1992).

On the positive side, there are two clear types of effective child protection interventions and outcomes. First, unknown numbers of seriously injured infants have grown up happily in successful adoptive families who would otherwise have faced further grave harm if they had been returned to their families of origin. Second, equally unknown numbers of infants who sustained serious suspicious injuries have been successfully reunified within their natural families/kinship carers with the help of appropriate therapeutic, support and supervisory services.

Given the profound consequences for children and families of positive and negative outcomes, we focus in this final chapter on two main areas. First, we argue that, in making the ultimate decision about the future of infants who have sustained serious suspicious injuries, courts should more explicitly take into account the 'reasonableness' and 'unreasonableness' of child protection interventions. Second, we consider the options that are available to the court at what is known as the 'disposal' or welfare concluding stage of care proceedings.

BEING REASONABLE

'Reasonableness' is an ancient legal concept describing a fictional person who, in any given circumstances, behaves appropriately with regard to those circumstances. It is against these imagined actions of the hypothetically reasonable person that the actual actions of an individual are adjudged to determine whether or not that individual was responsible, culpable or negligent. The question: *How would a reasonable person act under the circumstances?* is therefore central to legal judgments in many aspects of law.

In cases involving professional opinions and behaviour, the legal doctrine of the *reasonable professional* has developed. For example, if a doctor misdiagnoses a patient, the significant question is not so much whether the diagnosis was wrong as would a doctor acting under the same circumstances, with the knowledge available to the field at the time of the diagnosis, have concluded that the given diagnosis was reasonable? This signifies the importance of *peer review* as an important factor in evaluating the reasonableness of professional behaviour and judgments. This is an area where *children's guardians* and independent social work expert witnesses have a crucial role to play in care proceedings, especially where there are contentious disputes between families and local authorities. Just as grossly inappropriate professional (in)actions underlie many cases of avoidable child abuse fatality, equivalent inappropriate, disproportionate and unreasonable professional behaviour (in the name of 'child protection') can result in significant *iatrogenic* (system-generated) harm to children and families.

What is Reasonable?

The nature, quality, style and proportionality of child protection interventions fall within a continuum of reasonableness–unreasonableness. It is rare that this is addressed specifically in the child protection literature, although Ryburn (1994b) in the UK, and Crenshaw (2004) in the USA are exceptions:

> The reasonableness of parents can only be interpreted in the light of the reasonableness of those with a duty to offer services. Reasonableness is not a word that is applied to professional behaviour in the process of assessing the risk of harm. We should do so. (Ryburn 1994a, p. 197)

> Families cannot find justice . . . if the system around them is unjust, and the system cannot be just if it does more harm than good. (Crenshaw 2004, p. 2)

In the UK, government guidance such as the Assessment Framework (Department of Health 2000) does not consider the fact that the behaviour of families being assessed will, on occasion, be adversely affected by and misinterpreted through the perverse operation of the child protection system. Without this perspective, as we argued in Chapter 4, the myth is generally maintained that 'the system works as best as it can with serious cases' (Thoburn et al. 1995).

Child protection practice is subject to specific internal and interagency operational procedures (which are not always followed) as well as directions from professional regulatory bodies, such as the General Medical Council and the General Social Care Council. Such bodies set standards for professional conduct, and deal with complaints of malpractice. Parents and family members do not have explicit standards of conduct to observe while subject to child protection interventions. Parental behaviour is not prescribed, standardised, certificated, accredited, peer reviewed or subject to complaint and sanction by a regulatory or disciplinary body. Fortunately, from a civil liberties perspective, there is no *General Parenting Council*. However, like all citizens, parents involved in child protection interventions are expected to obey the law, and this will be one objective test of their reasonableness. Consequently, at the extreme, it is not difficult to construe parental behaviour that breaches the law (such as assaulting a social worker or not complying with a civil court order) as being unreasonable.

Families who become involved with child protection services respond to interventions with varying degrees of 'reasonableness' and 'unreasonableness'.

A complex interactional dynamic arises where the degree of 'reasonableness' of the behaviour of each 'side' influences the 'reasonableness' of the other. In such situations, what is 'reasonable given the circumstances' can be a matter of significant dispute. To ensure fair process, it is vital that courts specifically attend to the *reasonableness* of professional practice in hearings and when making judgments in contentious cases of serious suspicious injuries to infants.

Four types of reasonableness–unreasonableness dynamics between families and the child protection system can be portrayed:

(1) *Reasonable* child protection system encounters *reasonable* family.
(2) *Reasonable* child protection system encounters *unreasonable* family.
(3) *Unreasonable* child protection system encounters *reasonable* family.
(4) *Unreasonable* child protection system encounters *unreasonable* family.

We shall discuss and illustrate these scenarios in turn. We focus in rather more detail on the third dynamic, unreasonable child protection system encounters reasonable family, as this has received less attention in the child protection assessment literature (which mostly discusses parental risk factors and 'dangerousness').

Reasonable Child Protection System Encounters Reasonable Family

The process of child protection intervention where both parties behave reasonably reflects the ideal of 'partnership' between families and agencies as promoted in guidance stemming from the Children Act 1989 and the aspirations of the Assessment Framework (Department of Health 2000). In this dynamic, agency interventions are timely, skilled, proportionate and sensitive to the feelings of family members concerned. For example, it is understood that most parents will be anxious, upset or angry about an unexpected child protection intervention. Professionals do not automatically construe the expression of such feelings as being indicators of risk or lack of potential for cooperation. Skills to promote reasonableness in parents who are shocked, angry, or afraid are utilised, and professionals demonstrate attitudes of 'respectful uncertainty', as well as empathic and supportive compassion.

Being reasonable, family members recognise and accept that in situations where a serious suspicious injury to an infant has occurred, child protection agencies have a responsibility to make enquiries into the safety and welfare of children. In view of this, parents and family members cooperate with appropriate appointments, interviews and examinations, and are consistent in continuing contacts with their infant (for example in hospital or foster care). Family members behaving reasonably do not avoid, intimidate, threaten or assault professional staff.

Much of the skill (and professional responsibility) of family law solicitors is directed toward influencing their clients (especially when acting for parents) to behave reasonably in their dealings with social services and other professionals. In the privacy of the solicitor's office, encouraging (and sometimes firm) words are spoken to parents along these lines. This can be particularly important when the parents (and the solicitor) perceive the local authority to be acting unreasonably, and where the parents might have a propensity to respond to perceived provocation in a way that would reinforce the local authority's perspective that the parents are uncooperative and/or intractably hostile (and therefore of higher risk).

Toward the end of Chapter 6, we gave a number of illustrations from parents' perspectives of a 'reasonable–reasonable' dynamic between families and the child protection system, reflecting skilled, sensitive and proportionate child protection interventions. On this point, in a previous publication, we concluded:

> The public is much less aware that child protection systems which have developed over the past 30 years do, in fact, work well for thousands of children each year. Out of sight, skilled and diligent professionals arrange vital protection for vulnerable children and provide or organise effective support for their parents and wider families. Without this level of successful but hidden child protection practice, rates of serious and fatal child abuse in the UK would undoubtedly be substantially higher than they currently are. (Dale et al. 2002b, p. 68)

We also noted that such high-quality child protection practice does not have the high public profile that it deserves, and that this serves to demoralise child protection practitioners (in turn affecting the quality of services).

Reasonable Child Protection System Encounters Unreasonable Family

> A solicitor had a pay-phone wrenched off the wall and thrown at him. We are operating in a level of fear all the time ... (people are) unpredictable because of psychiatric and drug problems, some have very violent backgrounds. There is nothing like taking someone's child to make them angry. (Stanley & Goddard 2002, p. 97)

> The problem is that there are many reasons why people lie or distort the facts when talking to a social worker. Parents who are actually harming their child have powerful motives for concealing this.... Inquiry reports show the lengths abusive parents will go to to hide the truth and how successful that can be. (Munro 1999, p. 752)

In the 'reasonable child protection system encounters unreasonable family' scenario, child protection agency interventions are necessary and appropriate, but the responses of the family have to be construed as being unreasonable in the circumstances. Parents and other family members may behave in the following unreasonable ways:

- being violent, aggressive and intimidating professionals
- avoiding contact with professionals
- continually misleading professionals (especially in assessments) with untrue information about personal/family/social circumstances (being untruthful in denying domestic violence, concealing the continued presence of a violent adult, falsely denying continuing substance abuse, etc.)
- intimidating the other parent (for example when parents have separated)
- being intoxicated in contacts with children and/or professionals
- being significantly inconsistent in attending contact sessions
- manipulating their child psychologically and emotionally in detrimental ways during contact sessions (and even causing further physical harm)
- attempting to disrupt the foster/kinship placement and/or intimidating the foster/kinship carers
- attempting to 'snatch' children from substitute placements (and occasionally doing so)
- failing to utilise consistently appropriate services and advice in relation to mental health problems (such as depression, psychosis, substance-abuse related disinhibition and incapacity)
- failing to cooperate fully with drug-dependence services (e.g. not complying with hair-strand and urine testing)
- being unwilling to participate constructively in court-agreed assessment programmes.

The crucial question is to what extent parents and extended family members in these circumstances can engage in independent assessments, and whether there is potential for change regarding such 'unreasonable' behaviour, and over what timescale. Does this behaviour reflect transient, panic-like reactions at times of intense and unusual stress? Or, is it indicative of more fixed personality characteristics, mental health problems and disturbed relationships that have minimal prospect of change (or of any changes being sustained).

One Australian study provided graphic accounts of the extent of the disturbance and violence from parents that child protection workers can be subject to in the course of their work:

The worker reported that she had been threatened with a gun, had been assaulted once, had received numerous death threats, and had been twice threatened with a knife. (Stanley & Goddard 2002, p. 13)

A worker described an armed hold-up at her office. Another worker had been held hostage with a gun at her head. A number of files were stolen in the raid. The man believed to be responsible was still free and continued to 'stalk' and 'harass' workers. He had also threatened to 'take out' some workers. The protective services office was closed as a result of this hold-up and its effects on the protective workers. The workers were moved to a new location. (Stanley & Goddard 2002, p. 13)

From this the researchers concluded:

When a protective worker becomes involved with a violent family it is illogical to believe that the protective worker will be immune from this violence. The Victorian study demonstrates that the workers are not in fact exempt. Within a period of only six months, 9 of the 50 workers interviewed had been subjected to physical assaults, and four workers to assault by a person wielding an object. There were a total of 68 episodes of threatened assault. Thus, 35 of the 50 workers were victims of at least one major trauma, in the form of assault, attempted or threatened assault, a death threat, or another form of major intimidation. (Stanley & Goddard 2002, p. 151)

In what ways does being subject to such intimidation, fear and violence affect the behaviour and judgments of child protection professionals? Stanley & Goddard (2002) described a post-traumatic, 'hostage'-type response where, in accommodating to threats, practitioners underestimated the risks to children in such families and did not take necessary protective action. Their study (undertaken in the equivalent of social services in Victoria, Australia) also noted that support for practitioners affected in these ways was significantly absent on the part of their managers and employers.

While these are important findings in relation to the risks of child protection work, Stanley & Goddard (2002) did not analyse in an equivalent way the extent to which the 'unreasonableness' of the families in their sample was itself a reaction to 'unreasonable' child protection interventions. As we have already noted, one social worker in the study commented (perhaps with dry, Australian understatement): 'There is nothing like taking someone's child to make them angry.' Indeed. But such anger needs to be viewed and understood in the context of knowledge regarding whether the removal of the child was necessary and reasonable, or disproportionate and unreasonable. However, some parents *are* intractably hostile and psychopathically aggressive, and cannot (at this stage in their lives) be worked with constructively no matter what the skills level of the practitioners involved.

Unreasonable Child Protection System Encounters Reasonable Family

Research into parents' perceptions of child protection interventions (see Chapter 6) and some studies of child protection outcomes (see Chapter 4) illustrate child protection practice which is demonstrably unprofessional and unreasonable. In this third dynamic, the behaviour of parents remains reasonable in the face of unreasonable interventions; that is, dissatisfaction is communicated in civil and formal ways.

By any measure, unreasonable child protection processes occur which are negligent, inappropriate, inconsistent, contradictory, unpredictable, insensitive, intimidating, disproportionate, manifestly biased and even duplicitous. Unreasonable practice contributes to both major types of child protection error: underreacting (the highly visible false-negative error), and overreacting (the socially largely invisible false-positive error). Unreasonable child protection practice throughout the whole child protection process includes the following:

- inadequate *preventive* services and interventions
- failure to follow child protection *procedures* and to invoke care proceedings in serious cases
- inadequate *investigation* of suspected abuse and initial case management
- absent, inadequate and biased *assessment* of risk
- failure to implement *care plans* and to provide services
- inadequate professional *competence skills and resources*.

One common context of child protection tragedies is families experiencing major problems where known concerns either were not referred to social services or, when referred, were not properly considered. In some overburdened social services intake and assessment teams, a gatekeeping culture operates seeking rationales to dispose of referrals as 'no further action' at the earliest possible stage. A comment from a Part 8 Review into the death of a baby encapsulates such unreasonable professional practice:

> The general approach to practice at the point of referral appears to have been dominated by trying to find evidence to confirm that social work intervention was not needed, rather than a curious and enquiring approach as to what might have happened to a very young baby. (Pt 8 Review conclusion)

However, it is also important to acknowledge that many child protection professionals work in totally inadequate environments and face real risks in their work. The Laming inquiry into the death of Victoria Climbié reported that social workers are expected in some instances to carry out child protection tasks in the context of quite unreasonable administrative systems with deficient (and sometimes incompetent) management support and oversight of practice (Laming 2003). Pressures also increase for child protection professionals (as well as families) due to the general decline in preventive family support services in the UK in recent times (Laming 2003). As we have discussed, researchers also highlight the very stressful environments that many child protection practitioners have to work in, including threats to their personal safety.

What is often unreasonable about assessment practice? As we have discussed throughout this book, there is substantial research to indicate that:

● Assessments are not undertaken.
● Assessments can be inadequate.
● Assessments can be significantly biased.
● The style of assessments can be counter-productive.

The more fundamental the implications of the decisions to be taken, the more important it is that assessments influencing decisions are thorough, evidence-based, neutral, that they systematically identify risks and strengths, and utilise appropriate skills to explore potential for change. Assessment bias occurs when prejudgments, lack of knowledge, cognitive distortions, dominant belief systems and counter-transference affect the type of evidence that is elicited, how it is interpreted, and the conclusions that are drawn from it (Dale et al. 2002a,b; Holland 2004; Macdonald 2001; Munro 1999, 2002; Scott 1998).

Such bias may be over-optimistic (as shown in many fatal case reviews) when insufficient attention is paid to recognised risk factors. When serious suspicious injuries have been sustained by a very young infant, the real possibility of further harm to the injured child cannot sensibly be ignored and requires very careful assessment. Alternatively, the bias may be over-pessimistic and 'family-phobic' (Crenshaw 2004), where almost every facet of a family's attitudes, behaviour, relationships and culture is negatively construed, sometimes reflecting an almost paranoid professional perspective on risk.

Unreasonable Child Protection System Encounters Unreasonable Family

It should be noted that injuries were occurring to Luke constantly and it would have been unnecessarily burdensome to pursue each occurrence through procedural channels. (Internal management review report by social services for a Part 8 Review)

In Chapter 5, we noted this comment from a management report to a Part 8 Review after the death of a male infant. It is a startling explanation for a quite unreasonable failure to protect a very vulnerable infant who was known to be living in a very violent family.

There is a chicken-and-egg conundrum present with the 'unreasonable child protection system encounters unreasonable family' dynamic. Some professionals view some parents and families as being inconsistent, unco-operative, unreasonable, unpredictable, unreliable, divided, devious, deceitful and manipulative. Equally, some parents have exactly the same view of child protection professionals. While child protection workers must anticipate a range of emotional parental reactions, families have the right to expect that the professionals they encounter will be respectful, competent, consistent, transparent and well informed. This is by no means always the case.

Child protection workers (like professionals in all fields) have their fair share of personality peculiarities and stress responses that can affect clients' perceptions of their competence, humanity and humility. Child protection systems as a whole are also idiosyncratic. Like any complex group process, they develop inconsistencies, internal conflicts, hidden agendas and biases – compounded in many areas by the chronically undermining impact of seriously inadequate resources. This dynamic sometimes develops into an impasse of intractable mutual hostility. These are cases where independent assessments are particularly vital, and can be effective in ameliorating the mutual antagonism between families and the child protection agencies.

Demonstrating 'Reasonableness': Auditing Rationales for Child Protection Decisions and Professional Skills

In this book, we have addressed our concern about two major types of child protection errors (the false-negative and the false-positive). Some errors are unavoidable when dealing with uncertain, emotionally charged and complex situations. In human systems dealing with human behaviour, risks can never be totally eliminated. In child protection work there are no 'risk-free' solutions. A 'safety-first' response that subsequently turns out not to have been necessary may well be considered reasonable in the known circum-stances at the time. Adverse outcomes and even mistakes are not necessarily an indicator of unreasonable practice.

However, in child protection practice, the application of systematic thinking and analytic skills are notoriously lacking in assessments (Holland 2004;

Macdonald 2001; Munro 2002; Scott 1998). Assessments can be susceptible to significant cognitive and emotional bias (Dale et al. 2002b; Dale 2003). In this context, a requirement to record the thinking processes behind the taking of fundamental decisions would instigate practitioners, supervisors and managers to take much more consistent and carefully considered decisions. An audit trail of rationale could have a crucial effect on many key decisions such as the following:

- Is the removal of the child really necessary?
- Is the removal of siblings really necessary?
- Is the removal at birth of a new baby really necessary?
- Is placement with strangers really necessary?
- On what basis have the frequency, length and venue for contact sessions been determined?
- What is the justification for contact restrictions placed on siblings and extended family members?

We have noted on several occasions in this book that there is a significant inconsistency in the nature of such decisions. Decisions that are made seem to be highly influenced by chance factors (which particular staff happen to become involved) and pragmatic factors (such as availability of mother-baby foster placements, and resources to supervise and provide transport for contact). To record the rationale for these decisions would focus thinking in a systematic way, and also ensure that the evidence base of the decision would be transparent and available as a contemporary record in any subsequent dispute (such as a formal complaint or challenge to the proportionality of a decision in the course of care proceedings). Similarly, when 'unreasonable' behaviour of families is reported in evidence by social services in court proceedings, there should be a requirement also to report how this interpretation was made and what efforts were made to address and resolve such behaviour in a constructive way.

As mentioned in Chapters 6, 8 and 9, there is also a very important issue about the nature and levels of professional *skills* required to respond constructively to parents who are agitated and angry (and often very frightened) in the face of child protection interventions. We have discussed the traumatic impact on parents/carers of the circumstances of the injury, including the frightening immediate aftermath of medical, police and social service interventions, and the post-traumatic chronic anxiety experienced by families separated from their children during the many months before the final hearing in the care proceedings.

This begs a number of questions. Are social workers receiving sufficient training to deal with highly emotionally aroused people in the midst of such traumatic and post-traumatic situations? Are social workers in general trained as well as police officers and nurses in methods of calming and defusing highly stressful and conflictual incidents? As social work becomes an increasingly female profession, is there a particular issue in relation to effective skills in dealing with distressed, indignant and angry men? Do social workers have sufficient training and clinical supervision (i.e. supervision of their *practice* rather than monitoring of their administration) to recognise and respond constructively to moments of intense negative transference on the part of family members – that is to say, not taking *personally* expressions of anger by family members who are in the midst of a child protection crisis and its aftermath? Do social workers have sufficient skills to *surf* such negative transference – allowing both its expression and constructive containment rather than being emotionally triggered into their own counter-transference reactions such as fear, fight or flight?

On this point, we turn back to an example of highly effective child protection practice that was presented in Chapter 6. Readers will recall the mother in this case describing her angry and hostile behaviour toward the social worker:

> At first it was not very good – I kept losing my temper – which is bound to happen when they are threatening to take your son off you.... As it's gone along, things have got better... we've got more friendly – we talk to each other – instead of shouting and bawling at each other (laughs).... She actually stayed quite calm – she tried to calm me down. I just couldn't hold my temper back – I had to let it out. She either just sat there and let me say what I had to say – or she'd sit there and talk to me and tell me to calm down. (Ms Durgan, a mother, in Dale 2002c, p. 44)

Fortunately, the social worker concerned had the knowledge to understand that this behaviour was a traumatic response, and the skills to be able to allow its expression and gradual containment without feeling provoked into a personal defensive or persecutory reaction (and without taking her professional eye off the child protection 'ball'). This case might well have had a very different outcome if the mother had been unlucky enough to encounter a social worker who did not have such knowledge and skills, and who responded in a fearful or emotionally intensifying way, thereby provoking the intensity of the mother's anger. This example accords with the findings of several researchers (Fernandez 1996; MacKinnon 1998; Thorpe & Thomson 2003; Trotter 2004) who analysed the skills of child protection social workers in Australia:

> When workers made use of the various relationship skills the clients generally did better on the outcome measures. The clients saw the worker's ability to listen and understand their problems as particularly valuable. These qualities were also related to improved outcomes. When workers were judgmental and critical the outcomes were particularly poor. (Trotter 2004, p. 162)

Unknown proportions of parents who are 'written off' by social services *can* be worked with very productively when approached in specific ways (as described in Chapters 8 and 9). Many initially 'unreasonable' families can be influenced over time into a much more amenable and cooperative stance (Trotter 1999). The skill levels, experience and orientation of child protection professionals is a key factor in this; and it is important in individual cases that judges pay full attention to whether child protection interventions have met this criterion to a reasonable degree.

In the concluding section of this book, we address the options open to the court in making decisions that will profoundly affect children, siblings, parents and families for the rest of their lives.

'DISPOSALS'

At the 'disposal' or 'welfare' stage of care proceedings, the court has already made a 'finding of fact' at the causation stage that, on the balance of probabilities, the nature of the serious injuries constitutes significant harm. The court may or may not have been able to make a finding in respect of which parent/carer was responsible, and whether any relevant person 'failed to protect' the child from the significant harm that occurred.

At disposal hearings the court will consider a wider range of evidence relating to the child's family and social circumstances and will hear evidence from the family and a range of professional and expert witnesses in relation to proposals for subsequent placement of the child. The court will formally consider whether the welfare of the child requires a care order to be made, which would transfer parental authority to the local authority. In considering a recommendation by a local authority for a care order to be made, the court will give consideration to the 'care plan' of the local authority. The care plan is the local authority's statement of its intentions with regard to the child should the court make a care order. As was discussed in Chapter 4, for various reasons local authorities do not always implement the care plans presented to courts, and many family judges regret the loss of the wardship powers to monitor and compel the actions (and inactions) of local authorities in this respect.

In cases of serious suspicious injuries to infants, there are usually three main options for the court to consider:

- that the child is placed outside the family with a prospective adoptive family (compulsory adoption)
- that the child is moved from foster parents into the care of specified extended family/kinship carers (kinship care)
- that the child is returned (usually from foster parents) to the care of his/ her parent(s) (reunification).

During the disposal/welfare stage of care proceedings, significant differences of opinion can arise regarding the best interests of infants who have suffered serious suspicious injuries. Professionals have different views about the circumstances where it can be considered appropriate to take considered risks in relation to reunification, and the resources and timescales that are justifiable to facilitate parents making sufficient positive changes in their lives and relationships. To what extent should efforts be made to identify placements within the extended family and kinship network so that the infant is able to grow up as a member of his/her biological family with its specific cultural and social identity? Or, in what circumstances should placements be quickly found with prospective adoptive parents so that the child can benefit from the formation of new positive (more consistently responsive) attachments (and often the benefits of a socially advantageous new family environment)?

In addition to the professional knowledge and research base that is called upon to support these very different outcomes, judicial decisions since October 2000 have (more formally than before) had to consider explicitly the human rights of the children, parents and families concerned.

European Convention for the Protection of Human Rights and Fundamental Freedoms (1950) (ECHR), and the Human Rights Act 1998

The implementation (in October 2000) of the Human Rights Act 1998 requires the judiciary in the UK to be compliant with the ECHR. This affects judgments in contested childcare cases. The following articles of the European Convention for the protection of Human Rights and Fundamental Freedoms (1950) (ECHR) are particularly significant (emphasis added):

- Article 2(1): *'Everyone's **right to life** shall be protected by law.'*
- Article 3: *'No one shall be subjected to torture or to **inhuman or degrading treatment or punishment**.'*
- Article 6: *'In the determination of his civil rights and obligations or of any criminal charge against him, everyone is entitled to **a fair and public hearing** within a reasonable time by an independent and impartial tribunal established by law.'*
- Article 8(1): *'Everyone has the right to **respect for his private and family life**, his home and his correspondence.'*
- Article 8(2): *'There shall be **no interference by a public authority** with the exercise of this right **except** such as is in accordance with the law and is necessary in a democratic society in the interests of national security, public safety or the economic well-being of the country, for the prevention of disorder or crime, **for the protection of health or morals, or for the protection of the rights and freedoms of others.'***

Articles 2 and 3, 'right to life' and freedom from 'torture or to inhuman or degrading treatment or punishment', are fairly explicit rights for children not to be abused and re-abused by their parents/carers. In relation to Article 8(1) and Article 8(2), courts have to balance the tension between them when considering alternative proposals about the futures of suspiciously injured infants. In particular, courts must ensure that the proposed 'disposal' of the child is *proportionate* to the degree of harm experienced and the degree of identified future risk.

This *principle of proportionality* has become very significant in Human Rights Act adjudications, and is specifically applicable to professional opinions and legal judgments about the appropriate placements of suspiciously injured infants. Taking all relevant Articles of the Human Rights Act (1998) into account, and recognising the importance of proportionality, an eminent legal academic recently came to two important conclusions regarding cases of serious suspicious injuries to infants where the identity of the person who caused the harm remains uncertain:

> Proportionality in the face of uncertainty requires that the door is left open to a child's eventual reintegration with her family. This will normally, although not necessarily, be in the interests of the child. (Hayes 2004, p. 63)

> In an 'uncertain attribution' case where there would be a very serious risk to the child should she be looked after by the parent who harmed her, a care order with a care plan of fostering with supervised and relatively infrequent contact by either parent might be deemed necessary in order to protect the child from the real possibility of further significant harm. But a care plan of fostering with a view to the child's closed adoption would probably be a disproportionate response, even if otherwise thought best for the child. (Hayes 2004, pp. 84–5)

These are crucial points that should give considerable cause for reflection within many social services departments about a culture which advocates rapid compulsory adoption for infants (often without prior specialist assessment) at the disposal/welfare stage of care proceedings. Cases have arisen where such proposals have been made to courts without the local authority having made significant efforts to assess the potential for change in the family (and to provide services to promote such change). If reasonable efforts to facilitate the appropriate return of a child to his/her family are not made, local authorities are failing in their duty under s23(6) Children Act 1989 – 'Any local authority looking after a child shall make arrangements to enable them to live with a relative, friend or other person connected with him, unless that would not be reasonably practicable or consistent with his welfare' – and are not complying with the ECHR Article 8 requirement to promote family life. In this context, a senior member of the judiciary has expressed concern that local authorities do not fully recognise the implications for their practice that stem from the implementation of the Human Rights Act 1998 (Munby 2004).

Adoption

There are cases where infants who have sustained serious suspicious injuries cannot return to their parents or extended family/kinship carers with a reasonable degree of anticipated safety. These are likely to be situations involving combinations of the following factors:

- where serious suspicious injuries have occurred on several occasions
- where it appears that there was intent to cause harm and/or sadistic motivation
- where the injuries occurred in the context of significant child neglect
- where the parents' commitment to and attitudes toward the child are indicative of ambivalence and/or emotional rejection
- where parenting skills remain inadequate despite the opportunity for coaching interventions
- where the parents/carers have continuing significant intellectual impairment, mental health problems and/or personality disorder involving habitual aggression and poor impulse control
- where the parents/carers exhibit significant substance/alcohol dependence
- where domestic violence continues to be a significant feature of the parents' relationship
- where the parents continue to have an inherently unstable lifestyle (which itself would present dangers to an infant)
- where the parents are unable to move over time into a position of cooperation with reasonable professional assessment interventions (and to address areas of identified difficulties)
- where assessments indicate that there are no extended family members who are in a position to provide suitable, stable and secure substitute care.

When it is assessed that an infant cannot return to the parents or extended family members, long-term fostering is likely to be recommended in preference to an adoptive placement only in exceptional circumstances. This is in recognition of robust research evidence that for very young children, outcomes for adoption are likely to be superior to those of long-term fostering (Triseliotis 2002, 2003).

There have been several stages in the evolution of adoption philosophy and practice. At its inception in the UK (1926–30), adoption was predominantly the legal transfer of babies from shameful unmarried mothers to anonymous childless couples. The process was private (the relinquishing mother knew nothing about the adopters), secret (the adoptee was rarely informed of family history) and closed (all contact between natural parent(s) and the adopted infant was totally severed). It is now generally recognised that such practice was psychologically misguided, and across several decades commentators (e.g. Gupta 2003; Kirk 1964) have questioned the maladaptive effects on the development of individual identity of adopted children/adults who did not have full information about their family, and genetic and cultural backgrounds. Concerns about the consequences of such 'genealogical bewilderment' were raised (Sants 1964). Extensive research in the 1980s and 1990s raised further doubts about the social transplantation model of closed adoption in respect of healthy identity formation and stability of placements (e.g. Banks 1994; Fratter et al. 1991; Howe & Feast 2000; Smith & Logan 2004; Thoburn 1994).

Legal concerns have also arisen regarding the potential infringement of human rights and 'rights of the child' stemming from the legal fiction that adopted children do not have natural family members separate from their adoptive family. The review of adoption law in New Zealand in 2000 commented forcefully on this point: 'deeming an adopted child to have been born to adoptive parent *is a repugnant and an unnecessary distortion of reality*' (Law Commission of New Zealand 2000, pp. 43–4).

Compulsory Adoption

Infants may be subject to compulsory adoption if courts decide that it is not safe for them to be returned to the care of their parents or extended families. Compulsory closed adoption is a *draconian* measure (legal parlance derived from Draco, a lawgiver of Athens in 621 BC, whose measures were so severe they were said to be written in letters of blood):

> Adoptions made without family consent represent the loss of a lifetime for children and their original families. Many such placements have been made with far too little consideration for the gravity of the consequences for all parties involved, and far too little regard for a process that is fair and just. (Ryburn 1994a, p. 174)

In certain circumstances, it is difficult to envisage an alternative to compulsory adoption that could provide appropriately for the long-term security and safety of infants. We point readers' attention back to the case examples of sustained sadistic abuse of children reported in Chapter 2. In many such cases, there is negligible prospect of sufficient positive changes being made and sustained by parents that could result in their having a direct role in the future of their children. If the poor child had not died, it is difficult to imagine any circumstances in which Tangaroa Matiu could have been cared for again by his mother and stepfather, or indeed have any beneficial contact with them (see Chapter 2, page 10). The nature of parental personality disorders that are often associated with prolonged sadistic violence to children makes it likely that such parents' knowledge of their child's placement would put the substitute family at risk of manipulative, intimidating or violent behaviour. In such specific (but relatively rare) circumstances, compulsory adoption seems unavoidable.

We are concerned, however, that recommendations for compulsory adoption are increasingly made by social services and *children's guardians* in a much broader range of circumstances – what Thoburn (2003b) referred to as 'the calamity of over-hasty adoptions'. At the disposal/welfare stage of care proceedings, social services core assessments and care plans for compulsory adoption sometimes imply a contrast between irredeemably inadequate natural families and hypothetically perfect prospective adoptive parents. There is an inherent bias in such juxtapositions, given that:

> Research indicates that adoptive families are as prone to the insecurities and calamities of modern life as any other families. There is no clear-cut group of 'wonderpeople' waiting to be identified who will give children in need the total experience of love and security that all child care workers wish. (Jordan 1994, p. 17)

Thoburn (2003a) has noted that it is only in the USA and the UK that substantial numbers of children in care are placed for adoption – and that compulsory adoption is not common across most of Europe: 'The marked difference with other European countries is explained by differing views about whether it is ethically and legally possible to place children for adoption when birth parents do not agree' (Thoburn 2003a, p. 228).

Ryburn also addressed the relativity of cultural/racial norms and values regarding adoption:

> One of the factors which has most militated against the recruitment of permanent new families for children of minority ethnic groups is the belief that adoption is necessarily the most desirable form of substitute care. This is coupled with the assumption that because formal legal adoption finds acceptance in the non-black community it is right for all communities. Permanent and long-term substitute care for children, where links with original family are usually maintained, are common in many societies. The concept of a legal severance and the complete transfer of a child from one family to another may be an alien concept for many ethnic groups in Britain, and in Muslim countries, for example (with the exception of Tunisia) it does not exist. (Ryburn 1994a, p. 165)

Adoption Outcomes and Open Adoptions

> Closed stranger adoption can now be seen for what it was – a social experiment with unknown and uninvestigated outcomes conducted on a massive scale. (Else 1991, p. 197)

> The courts have spent the last 20 years or more hearing from the 'experts' that adoption with no contact with the natural family was best for children and that life story books were enough. They need to be shown different models of adoption, and be convinced that they are workable and in the best interests of the child with whom they are concerned. (Lawson 1994, p. 49)

It is surprising, given the draconian nature of compulsory adoption, that there is actually minimal outcome evaluation to support a policy of total and compulsory severance of all natural family links (Ryburn 1996). It is also important to note that there is very little research focused specifically on outcomes for very young children who have been adopted as a consequence of abuse and neglect (Rushton 2004).

Outcome measures for adoption in general are problematic (Quinton et al. 1997; Thoburn 2003c). Placement 'breakdown rate' is a crude measure and does not provide information about the quality of adoptions that do not actually reach the extreme point of breakdown. For example, in a major study of nearly 400 adult adoptees (whose placements did not break down), 7% of those who had been placed before the age of 1 year rated their experience of growing up adopted in a negative way, and 32% of the same group had mixed negative and positive feelings about their adopted childhoods (Howe & Feast 2000). It is also difficult to establish whether the 'successes' identified in adoption research are related to adoption itself – or the fact that most compulsory adoptions involve a social stratification shift between working-class and middle-class families and communities:

> Children who will be adopted against the wishes of their families are highly likely to be children of the poor. Our adoption and statutory substitute family placement practice has always been of the transfer of children across wealth and class barriers. (Ryburn 1994a, pp. 190–1)

Over recent years, the philosophical and policy insistence on the benefit of closed adoptions has significantly weakened in response to accumulating evidence that having adopted children maintain varying forms of knowledge of and contact with their natural families can actually enhance the success of adoptive placements. It is increasingly recognised that for substitute parenting to be emotionally and developmentally optimal two factors are crucial. First, children need legal security (sense of permanence) with their primary carers. Second, children need a genuine sense of personal and cultural identity. To minimise the prospect of longer-term identity confusion, children benefit from accurate knowledge of and continuing contact with (where safe) significant members of their families of origin (Fahlberg 1991; Thoburn 1996). As Ryan noted:

> Recognising that there are cases where children need to be cared for on a long-term basis by a new family, and, in some of those cases, that an order must be permanent and irrevocable, does not lead logically to the conclusion that such children have to lose their legal relationship with their families of origin in order for permanence to be established. (Ryan 1994, p. 21)

'Open' adoption refers to practice in adoption placements that do not follow the traditional model of a child being placed with strangers without natural and adoptive parents having contact with each other (or much mutual knowledge), and with no subsequent contact between the families. Opinion from research (e.g. Sellick & Thoburn 1996; Quinton et al. 1997) is now fairly consistent that for children who are adopted, direct contact with parents, siblings and significant extended family members contributes to the stability of the placement, or has neutral effect (that is, such contact does not have a negative effect). The influence of such research has reversed policy underlying the openness of adoption to the current position where, when adoption is indicated, the presumption is that this will involve some form of continuing contact with the natural family unless it is demonstrably not in the child's best interests (Adcock et al. 1993; Ryburn 1994b; Thoburn 1996, 2003c).

Exceptions to the presumption of direct contact apply mainly in situations where a child is old enough to express a genuine view that this is not desired, where a child is afraid of natural family members, where there is a significant risk of the child being abducted as a consequence of such contact, and where the natural family appear determined to undermine the stability of the placement.

From this perspective, the *rights* of each child concerned must be considered of paramount importance, including the right to an authentic sense of personal identity moulded by nature (natural family characteristics) as well as nurture (influence of adoptive family). The issue of *children's rights* has become an increasingly prominent factor supportive of open adoption. Both the 1989 United Nations Convention on the Rights of the Child and the Human Rights Act 1998 provide specific rights to children to maintain personal relations and direct contact with both parents on a regular basis (unless this is contrary to the child's best interests). Article 8 of the Human

Rights Act approaches the same issue from the opposite direction, providing parents with 'the right to respect for his private and family life, his home and his correspondence'.

In this context, future successful adopters (such as foster parents) will increasingly be able to accept, maintain and promote meaningful relationships between their adopted children and their natural families, while having primary (but not sole) responsibility for the child's upbringing, welfare and development. This raises important training and support issues for prospective and actual adoptive parents:

> Since some form of continuing contact with birth family members will be a part of most adoptions, the ability to empathise not only with the child but also with the child's (often distressing) history, and with the birth parents themselves, will be much in demand as a characteristic for the successful adopter of the future. (Thoburn 2003a, p. 231)

Adoption and Children Act 2002

In a major reform of adoption legislation, the Adoption and Children Act 2002 introduces a new legal status, separate from adoption, of special guardianship. This is a response to many of the concerns about traditional adoption outlined above, and a recognition that legal adoption is not wanted and is not appropriate or necessary in various circumstances. As an alternative way of securing permanent status for children in need of substitute care, special guardianship provides the carer with legal parental responsibility for the child (meaning that the child is no longer 'looked after' by the local authority). Special guardianship cements the relationship between a child and the carer, who may be a foster carer or an adult with a residence order (for example, a member of the child's extended family).

Local authorities are responsible for preparing reports for courts assessing the suitability of people for the role of special guardians, and also assessing needs for continuing support (which may be financial or therapeutic) in relation to the special guardianship arrangement. At the time of writing, it remains to be seen to what extent the *special guardianship order* will create a practical and valuable third option for infants whose needs for alternative safe and secure substitute parenting arrangements lie between the uncertainties of long-term fostering and the absoluteness of adoption.

The potential benefits of special guardianship are increased security for children within more flexible, shared parenting relationships than was traditionally possible with adoption, specifically facilitating the preservation of the child's links with his/her birth family. Moreover, unlike adoption orders, special guardianship orders can be varied or brought to an end – a recognition that circumstances can change significantly over time and that parenting arrangements need to have more flexibility than adoption to accommodate such changes (especially when children are old enough to express their own wishes and feelings).

Concurrent and Parallel Planning

Concern is generally expressed about the length of time infants may remain in temporary foster care placements before definite decisions are made by courts about their future. These problems are exacerbated in cases where infants have several placements during this period of uncertainty. In attempts to reduce the disadvantage (and damage) to infants caused by extended periods of uncertainty (and multiple placements), social services case-management processes of concurrent and parallel planning have become established (Cousins et al. 2003; Katz et al. 1994).

In concurrent planning, the primary intention is that the baby should be returned home. Foster carers look after the infant on this basis and often support parents in achieving this goal. However, should this not proceed, the current foster parents are committed to keeping the child with a view to adoption. On this basis, the child does not have a further move should the attempt at reunification fail.

In contrast, parallel planning (often also referred to as 'twin-track planning') involves social services searching at an early stage for an adoptive placement during the assessment of the potential for reunification. If the child is not reunified, prospective adoptive parents will already have been identified, and the child will be quickly moved into their care (from the temporary foster home). In this way, previous delays in identifying prospective adoptive parents are minimised, and the infant is able to move into the adoptive home at an earlier age than otherwise would have been the case (which is advantageous for the forming of attachments with the adoptive parents).

Increasingly, in cases of infants who have suffered serious suspicious injuries and 'removals at birth', local authorities are implementing these case-management practices. In the UK, there are pilot concurrent planning projects under way in London, Brighton and Manchester. An initial evaluation concluded that concurrent planning had undoubtedly contributed to decisions about infants' placements being made more quickly, and to reductions in the numbers of placements (Monck 2004).

While the principles underlying concurrent/parallel planning (to minimise delay and multiple placements) are valid, there are several potential unintended negative consequences that must be taken into account. In theory, social workers undertake intensive assessment and support work with the natural parents, while at the same time helping the foster parents to prepare either to adopt or to relinquish the child (Gray 2003). One significant concern is whether the professional commitment and resources will be forthcoming from social services to invest in constructive assessments with natural parents, and to explore appropriately and cultivate extended family/kinship care resources. Or will this focus be unreasonably minimal, with parents inadvertently being set up to fail – as social services take the safer, cheaper and professionally simpler route of identifying prospective adoptive parents?

Placement with Extended Family/Kinship Carers

Utilisation of extended family and kinship resources has been an underdeveloped resource in UK child protection policy and practice. It is, however, a significant aspect of statutory child care in many other countries including the USA and New Zealand. In New Zealand in the 1960s, it had become common for Maori children to be compulsorily adopted into white families, a practice that adversely affected the mental health of adult Maori adoptees. Since then, New Zealand childcare practice has enshrined in law the recognition and utilisation of the value of Maori kinship practices and resources (*whangai*) by means of family group conferences. New Zealand also leads the world in the implementation of open adoption practice, recognising that 'the legal transfer and severance of a child's heritage is foreign to Maori' (Goldson 2003, p. 247).

When it cannot be considered safe for infants who have sustained serious suspicious injuries to return to the parents/carers who were responsible for their care at the time of the injuries, it is a requirement of the Children Act 1989 and the Human Rights Act 1998 that local authorities actively consider whether there are appropriate alternative carers within the extended families/kinship networks of the infants concerned. Often the first matter to be explored is the circumstances of the grandparents, aunts and uncles of the infant concerned. This raises a fundamental question: what are the nature of the 'hurdles' that extended family members have to jump to convince social services, *children's guardians* and judges that they are fit, suitable and appropriate people to look after the child? Do extended family members have to be assessed to the same standards as stranger foster parents? At what age are grandparents considered to be too old to be primary carers for their grandchild?

It can appear to families at times that a double standard operates, so that, if the infant had been orphaned by a tragic accident to his/her parents, social services would welcome and encourage grandparents to assume care, but after a serious suspicious injury the grandparents may be excluded, ostensibly on grounds of age (e.g. early 50s) or may have to match the criteria of hypothetical adoptive parents. On this point, grandparents and other extended family members express strong feelings about ways in which they feel discriminated against in assessments by social services and treated unfairly in courts (grandparents often cannot get legal aid for representation in care proceedings). Another grievance is the variable (often poor) levels of support they receive if they do ultimately assume care of the child (Clarke & Cairns 2001; Jenkins 2001; Laws 2001; Nixon 2001; Ryburn 1994b; Tapsfield 2001; Tingle 1994).

Extended family/kinship care, however, is not a panacea. When an infant has sustained a serious suspicious injury and the local authority has been given parental authority (through an interim care order, or care order), the local authority has a heavy responsibility to ensure (so far as is ever possible) that the subsequent permanent caring arrangements for the infant are safe and appropriate. While in many cases extended families/kinship carers do offer such outcomes, not all grandparents and extended family members are suitable alternative carers.

Assessments must establish to what extent parenting problems (that resulted in the serious injury to the infant) are intergenerational. To what extent are the problems of the current parents related to highly unsatisfactory and/or abusive parenting they received from their parents (the infant's grandparents)? To what extent do grandparents and extended family members have significant mental health problems, alcohol/substance misuse problems, domestic violence, unstable relationships and lifestyles, and perhaps relevant criminal histories? What is the nature of current family dynamics? In particular, how would the infant's mother and father react to an extended family member becoming their child's primary parent/carer? While this may be with a sense of relief (if it avoids compulsory out-of-family adoption), it may also generate powerful feelings of resentment and hostility. If so, how might this affect the stability and security of the placement over time?

These are all factors that have to be taken into account, meaning that extended family/kinship care cannot be a presumed 'disposal' outcome simply on the basis of family members putting themselves forward. However, when appropriate extended family/kinship care placements are made – and necessary professional (and financial) support is offered and sustained – outcomes are generally good (Broad 2001; Farmer 2001; Hunt 2001; McGill 2003; Waterhouse 2001).

Reunification with Parents/Carers

There are two main ways in which infants who have sustained serious suspicious injuries may be reunified with their parents after periods of assessment. First, the child may return to the same household within which the injuries occurred. Second, the parents/carers may have separated, and the child may be returned to one of them as a single parent (invariably with extended family support, and sometimes with a new partner). In the latter scenario, assessment questions will arise regarding the new partner, and appropriate contact arrangements with the parent/carer who is no longer the custodial parent.

We noted in Chapter 8 that the making of recommendations for or against reunification in cases of serious suspicious injuries to infants requires a balancing act of the significance of risk factors, the degree to which risk factors can be ameliorated, the identification of family strengths, and the availability of appropriate resources for a specific risk-management strategy. While caution is always indicated, it is clear that there are cases of successful reunifications after serious injuries to infants with unsatisfactory explanations. In our view, this is most likely in the cases following:

- The injuries were not inflicted on multiple occasions.
- The injuries were unlikely to reflect intentional or sadistic motivation.
- The injuries occurred in a context of identified stressors.
- The injuries occurred in a context of otherwise good parenting.
- The infant does not present any exceptionally difficult parenting challenges.
- There is an absence of serious parental mental health concerns, alcohol/drug abuse and domestic violence.
- There is the presence of committed extended family support.
- Parents have engaged (and continue to engage) with professional services, focusing on assessment, stress management, child management and any identified therapeutic issues.

Systematically gathered follow-up information about outcomes after reunification in cases of serious suspicious injuries to infants is virtually non-existent. Neither social services nor courts have systems for capturing long-term outcomes in such cases. Specialist assessment and therapeutic services invariably have very limited evaluation resources (systematic follow-up evaluation can be far more expensive than actually providing the services). Reports of a number of clinical specialist treatment centres indicate that, over time, varying proportions of seriously injured children are returned home. Reported reunification rates are 95% (Baher et al. 1976), 88% (Lynch & Roberts 1982), 70% (Asen et al. 1989), 65% (Dale et al. 1986) and 52% (Miller et al. 1999). None of these samples were subject to extended follow-up, so that rates of re-injury and general welfare outcomes over a long period of time are simply not known.

As discussed in Chapter 4, research has more systematically evaluated re-abuse outcomes from *general* child protection system case management. These findings (incorporated in the *Messages from Research* conclusions) indicate that between one-third and one-quarter of children were known to have been re-abused after they had come to the notice of child protection agencies (Cleaver & Freeman 1995; Farmer & Owen 1995; Gibbons et al. 1995; Terling 1999). These studies also noted that when re-injuries did occur, the proportion that were severe was very low. This was recently confirmed by the extensive 3-year follow-up study in Wales of a large sample of reunified babies who had suffered non-accidental injuries (Ellaway et al. 2004) from which a *serious* re-injury rate of 2% can be deduced (see discussion of this study in Chapter 4).

The defining feature of the assessments we have been concerned about in this book is that parent/carer explanations for a serious injury or injuries to their infant is either absent, inconsistent or discrepant with expert medical opinion. We have discussed in Chapter 7 the complexities facing courts in determining whether, on the balance of probabilities, an injury was due to abuse (and who was responsible), or whether there was an alternative non-abuse explanation or unknown (improbable) non-abuse event. In Chapter 6, we also noted that some parents feel that judgments made on the 'balance of probability' by a single judge is an unreasonable basis for decisions to be taken about the future of children that will have profound, lifelong family consequences.

Nevertheless, after the causation hearing and 'findings of fact' about the injuries, assessments will explore with parents/carers (and wider family members) the finding that has been made as to who, on the balance of probability, was responsible for the injuries. Assessments of future risk have to be based on such judgments. It is not common, however, that 'findings of fact' change the beliefs of significant family members about how injuries were caused (and we noted in Chapter 5 that 'confessions' rarely emerge subsequently in such cases).

The nature and severity of injury is one important factor to take into account in child protection assessments, but it is not the determining factor. If this were so, no infants who have suffered multiple fractures and/or brain injuries (or later siblings of infants who have been killed) would ever successfully return to their families, and this is not the case. There is clinical and research evidence that demonstrates that successful reunifications do occur in some cases after serious injuries to infants where there are absent, inadequate or discrepant explanations (Asen et al. 1989; Bentovim 2003; Dale et al. 2002a,b; Ellaway et al. 2004; Essex et al. 1995; Robinson & Whitney 1999; Turnell & Edwards 1999).

Consequently, in principle, and in general child protection practice, the fact that a serious injury to an infant remains unexplained or in dispute is not, in itself, a barrier to some such children being returned home in the context of protection plans involving appropriate monitoring, family support and therapeutic services.

REFERENCES

Adams, R.D. & Victor, M. (1989) *Principles of Neurology* (4th edn). New York: McGraw-Hill Information Services.

Adcock, M., Kaniuk, J. & White, R. (1993) *Exploring Openness in Adoption*. Croydon: Significant Publications.

Adshead, G. (2003) Dangerous and severe parenting disorder? Personality disorder, parenting and new legal proposals. *Child Abuse Review* 12, 227–237.

Ainsworth, M.D.S., Blehar, M.C., Waters, E. & Wall, S. (1978) *Patterns of Attachment: A Psychological Study of the Strange Situation*. Hillsdale, NJ: Erlbaum.

Alaszewski, A. & Manthorpe, J. (1991) Literature review: meaning and managing risk in social welfare. *British Journal of Social Work* 21, 277–290.

American Academy of Pediatrics (1993) Shaken baby syndrome: inflicted cerebral trauma. *Pediatrics* 92, 872–875.

American Psychiatric Association (APA) (1994) *Diagnostic and Statistical Manual of Mental Disorders (DSM-1V)*. Washington, DC: APA.

Archer, J. (2000) Sex differences in aggression between heterosexual partners: a meta-analytic review. *Psychological Bulletin* 126, 651–680.

Arthurs, Y. & Ruddick, J. (2001) *An Analysis of Child Protection 'Part 8' Reviews Carried Out Over a Two-Year Period in the South-East Region of the NHS*. NHS Executive.

Asen, K., George, E., Piper, R. & Stevens, A. (1989) A systems approach to child abuse: management and treatment issues. *Child Abuse and Neglect* 13, 45–57.

Baher, E., Hyman, C., Jones, C., Jones, R., Kerr, A. & Mitchell, R. (1976) *At Risk: An Account of the Work of the Battered Child Research Department, NSPCC*. London: Routledge & Kegan Paul.

Baker, T. (2003) What is the relevance of attachment to parenting assessments? In: P. Reder, S. Duncan & C. Lucey (eds) *Studies in the Assessment of Parenting*. Hove: Brunner-Routledge.

Banks, N. (1994) Issues of attachment, separation and identity in contested adoptions. In: M. Ryburn (ed.) *Contested Adoptions: Research, Law, Policy and Practice*. Aldershot: Arena, Ashgate.

Barlow, K.M. & Minns, R.A. (2000) Annual incidence of shaken impact syndrome in young children. *Lancet* 356, 1571–1572.

Barr, R.G. (1990) The normal crying curve: what do we really know? *Developmental Medicine and Child Neurology* 32, 356–362.

Batt, J. (2004) *Stolen Innocence: A Mother's Fight for Justice, The Story of Sally Clark*. London: Ebury Press.

Baum, J.D. & Bulpitt, C.J. (1970) Retinal and conjunctival haemorrhage in the newborn. *Archives of Disease in Childhood* 45, 344–349.

Beck, A.T. (1976) *Cognitive Therapy and Emotional Disorders.* New York: New American Library.

Benger, J.R. & Pearce, V. (2002) Simple intervention to improve detection of child abuse in emergency departments. *British Medical Journal* 324, 780.

Bentovim, A. (1992) *Trauma-Organised Systems: Physical and Sexual Abuse in Families.* London: Karnac Books.

Bentovim, A. (2003) Is it possible to work with parental denial? In: P. Reder, S. Duncan & C. Lucey (eds) *Studies in the Assessment of Parenting.* Hove: Brunner-Routledge.

Bentovim, A., Elton, A. & Tranter, M. (1987) Prognosis for rehabilitation after abuse. *Adoption and Fostering* 11, 26–31.

Bentovim, A. & Tranter, M. (1984) A family therapy approach to decision-making. *Adoption and Fostering* 8, 25–32.

Bolen, R.M. (2000) Validity of attachment theory. *Trauma, Violence and Abuse* 1, 2128–2153.

Bolen, R.M. (2002) Child sexual abuse and attachment theory: are we rushing headlong into another controversy? *Journal of Child Sexual Abuse* 11, 95–124.

Bowlby, J. (1951) *Maternal Care and Mental Health.* WHO Monograph Series No. 2. Geneva: World Health Organization.

Bowlby, J. (1969) *Attachment and Loss,* vol. 1. *Attachment.* New York: Basic Books.

Bowlby, J. (1973) *Attachment and Loss,* vol. 2. *Separation, Anxiety and Anger.* London: Hogarth Press.

Bowlby, J. (1980) *Attachment and Loss,* vol. 3. *Loss, Sadness and Depression.* London: Hogarth Press.

Bradford, J.W. & Smith, S.M. (1979) Amnesia and homicide: the Padola case and a study of thirty cases. *Bulletin of the American Academy of Psychiatry and the Law* 7, 218–231.

Brandon, M. & Lewis, A. (1996) Significant harm and children: experiences of domestic violence. *Child and Family Social Work* 1, 33–42.

Brophy, J. (2001) *Child Psychiatry and Child Protection Litigation.* London: Gaskell.

Brophy, J. & Bates, P. (1998) The position of parents using experts in care proceedings: a failure of 'partnership'? *Journal of Social Welfare and Family Law* 20, 23–48.

Broad, B. (ed.) (2001) *Kinship Care: The Placement Choice for Children and Young People.* Lyme Regis: Russell House.

Buckley, H., Skehill, C. & O'Sullivan, E. (1997) *Child Protection Practices in Ireland: A Case Study.* Dublin: Oak Tree Press.

Butler-Sloss, L.J. (1996) Re: M and R (Child abuse evidence) 2 FLR 195, p. 205.

Buttram, H.E. & Yazbak, E.F. (2000) Shaken baby syndrome or vaccine-induced encephalomyelitis? The story of baby Alan. *Journal of the International Chiropractic Association* Nov/Dec. www.woodmed.com/ShakenBabyAlan.htm.

Byrne, J.G., O'Connor, T.G., Marvin, R.S. & Whelan, W.F. (2005) Practitioner review: the contribution of attachment theory to child custody assessments. *Journal of Child Psychiatry and Psychology* 46, 115–127.

Caffey, J. (1972) On the theory and practice of shaking infants. Its potential residual effects of permanent brain damage and mental retardation. *American Journal of Diseases of Children* 124, 161–169.

Carpenter, R.G., Waite, A., Coombs, R.C., Daman-Williams, C., McKenzie, A., Hubert, J., et al. (2005) Repeat sudden unexpected and unexplained infant deaths: natural or unnatural. *Lancet* 365, 29–35.

Carty, H. & Ratcliffe, J. (1995) The shaken infant syndrome. *British Medical Journal* 310, 344–345.

Cassell, D. & Coleman, R. (1995) Parents with psychiatric problems. In: P. Reder & C. Lucey (eds) *Assessment of Parenting: Psychiatric and Psychological Contributions.* London: Routledge.

Cawson, P., Wattam, C., Brooker, S. & Kelly, G. (2000) *Child Maltreatment in the United Kingdom.* London: NSPCC.

Chadwick, D.L., Chin, S., Salerno, C., Landsverk, J. & Kitchen, L. (1991) Deaths from falls in children: how far is fatal? *Journal of Trauma* 31, 1353–1355.

Chaplin, J. (1988) *Feminist Counselling in Action.* London: Sage.

Cima, M., Nijman, H., Merckelbach, H., Kremer, K. & Hollnack, S. (2004) Claims of crime-related amnesia in forensic patients. *International Journal of Law and Psychiatry* 27, 215–221.

Clarke, L. & Cairns, H. (2001) Grandparents and the care of children: the research evidence. In: B. Broad (ed.) *Kinship Care: The Placement Choice for Children and Young People.* Lyme Regis: Russell House.

Cleaver, H. & Freeman, P. (1995) *Parental Perspectives in Cases of Suspected Child Abuse.* London: HMSO.

Cleaver, H., Wattam, C. & Cawson, P. (1998) *Assessing Risk in Child Protection* London: NSPCC Policy Practice Research Series.

Clemetson, C.A.B. (2002) Barlow's disease. *Medical Hypotheses* 59, 52–56.

Cobley, C. (2004) 'Working together?': admissions of abuse in child protection proceedings and criminal prosecutions. *Child and Family Law Quarterly* 16, 175–187.

Cobley, C. & Sanders, T. (2003) 'Shaken baby syndrome': child protection issues when children sustain a subdural haemorrhage. *Journal of Social Welfare and Family Law* 25, 101–119.

Coleridge, J. (2003) Comment: Another big bang. *Family Law* 33, 799.

Coleman, R. & Cassell, D. (1995) Parents who misuse drugs and alcohol. In: P. Reder & C. Lucey (eds) *Assessment of Parenting: Psychiatric and Psychological Contributions.* London: Routledge.

Coles, E.M. & Veiel, H.O.F. (2001) Expert testimony and pseudoscience: how mental health professionals are taking over the courtroom. *International Journal of Law and Psychiatry* 24, 607–625.

Corby, B., Miller, M. & Pope, A. (2002) Out of the frame. *Community Care,* 12–18 September, 40–41.

Cordess, C. (2003) Can personality-disordered parents adequately care? In: P. Reder, S. Duncan & C. Lucey (eds) *Studies in the Assessment of Parenting.* Hove: Brunner-Routledge.

Cousins, C. (2002) Where the explanation doesn't fit the injury. *NCPC Newsletter* 11, 4–13.

Cousins, J., Morrison, M. & de Sousa, S. (2003) *Right from the Start: Best Practice on Adoption Planning for Babies and Other Children.* London: BAAF.

Creighton, S.J. (1995) Fatal child abuse – how preventable is it? *Child Abuse Review* 4, 318–328.

Crenshaw, W. (2004) *Treating Families and Children in the Child Protective System.* New York: Brunner-Routledge.

Crittenden, P.M. (1992) Children's strategies for coping with adverse home environments: and interpretation using attachment theory. *Child Abuse and Neglect* 16, 329–343.

Crittenden, P.M. (2000) *The Organization of Attachment relationships: Maturation, Culture and Context.* Cambridge: Cambridge University Press.

Crompton, S. (2004) Bursting the happy bubble. *The Times,* 18 September.

Dale, P. (1991) Dangerous families revisited. *Community Care,* 14 November.

Dale, P. (1998) Protection or prevention? An integrated approach to services for children and parents. Keynote paper: Kids first: protecting children – problems and solutions. Melbourne Convention Centre, Melbourne, Australia (2–3 April).

Dale, P. (1999) *Adults Abused as Children: Experiences of Counselling and Psychotherapy*. London: Sage.

Dale, P. (2002a) Benefits of therapy with adults who were abused as children: some issues from evaluation of counselling services. In: C. Feltham (ed.) *What's the Good of Counselling and Psychotherapy?* London: Sage.

Dale, P. (2002b) A Social Services Department Intake and Assessment Team File Review Audit. Unpublished report.

Dale, P. (2002c) *Parents' Perceptions of the Child Protection Process – Final Report*. Derbyshire County Council: Best Value Review.

Dale, P. (2003) Serious injuries to infants with discrepant explanations: specialist assessment issues. *Family Law* 33, 668–673.

Dale, P. (2004) 'Like a fish in a bowl': parents' perceptions of child protection services. *Child Abuse Review* 13, 137–157.

Dale, P., Davies, M., Morrison, T. & Waters, J. (1986) *Dangerous Families: Assessment and Treatment of Child Abuse*. London: Routledge.

Dale, P. & Fellows, R. (1999) Independent child protection assessments: incorporating a therapeutic focus from an integrated service context. *Child Abuse Review* 8, 4–14.

Dale, P., Green, R. & Fellows, R. (2002a) Serious and fatal injuries to infants with discrepant parental explanations: some assessment and case management issues. *Child Abuse Review* 11, 296–312.

Dale, P., Green, R. & Fellows, R. (2002b) *What Really Happened? Child Protection Case Management of Infants with Serious Injuries and Discrepant Parental Explanations*. London: NSPCC.

David, T.J. (1999) Shaken baby (shaken impact) syndrome: non-accidental head injury in infancy. *Royal Society of Medicine* 99, 556–561.

David, T.J. (2004a) Avoidable pitfalls when writing medical reports for court proceedings in cases of suspected child abuse. *Archives of Disease in Childhood* 89, 799–804.

David, T.J. (2004b) Medical experts in cases of suspected child abuse. Paper presented to Children, Law and Practice Conference. London, 17 March.

De Jong, P. & Insoo Kim Berg (2002) *Interviewing for Solutions* (2nd edn). New York: Brooks/Cole.

Department of Health (1991) *Child Abuse: A Study of Inquiry Reports 1980–1989*. London: HMSO.

Department of Health (1995) *Child Protection: Messages from Research*. London: HMSO.

Department of Health, Home Office and Department of Education and Employment (2000) *Framework for the Assessment of Children in Need and their Families*. London: HMSO.

DHSS (1988) *Report of the Inquiry into Child Abuse in Cleveland 1987, Butler-Sloss report*. London: HMSO.

Dobash, R. & Dobash, R. (1992) *Women, Violence and Social Change*. London: Routledge.

Dominelli, L. & McLeod, E. (1989) *Feminist Social Work*. Basingstoke: Macmillan Education.

d'Orban, P.T. (1979) Women who kill their children. *British Journal of Psychiatry* 134, 560–571.

Duhaine, A.C., Christian, C.W., Rorke, L.B. & Zimmerman, R.A. (1998) Nonaccidental head injury in infants – the 'shaken-baby syndrome'. *New England Journal of Medicine* 338, 1822–1829.

Dutton, R. (1995) *The Batterer*. New York: Basic Books.

Edleson, J.L. (1999) Children's witnessing of adult domestic violence. *Journal of Interpersonal Violence* 14, 839–870.

Egeland, B. (1988) Breaking the cycle of abuse: implications for prediction and intervention. In: K. Browne, C. Davies & P. Stratton (eds) *Early Prediction and Prevention of Child Abuse*. Chichester: Wiley.

Ellaway, B.A., Payne, E.H., Rolfe, K., Kemp, A.M., Butler, I. & Sibert, J.R. (2004) Are abused babies protected from further abuse? *Archives of Disease in Childhood* 89, 845–846.

Else, A. (1991) *Closed Stranger Adoption*. Wellington: Bridget Williams Books.

Erskine, R.G. & Moursund, J.P. (1988) *Integrative Psychotherapy in Action*. London: Sage.

Essex, S. & Gumbleton, J. (1999) 'Similar but different' conversations: working with denial in cases of severe child abuse. *Australian and New Zealand Journal of Family Therapy* 20, 139–148.

Essex, S., Gumbleton, J. & Luger, C. (1995) 'Resolutions': working with families where responsibility for abuse is denied. *Child Abuse Review* 5, 191–202.

Fahlberg, V. (1991) *A Child's Journey Through Placement*. London: BAAF.

Falkov, A. (1996) *A Study of Working Together 'Part 8' Reports: Fatal Child Abuse and Parental Psychiatric Disorder*. London: Department of Health.

Farmer, E. (1997) *Child Protection and Child Welfare: Striking the Balance*. London: Routledge.

Farmer, E. (2001) Children reunited with their parents: a review of research findings. In: B. Broad (ed.) *Kinship Care: The Placement Choice for Children and Young People*. Lyme Regis: Russell House.

Farmer, E. & Owen, M. (1995) *Child Protection Practice, Private Risks and Public Remedies*. London: HMSO.

Fenwick, P. (1990) Automatism, medicine and the law. *Psychological Medicine. Monograph Supplement* 17, 1–27.

Ferguson, H. & O'Reilly, M. (2001) *Keeping Children Safe: Child Abuse, Child Protection and the Promotion of Welfare*. Dublin: A. & A. Farmar.

Fernandez, E. (1996) *Significant Harm – Unravelling Child Protection Decisions and Substitute Care Careers of Children*. Aldershot: Avebury.

Finlay, A. (2002) Delay and challenges of the Children Act. In: L.J. Thorpe & C. Cowton (eds) *Delight and Dole: The Children Act 10 years on*. Bristol: Jordan.

Fitzpatrick, G. (1995) Assessing treatability. In: P. Reder & C. Lucey (eds) *Assessment of Parenting: Psychiatric and Psychological Contributions*. London: Routledge.

Fitzgerald, K.M. & McGregor, K.J. (1995) Specialist assessment services for child abuse and neglect. *Child Abuse Review* 4, 177–190.

Fleming, P., Blair, P., Bacon, C. & Berry, J. (2000) *Sudden Unexpected Deaths in Infancy: The CESDI SUDI Studies 1993–1996*. London: HMSO.

Florida Legislature (1998) *Review of the Effect of Child Protective Investigations on Families*. Florida: Office of Program Policy Analysis and Government Accountability.

Fox Harding, L.M. (1997) *Perspectives in Child Care Policy* (2nd edn). Harlow: Pearson Education Limited.

Fratter, J., Rowe, J., Sapsford, D. & Thoburn, J. (1991) *Permanent Family Placement: A Decade of Experience*. London: BAAF.

Freeman, P. & Hunt, J. (1999) *Parental Perspectives on Care Proceedings*. London: HMSO.

Gallwey, P. (1997) Bad parenting and pseudo-parenting. In: N. Wall (ed.) *Rooted Sorrows: Psychoanalytic Perspectives on Child Protection, Assessment, Therapy and Treatment*. Bristol: Jordan.

Geddes, J.F. & Plunkett, J. (2004) The evidence base for shaken baby syndrome. *British Medical Journal* 328, 719–720.

Geddes, J.F., Vowles, G.H., Hackshaw, A.K., Nickols, C.D., Scott, I.S. & Whitwell, H.L. (2001) Neuropathology of inflicted head injury in children. II. Microscopic brain injury in infants. *Brain* 124, 1299–1306.

Gelso, C.J. (1979) Research in counselling: methodological and professional issues. *Counselling Psychologist* 4, 7–36.

Giarretto, H. (1982) A comprehensive child sexual abuse treatment program. *Child Abuse and Neglect* 6, 263–278.

Gibbons, J., Gallagher, B., Bell, C. & Gordon, D. (1995) *Development after Physical Abuse in Early Childhood*. London: HMSO.

Gillen, J. (2002) Achieving best practice to secure the best interests of children. *Child Care in Practice* 8, 295–304.

Gleeson, J., Bakos, J., Thomas, S. & Moran, J. (2001) 'Life has got better since child protection became involved' – fact or fiction? Paper presented at Australasian Child Abuse and Neglect Conference, Melbourne, Australia.

Goldson, J. (2003) Adoption in New Zealand: an international perspective. In: A. Douglas & T. Philpot (eds) *Adoption: Changing Families, Changing Times*. London: Routledge.

Gray, G. (2003) Avoiding disruption: concurrent planning. In: A. Douglas & T. Philpot (eds) *Adoption: Changing Families, Changing Times*. London: Routledge.

Green, J. (2004) Concepts of child attachment. In: L.J. Thorpe & J. Cadbury, J. (eds) *Hearing the Children*. Bristol: Jordan.

Green, R. (1997) *Long Term Problems – Short Term Solutions: Parents in Contact with Mental Health Services. A Report for the Department of Health and the Brent Area Child Protection Committee*. London: Brent ACPC/NSPCC.

Green, J.M., Stanley, C., Smith, V. & Goldwyn, R. (2000) A new method of evaluating attachment representations on young school age children – the Manchester Child Attachment Story Task. *Attachment and Human Development* 2, 42–64.

Greenes, D.S. & Schutzman, S.A. (1998) Occult intracranial injury in infants. *Annals of Emergency Medicine* 32, 680–686.

Greenland, C. (1980) Lethal family situations: an international comparison of deaths from child abuse. In: E.J. Anthony (ed.) *The Child in His Family: Preventive Child Psychiatry in an Age of Transition*. New York: Wiley.

Gullestad, S.E. (2001) Attachment theory and psychoanalysis: controversial issues. *Scandinavian Psychoanalytic Review* 24, 3–16.

Gupta, A. (2003) Adoption, race and identity. In: A. Douglas & T. Philpot (eds) *Changing Families, Changing Times*. London: Routledge.

Guthkelch, A.N. (1971) Infantile subdural haematoma and its relationship to whiplash injuries. *British Medical Journal* 2, 430–431.

Harding, B., Risdon, R.A. & Krous, H.F. (2004) Shaken baby syndrome. *British Medical Journal* 328, 720–721.

Hare, R.D. (1993) *Without Conscience*. New York: Pocket Books.

Harvey, A.G. & Bryant, R.A. (2002) Acute stress disorder: a synthesis and critique. *Psychological Bulletin* 128, 886–902.

Harwin, J. & Owen, M. (2002) A study of care plans and their implementation and relevance for Re W and B and Re W (care plan). In: L.J. Thorpe & C. Cowton (eds) *Delight and Dole: The Children Act 10 Years On*. Bristol: Jordan.

Hayes, M. (2004) Re O and N; Re B – uncertain evidence and risk-taking in child protection cases. *Child and Family Law Quarterly* 16, 63–86.

Hester, M., Pearson, C. & Harwin, N. (2000) *Making an Impact – Children and Domestic Violence: A Reader*. London: Jessica Kingsley.

Hobbs, C. (1984) Skull fractures and the diagnosis of abuse. *Archives of Disease in Childhood* 59, 246–252.

Hobbs, C.J. & Wynne, J.M. (1996) Fractures in infancy: are the bones brittle? *Current Paediatrics* 6, 183–188.

Hobbs, J., Hanks, H.G.I. & Wynne, L. (1999) *Child Abuse and Neglect: A Clinicians' Handbook*. London: Churchill Livingstone.

Hobson, R. (1985) *Forms of Feeling: The Heart of Psychotherapy*. London: Routledge.

Holland, S. (2000) The assessment relationship: interactions between social workers and parents in child protection assessments. *British Journal of Social Work* 30, 149–163.

Holland, S. (2004) *Child and Family Assessment in Social Work Practice*. London: Sage.

Hollis, F. (1965) *Casework: A Psychosocial Therapy*. New York: Random House.

Holmes, J. (1993) *John Bowlby and Attachment Theory*. London: Routledge.

Hood, L. (2001) *A City Possessed: The Christchurch Civic Creche Case*. Dunedin: Longacre.

Horwath, J. (2000) *The Child's World: Assessing Children in Need*. NSPCC/University of Sheffield.

Hoskote, A., Richards, P., Anslow, P. & McShane, T. (2002) Subdural haematoma and non-accidental head injury in children. *Childs Nervous System* 18, 311–317.

Hoskote, A.U., Martin, K., Hormbrey, P. & Burns, E.C. (2003) Fractures in infants: one in four is non-accidental. *Child Abuse Review* 12, 384–391.

House of Lords (2002) *Judgments – In Re S (FC) In Re S and Others In RE W and Others (First Appeal) (FC) In Re W and Others (Second Appeal) (Conjoined Appeals)*. United Kingdom Parliament.

Howard, M.A., Bell, B.A. & Uttley, D. (1993) The pathophysiology of infant subdural haematomas. *British Journal of Neurosurgery* 4, 355–365.

Howe, D. (ed.) (1996) *Attachment and Loss in Child and Family Social Work*. Aldershot: Ashgate.

Howe, D., Brandon, M., Hinings, D. & Schofield, G. (1999) *Attachment Theory, Child Maltreatment and Family Support*. Basingstoke: Macmillan.

Howe, D. & Feast, J. (2000) *Adoption, Search and Reunion. The Long-term Experience of Adopted Adults*. London: Children's Society.

Howitt, D. (1992) *Child Abuse Errors: When Good Intentions Go Wrong*. London: Harvester Wheatsheaf.

Hunt, J. (2001) Kinship care, child protection and the courts. In: B. Broad (ed.) *Kinship Care: The Placement Choice for Children and Young People*. Lyme Regis: Russell House.

Hunt, J. & Macleod, A. (1999) *The Best Laid Plans: Outcomes of Judicial Decisions in Child Protection Cases*. London: HMSO.

Hunt, J., Macleod, A. & Thomas, C. (1999) *The Last Resort: Child Protection, the Courts and the 1989 Children Act*. London: HMSO.

Hymel, K.P., Jenny, C. & Block, R.W. (2002) Intracranial hemorrhage and rebleeding in suspected victims of abusive head trauma: addressing the forensic controversies. *Child Maltreatment* 7, 329–348.

Innis, M.D. (2004) Retinal haemorrhages and SBS. Fact or Fantasy? *British Medical Journal* on-line rapid response. 13 April.

James, G. (1994) *A Study of Working Together 'Part 8' Reports*. London: Department of Health.

Janet, P. (1889) *L'Automatisme psychologique*. Paris: Alcan.

Jayawant, S., Rawlinson, A., Gibbon, F., Price, J., Schulte, J., Sharples, P., et al. (1998) Subdural haemorrhages in infants: population based study. *British Medical Journal* 317, 1558–1561.

Jehu, D. (1988) *Beyond Sexual Abuse: Therapy with Women Who Were Childhood Victims*. Chichester: Wiley.

Jenkins, J. (2001) Overview of the legal position of grandparents as kinship carers. In B. Broad (ed.) *Kinship Care: The Placement Choice for Children and Young People*. Lyme Regis: Russell House.

Johnson, K. (2002) Radiological aspects of shaken baby syndrome. Paper presented at BASPCAN National Study Day: Multi-Agency Investigation and Management of Shaken Babies – Subdural Bleeds, Birmingham Children's Hospital.

Jones, D.P.H. (1987) The untreatable family. *Child Abuse and Neglect* 11, 409–420.

Jordan, B. (1994) Contested adoptions and the role of the state in family matters. In: M. Ryburn (ed.) *Contested Adoptions: Research, Law, Policy and Practice*. Aldershot: Arena, Ashgate.

Kalokerinos, A. (1981) *Every Second Child*. Melbourne: Thomas Nelson (Australia).

Karandikar, S., Coles, L., Jayawant, S. & Kemp, A.M. (2004) The neurodevelopmental outcomes in infants who have sustained a subdural haemorrhage from non-accidental head injury, *Child Abuse Review* 13, 178–187.

Katz, L., Spoonermore, N. & Robinson, C. (1994) *Concurrent Planning*. Lutheran Social Services of Washington and Idaho.

Kaufman, J. & Zigler, E. (1987) Do abused children become abusive parents? *American Journal of Orthopsychiatry* 57, 186–192.

Kemp, A.M. (2002) Investigating subdural haemorrhage in infants. *Archives of Disease in Childhood* 86, 98–102.

Kemp, A. & Coles, L. (2003) The role of health professionals in preventing non-accidental head injury. *Child Abuse Review* 12, 374–383.

Kemp, A. M., Stoodley, N., Cobley, C., Coles, L. & Kemp, K.W. (2003) Apnoea and brain swelling in non-accidental head injury. *Archives of Disease in Childhood* 88, 472–476.

Kennedy, H. (2004) *Sudden Unexpected Death in Infancy: A Multi-agency Protocol for Care and Investigation*. London: Royal College of Pathologists and Royal College of Paediatrics and Child Health.

Kennedy, R. (1997) *Child Abuse, Psychotherapy and the Law*. London: Free Association Books.

Kennedy, R. (2002) Assessment of families. *Family Law* 32, 843–847.

King, M. & Trowell, J. (1992) *Children's Welfare and the Law: The Limits of Legal Intervention*. London: Sage.

Kirk, D. (1964). *Shared Fate*. Toronto: Collier-Macmillan.

Kopelman, M.D. (1997) Anomalies of autobiographical memory: retrograde amnesia, confabulation, delusional memory, psychogenic amnesia, and false memories. In D. Read & S. Lindsay (eds) *Recollections of Trauma: Scientific Research and Clinical Practice*. New York: Plenum, pp. 273–297.

Krugman, R.D. (1985) Fatal child abuse: analysis of 24 cases. *Pediatrician* 12, 68–72.

Lambert, M.J. (2003) *Bergin and Garfield's Handbook of Psychotherapy and Behavior Change, 5th Edition*. NewYork: Wiley.

Laming, H. (2003) *The Victoria Climbié Inquiry: Report by Lord Laming. Cm. 5730.* London: HMSO.

Law Commission of New Zealand (2000) *Adoption and Its Alternatives: A Different Approach and a New Framework,* Report 65, Wellington, New Zealand Law Commission.

Laws, S. (2001) Looking after children within the extended family: carers' views. In B. Broad (ed.) *Kinship Care: The Placement Choice for Children and Young People.* Lyme Regis: Russell House.

Lawson, E. (1994) Contested adoption proceedings: a barrister's perspective. In: M. Ryburn (ed.) *Contested Adoptions: Research, Law, Policy and Practice.* Aldershot: Arena.

Lefanu, J. & Edwards-Brown, R. (2004) Subdural and retinal haemorrhages are not necessarily signs of abuse. *British Medical Journal* 328, 767.

Leventhal, J.M. (2000) Thinking clearly about evaluations of suspected child abuse. *Clinical Child Psychology and Psychiatry* 5, 139–147.

Levine, M., Freeman, J. & Compaan, C. (1994) Maltreatment-related fatalities: issues of policy and prevention. *Law and Policy* 16, 449–471.

Levine, R.A. & Miller, P.M. (1990) Commentary. *Human Development* 33, 73–80.

Lewin, K. (1951) *Field Theory in Social Science.* New York: Harper and Row.

Lindley, B. (1994) *On the Receiving End: Families' Experiences of the Court Process.* London: Family Rights Group.

Lindley, B. & Richards, R. (2002) *Protocol on Advice and Advocacy for Parents (Child Protection).* Cambridge: University of Cambridge, Centre for Family Research.

Lindley, B., Richards, M. & Freeman, P. (2001) *Advice and Advocacy for Parents in Child Protection Cases – What Is Happening in Current Practice? Child and Family Law Quarterly* 13, 167–195.

Lishman, J. (1978) A clash in perspective? A study of worker and client perceptions of social work. *British Journal of Social Work* 8, 301–311.

Lomas, P. (1994) *Cultivating Intuition: An Introduction to Psychotherapy.* Harmondsworth: Penguin.

Luborsky, L., Singer, B. & Luborsky, L. (1975) Comparative studies of psychotherapies: is it true that 'everyone has won and all must have prizes'? *Archives of General Psychiatry* 32, 995–1008.

Lusk, A. (1996) Rehabilitation without acknowledgement. *Family Law* 742–745.

Lynch, M. & Roberts, J. (1982) *Consequences of Child Abuse.* London: Academic Press.

Macdonald, G. (2001) *Effective Interventions for Child Abuse and Neglect: An Evidence-Based Approach to Planning and Evaluating Interventions.* London: Wiley.

MacKinnon, L.K. (1998) *Trust and Betrayal in the Treatment of Child Abuse.* New York: Guilford Press.

Maguire, S., Mann, M.K., Sibert, J. & Kemp, A. (2005) Can you age bruises accurately in children? A systematic review. *Archives of Diseases in Childhood* 90, 187–189.

Main, M. & Solomon, J. (1986) Discovery of an insecure-disorganized/disoriented attachment pattern. In: T. Brazelton & M. Yogman (eds) *Affective Development in Infancy.* Norwood, NJ: Ablex.

Male, I., Kenney, I., Appleyard, C. & Evans, N. (2000) Neoplasia masquerading as physical abuse. *Child Abuse Review* 9, 142–147.

Maluccio, A.N. (1979) *Learning From Clients: Interpersonal Helping as Viewed by Clients and Social Workers.* New York: Free Press.

Martin, H. (1970) Antecedents of burns and scalds in children. *British Journal of Medical Psychology* 43, 39–47.

Matthews, T. (2005) Sudden unexpected infant death: infanticide or SIDS? *Lancet* 365, 3–4.

Mayer, J.E. & Timms, N. (1970) *The Client Speaks: Working Class Impressions of Casework*. London: Routledge & Kegan Paul.

Mayou, R., Ehlers, A. & Hobbs, M. (2000) Psychological debriefing for victims of road traffic accidents: three year follow-up of a randomised controlled trial. *British Journal of Psychiatry* 176, 589–593.

McGill, P. (2003) Kinship care: a child in the family. In: A. Douglas & T. Philpot (eds) *Adoption: Changing Families, Changing Times*. London: Routledge.

McLeod, H.J., Byrne, K.B. & Aitken, R. (2004) Automatism and dissociation: disturbances of consciousness and volition from a psychological perspective. *International Journal of Law and Psychiatry* 27, 471–487.

McSherry, B. (1998) Getting away with murder? Dissociative states and criminal responsibility. *International Journal of Law and Psychiatry* 21, 163–176.

McSherry, B. (2003) Voluntariness, intention, and the defence of mental disorder: toward a rational approach. *Behavioral Science and the Law* 21, 581–599.

Meadow, R. (1997) Fatal abuse and smothering. In: R. Meadow (ed.) *ABC of Child Abuse* (3rd edn). London: BMJ Publishing Group.

Milham, S., Bullock, R., Hosie, K. & Haak, M. (1986) *Lost in Care: The Problems of Maintaining Links Between Children in Care and Their Families*. Aldershot: Gower.

Miller, B., Fox, B. & Garcia-Beckwith, L. (1999) Intervening in severe physical child abuse cases: mental health, legal and social services. *Child Abuse and Neglect* 23, 905–914.

Miller, M.E. (1999) Temporary brittle bone disease, a true entity? *Seminars in Perinatology* 23, 174–182.

Minuchin, S. (1977) *Families and Family Therapy*. London: Routledge.

Monck, E. (2004) Concurrent planning: meeting the needs of younger looked after children. *ChildRight* (April) 9–11.

Munby, J. (2004) Making sure the child is heard. II. Representation. *Family Law* 34, 427–35.

Munro, E. (1999) Common errors of reasoning in child protection work. *Child Abuse and Neglect* 23, 745–758.

Munro, E. (2002) *Effective Child Protection*. London: Sage.

Newham Area Child Protection Committee (2002) *'Ainlee': Chapter 8 Review*. London: Newham ACPC.

Nixon, P. (2001) Making kinship partnerships work: examining family group conferences. In: B. Broad (ed.) *Kinship Care: The Placement Choice of Children and Young People*. Lyme Regis: Russell House.

NSPCC (2001) *Out of Sight: NSPCC Report on Child Deaths from Abuse* (2nd edn). London: NSPCC.

NSPCC (2002) Which of You Did It? Conference. Cambridge University, 2 November.

NSPCC (2003) *The NSPCC Review of Legislation Relating to Children in Family Proceedings*. London: NSPCC.

NSW Child Death Review Team (2004) *2003–2004 Report*. NSW Commission for Children and Young People, Sydney, Australia.

O'Connell, M. (1960) Amnesia and homicide. *British Journal of Delinquency*, 10, 262–276.

O'Hagan, K. (1997) The problem of engaging men in child protection work. *British Journal of Social Work* 27, 25–42.

O'Keefe, M. (1995) Predictors of child abuse in maritally violent families. *Journal of Interpersonal Violence* 10, 3–25.

Oliver, J.E. (1993) Intergenerational transmission of child abuse: rates, research, and clinical implications. *American Journal of Psychiatry* 150, 1315–1324.

Oudesluys-Murphy, A.M. (2004) *British Medical Journal* on-line rapid response. 7 April.

Parwatiker, S.D., Holcomb, W.R. & Menninger, K.A. (1985) The detection of malingered amnesia in accused murderers. *Bulletin of the American Academy of Psychiatry and the Law* 13, 97–103.

Paterson, C. (1997) The child with unexplained fractures. *New Law Journal* 147, 648–652.

Pendergrast, M. (1995) *Victims of Memory: Sex Abuse Accusations and Shattered Lives*. Hinesburg, VT: Upper Access.

Piercy, M. (2004) Intractable contact disputes. *Family Law* 34, 815–919.

Pizzey, E. (1982) *Prone to Violence*. London: Hamlyn.

Pizzey, E. (1998) *The Emotional Terrorist and the Violent Prone*. Commoners www.bennett.com/ptv.

Plunkett, J. (2001) Fatal pediatric head injuries caused by short-distance falls. *American Journal of Forensic Medical Pathology* 22, 1–12.

Porter, S., Birt, A.R., Yuille, J.C. & Herve, H.F. (2001) Memory for murder: a psychological perspective on dissociative amnesia in legal contexts. *International Journal of Law and Psychiatry* 24, 23–42.

Pritchard, C. & Stroud, J. (2002) A reply to Helen Barnes' comment of child homicide: a review and empirical approach: the importance of values and evidence in practice. *British Journal of Social Work* 32, 369–373.

Prosser, J. (1992) *Child Abuse Investigations: The Families' Perspective*. Stanstead, Essex: Parents Against Injustice.

Puri, B.K. (1995) *Saunders' Pocket Essentials of Psychiatry*. London: W.B. Saunders.

Quinton, D., Rushton, A., Dance, D. & Mayes, D. (1997) Contact between children placed away from home and their birth parents: research issues and evidence. *Clinical Child Psychology and Psychiatry* 2, 393–413.

Raiha, H., Lehtonen, L., Huhtala, V., Saleva, K. & Korvenranta, H. (2002) Excessively crying infant in the family: mother–infant, father–infant and mother–father interaction. *Child Care, Health and Development* 28, 419–429.

Read, D. & Lindsay, S. (eds) (1997) *Recollections of Trauma: Scientific Research and Clinical Practice*. New York: Plenum, pp. 273–297.

Reder, P. & Duncan, S. (1999) *Lost Innocents: A Follow-Up Study of Fatal Child Abuse*. London: Routledge.

Reder, P., Duncan, S. & Gray, M. (1993) *Beyond Blame: Child Abuse Tragedies Revisited*. London: Routledge.

Reder, P. & Lucey, C. (eds) (1995) *Assessment of Parenting: Psychiatric and Psychological Contributions*. London: Routledge.

Reece, R.M. (2004) The evidence base for shaken baby syndrome: responses to editorial from 106 doctors. *British Medical Journal* 328, 1316–1317.

Reece, R.M. & Sege, R. (2000) Childhood head injuries: accidental or inflicted? *Archives of Pediatrics and Adolescent Medicine* 154, 11–15.

Resnick, P.J. (1969) Child murder by parents – a psychiatric review of filicide. *American Journal of Psychiatry* 126, 325–333.

Rivara, F.P., Kamitsuka, M.D. & Quan, L. (1988) Injuries to children younger than 1 year of age. *Pediatrics* 81, 93–97.

Robertson, J. (1953) Some responses of young children to loss of maternal care. *Nursing Times* 49, 382–386.

Robertson, J. (1970) *Young Children in Hospital* (2nd edn). London: Tavistock.

Robinson, G. & Whitney, L. (1999) Working systemically following abuse: exploring safe uncertainty. *Child Abuse Review* 8, 264–274.

Rogers, C.R. (1957) The necessary and sufficient conditions of therapeutic personality change. *Journal of Consulting Psychology* 21, 95–103.

Rushton, A. (2004) A scoping and scanning review of research on the adoption of children placed from public care. *Clinical Child Psychology and Psychiatry* 9, 89–106.

Rutter, M. (1981) *Maternal Deprivation Reassessed*. London: Penguin.

Rutter, M. (1995) Clinical implications of attachment concepts: retrospect and prospect. *Journal of Child Psychology and Psychiatry* 36, 549.

Ryan, M. (1994) Contested proceedings: justice and the law. In: M. Ryburn (ed.) *Contested Adoptions: Research, Law, Policy and Practice*. Aldershot: Arena, Ashgate.

Ryburn, M. (1994a) Contested adoptions in context. In: M. Ryburn (ed.) *Contested Adoptions: Research, Law, Policy and Practice*. Aldershot: Arena, Ashgate.

Ryburn, M. (ed.) (1994b) *Contested Adoptions: Research, Law, Policy and Practice*. Aldershot: Arena, Ashgate.

Ryburn, M. (1994c) Contested adoption: the perspective of birth parents. In: M. Ryburn (ed.) *Contested Adoptions: Research, Law, Policy and Practice*. Aldershot: Arena, Ashgate.

Ryburn, M. (1996) A study of post-adoption contact in compulsory adoption. *British Journal of Social Work* 26, 627–646.

Sainsbury, E. (1987) Client studies: their contribution and limitations in influencing social work practice. *British Journal of Social Work* 17, 635–644.

Sanders, S., Colton, M. & Roberts, S. (1999) Child abuse fatalities and cases of extreme concern: lessons from reviews. *Child Abuse and Neglect* 23, 257–268.

Sanders, T., Cobley, C., Coles, C. & Kemp, A. (2003) Factors affecting clinical referral of young children with a subdural haemorrhage to child protection agencies. *Child Abuse Review* 12, 358–373.

Sants, H.J. (1964) Genealogical bewilderment in children with substitute parents. *British Journal of Medical Psychology* 37, 133–141.

Scheibner, V. (1998) The shaken baby syndrome, the vaccination link. *Nexus* 87, 35–37.

Scheibner, V. (2001) Shaken baby syndrome diagnosis on shaky ground. *Journal of Australasian College of Nutritional and Environmental Medicine* 20, 2.

Scott, D. (1998) A qualitative study of social work assessment in cases of alleged child abuse. *British Journal of Social Work* 28, 73–88.

Scott, P.D. (1973) Parents who kill their children. *Medicine, Science, and the Law* 13, 120–126.

Scottish Executive (2002) *It's Everyone's Job to Make Sure I'm Alright*. Edinburgh: Scottish Executive.

Secretary of State (1974) *Report of the Committee of Inquiry into the Care and Supervision Provided in Relation to Maria Colwell*. London: HMSO.

Sellick, C. & Thoburn, J. (1996) *What Works in Child and Family Placement*. London: BAAF.

Shaver, P.R. & Mikulincer, M. (2002) Psychodynamics of adult attachment: a research perspective. *Attachment and Human Development* 4, 133–161.

Sheldrick, C. (1998) Child psychiatrists in court: their contribution as experts in child care proceedings. *The Journal of Forensic Psychiatry* 9, 249–266.

Sibert, J.R., Payne, E.H., Kemp, A.M., Rolfe, K., Morgan, R.J.H., Lyons, R.A., et al. (2002) The incidence of severe physical child abuse in Wales. *Child Abuse and Neglect* 26, 267–276.

Sinclair, R. & Bullock, R. (2002) *Learning from Past Experience: A Review of Serious Case Reviews*. London: Department of Health.

Smith, C. & Logan, J. (2004) *After Adoption: Direct Contact and Relationships*. London: Routledge.

Southall, D.P., Plunkett, M.C.B., Banks, M.W., Falkov, M.P. & Samuels, M.P. (1997) Covert video recordings of life-threatening child abuse: lessons for child protection. *Pediatrics* 100, 735–760.

Southall, D.P., Samuels, M.P. & Golden, M.H. (2003) Classification of child abuse by motive and degree rather than type of injury. *Archives of Disease in Childhood* 88, 101–104.

Spinelli, M.G. (2003) *Infanticide: Psychosocial and Legal Perspectives on Mothers Who Kill*. Washington, DC: American Psychiatric Publishing, Inc.

Spratt, T. & Callan, J. (2004) Parents' views on social work interventions in child welfare cases. *British Journal of Social Work* 34, 199–224.

Stainton Rogers, W. (1998) Book review: R. Kennedy, Child Abuse, Psychotherapy and the Law. *Child Abuse Review* 7, 212–213.

Stanley, J. & Goddard, C. (2002) *In the Firing Line: Violence and Power in Child Protection Work*. Chichester: Wiley.

Steele, B.F. & Pollock, C.B. (1968) A psychiatric study of parents who abuse infants and small children. In: R.F. Helfer & C.H. Kempe (eds) *The Battered Child*. Chicago: University of Chicago Press.

Stevenson, J. (2002) Delay in proceedings? – the use and over-use of expert witnesses. In: L.J. Thorpe & C. Cowton (eds) *Delight and Dole: The Children Act 10 Years On*. Bristol: Jordan.

Stroud, J. (1997) Mental disorder and homicide of children: a review. *Social Work and Social Sciences Review* 6, 149–162.

Stroud, J. & Pritchard, C. (2001) Child homicide, psychiatric disorder and dangerousness: a review and an empirical approach. *British Journal of Social Work* 31, 249–269.

Sturge, C. (2000) Contact and domestic violence – the experts' court report. *Family Law* 30, 615–629.

Swihart, G., Yuille, J. & Porter, S. (1999) The role of state-dependent memory in 'red-outs'. *International Journal of Law and Psychiatry* 22, 199–212.

Takahashi, K. (1990) Are the key assumptions of the 'Strange Situation' procedure universal? A view from Japanese research. *Human Development* 33, 23–30.

Tapsfield, R. (2001) Kinship care: a family rights group perspective. In: B. Broad (ed.) *Kinship Care: The Placement Choice for Children and Young People*. Lyme Regis: Russell House.

Taylor, P.J. & Kopelman, M.D. (1984) Amnesia for criminal offenses. *Psychological Medicine*, 14, 581–588.

Terling, T. (1999) The efficacy of family reunification: re-entry rates and correlates of re-entry for abused and neglected children reunited with their families. *Child Abuse and Neglect* 23, 1359–1370.

Thoburn, J. (1994) Uses and abuses of research findings in contested cases. In: M. Ryburn (ed.) *Contested Adoptions: Research, Law, Policy and Practice*. Aldershot: Arena, Ashgate.

Thoburn, J. (1996) Psychological parenting and child placement: 'but we want to have our cake and eat it'. In: D. Howe (ed.) *Attachment and Loss in Child and Family Social Work*. Aldershot: Avebury.

Thoburn, J. (2003a) Home news and abroad: comparing UK trends elsewhere. In: A. Douglas & T. Philpot (eds) *Adoption: Changing Families, Changing Times*. London: Routledge.

Thoburn, J. (2003b) Keynote address: BASPCAN Fifth National Congress. Strengthening the links – research, policy and practice. University of York, 20–23 July 2003.

Thoburn, J. (2003c) The risks and rewards of adoption for children in public care. *Child and Family Law Quarterly* 15, 391–401.

Thoburn, J., Lewis, A. & Shemmings, D. (1995) *Paternalism or Partnership? Family Involvement in the Child Protection Process.* London: HMSO.

Thorpe, J. & Clarke, E. (1998) *Divided Duties: Care Planning for Children Within the Family Justice System.* Bristol: Jordan.

Thorpe, L.J. (2003) How does a judge weigh up a case? In P. Reder, S. Duncan & C. Lucey (eds) *Studies in the Assessment of Parenting.* Hove: Brunner-Routledge.

Thorpe, L.J. & Cadbury, J. (eds) (2004) *Hearing the Children.* Bristol: Jordan.

Thorpe, L.J. & Cowton, C. (eds) (2002) *Delight and Dole: The Children Act 10 Years On.* Bristol: Jordan.

Thorpe, L.J., Hale, J. & Clarke, E. (2000) *No Fault or Flaw: The Future of the Family Law Act.* Bristol: Jordan.

Thorpe, R. (2003) Stopping the drift: improving the lives of Queensland's children and young people in long-term care. Response to Community Consultation.

Thorpe, R. & Thomson, J. (2003) The importance of parents in the lives of children in the care system. *Children Australia* 28, 25–31.

Tingle, N. (1994) A view of wider family perspectives in contested adoptions. In: M. Ryburn (ed.) *Contested Adoptions: Research, Law, Policy and Practice.* Aldershot: Arena.

Tolson, R. (2004) Latest developments in public law children cases. Paper given at Children Law and Practice Conference, Family Law, London, 17 March 2004.

Tomison, A. (2000) Exploring family violence: linking child maltreatment and domestic violence. Australian National Child Protection Clearing House Issues Paper No. 13.

Triseliotis, J. (2002) Long term foster care or adoption? The evidence examined. *Child and Family Social Work* 7, 23–35.

Triseliotis, J. (2003) Long term foster care or adoption? In: P. Reder, S. Duncan & C. Lucey (eds) *Studies in the Assessment of Parenting.* Hove: Brunner Routledge.

Trotter, C. (1999) *Working with Involuntary Clients.* New South Wales, Australia: Allen & Unwin.

Trotter, C. (2004) *Helping Abused Children and Their Families.* New South Wales, Australia: Allen & Unwin.

Turnell, A. & Edwards, S. (1999) *Signs of Safety: A Safety and Solution and Oriented Approach to Child Protection Casework.* New York: W.W. Norton.

van Deurzen-Smith, E. (1988) *Existential Counselling in Action.* London: Sage.

van Ijzendoorn, M.H. & Kroonenberg, P.M. (1988) Cross-cultural patterns of attachment: a meta-analysis of the strange situation. *Child Development,* 59, 147–156.

Vetere, A. (2002) The over-use of expert witnesses?: a psychological perspective. In: L.J. Thorpe & C. Cowton (eds) *Delight and Dole: The Children Act 10 Years On.* Family Law, Bristol: Jordan.

Victoria Child Death Review Committee (2004) *Annual Report of Inquiries into Child Deaths.* Melbourne: Victorian Government Publishing Service.

Wall, J. (1997) *Rooted Sorrows: Psychoanalytic Perspectives on Child Protection, Assessment, Therapy and Treatment.* Bristol: Jordan.

Wall, N. (2000) *A Handbook for Expert Witnesses in Children Act Cases.* Bristol: Jordan.

Waller, B. (1997) A social services view of the Dartington conference. In J. Wall (ed.) *Rooted Sorrows: Psychoanalytic Perspectives on Child Protection, Assessment, Therapy and Treatment.* Bristol: Jordan.

Warner, R., Appleby, L., Whitton, A. & Faraghen, B. (1996) Demographic and obstetric risk factors for postnatal psychiatric morbidity. *British Journal of Psychiatry* 168, 607–611.

Warrington, S.A. & Wright, C.M. (2001) Accidents and resulting injuries in premobile infants: data from the ALSPAC study. *Archives of Disease in Childhood* 85, 104–107.

Waterhouse, S. (2001) Keeping children in kinship placements within court proceedings. In: B. Broad (ed.) *Kinship Care: The Placement Choice for Children and Young People*. Lyme Regis: Russell House.

Whitby, E.H., Griffiths, P.D., Rutter, S., Smith, M.F., Sprigg, A., Ohadike, P., et al. (2004) Frequency and natural history of subdural haemorrhages in babies and relation to obstetric factors. *Lancet* 2004; 363, 846–851.

Wilczynski, A. (1995) Child killing by parents: a motivational model. *Child Abuse Review* 4, 365–370.

Wilczynski, A. (1997) *Child Homicide*. London: Greenwich Medical Media.

Wilkins, B. (1997) Head injury – abuse or accident? *Archives of Disease in Childhood* 76, 393–397.

Willman, K.Y., Bank, D.E., Senac, M. & Chadwick, D.L. (1997) Restricting the time of injury in fatal inflicted head injuries. *Child Abuse and Neglect* 21, 929–940.

World Health Organisation (1992) *The ICD-10 Classification of Mental and Behavioural Disorders: Clinical Descriptions and Diagnostic Guidelines*. Geneva: World Health Organisation.

INDEX

Note: Page references in *italics* refer to tables.

DATE DUE

JAN 19 '07			

#47-0108 Peel Off Pressure Sensitive